CHRIS BUSH

Chris Bush is an award-winning playwright, lyricist and theatre-maker. Past work includes *The Odyssey* (National Theatre: Olivier), *Rock / Paper / Scissors* (Sheffield Theatres), *Jane Eyre* (Stephen Joseph Theatre/New Vic Theatre), *Fantastically Great Women Who Changed the World* (Kenny Wax, UK tour), *Hungry* (Paines Plough), *~~Kein~~ Weltuntergang / ~~Not~~ the End of the World* (Schaubühne, Berlin), *Standing at the Sky's Edge* (Sheffield Theatres/National Theatre/West End), *Nine Lessons and Carols: Stories for a Long Winter* (Almeida Theatre), *Faustus: That Damned Woman* (Headlong/Lyric Hammersmith/Birmingham Rep), *The Last Noël* (Attic Theatre/UK tour), *The Assassination of Katie Hopkins* (Theatr Clwyd), *Pericles* (National Theatre: Olivier), *The Changing Room* (NT Connections), *The Band Plays On*, *Steel*, *What We Wished For, A Dream, The Sheffield Mysteries* (all Sheffield Theatres), *Scenes from the End of the World* (Yard/Central School), *A Declaration from the People* (National Theatre: Dorfman) and *Larksong* (New Vic, Stoke-on-Trent). Awards include an Olivier Award for Best New Musical, a South Bank Sky Arts Award, three UK Theatre Awards, the Perfect Pitch Award, a Brit Writers' Award and the Theatre Royal Haymarket Writers' Award.

Other Playwright Collections from Nick Hern Books

Mike Bartlett

Jez Butterworth

Alexi Kaye Campbell

Caryl Churchill

Ayub Khan Din

David Edgar

Kevin Elyot

James Fritz

Ella Hickson

Robert Holman

Stephen Jeffreys

Deirdre Kinahan

Lucy Kirkwood

Liz Lochhead

Kenneth Lonergan

Conor McPherson

Mark O'Rowe

Evan Placey

Jack Thorne

debbie tucker green

Enda Walsh

Steve Waters

Nicholas Wright

CHRIS BUSH

Plays: One

Steel
Faustus: That Damned Woman
Nine Lessons and Carols
Hungry
~~Not~~ the End of the World

with an Introduction by the author

NICK HERN BOOKS
London
www.nickhernbooks.co.uk

A Nick Hern Book

Chris Bush Plays: One first published in Great Britain as a paperback original in 2024 by Nick Hern Books Limited, The Glasshouse, 49a Goldhawk Road, London W12 8QP

Cover image (right to left): Mel Lowe (as Bex) and Eleanor Sutton (as Lori) in the 2022 production of *Hungry* (Paines Plough at Soho Theatre, London). Photo by The Other Richard/ArenaPAL (www.arenapal.com)

Designed and typeset by Nick Hern Books, London
Printed in Great Britain by Mimeo Ltd, Huntingdon, Cambridgeshire PE29 6XX

ISBN 978 1 83904 297 3

www.nickhernbooks.co.uk/environmental-policy

For Roni, of course

Contents

Introduction

These plays were first performed in the three-year period between autumn 2018 and autumn 2021, a period which, I think we can all agree, was generally fairly quiet and uneventful on a global scale. They don't represent the beginning of my writing career, but do mark the point where I was increasingly able to make the work I wanted to, pursue the ideas I found most interesting, and stretch my theatrical muscles in new and exciting directions.

I wrote my first play when I was thirteen. It is not included in this volume. I sincerely hope that no one will ever have to read it again. Even so, I knew pretty much from that point that I wanted to write theatre for a living, and started to plan accordingly. Growing up in Sheffield, theatre was never presented to me as something rarefied or inaccessible. The Crucible remains the best theatre anywhere on the planet, and there was nowhere better to fall in love with the form. I studied at the University of York, primarily because of the reputation of its drama society, and took my first show to the Edinburgh Fringe in 2006 (which spectacularly sank without a trace). I fared far better the following year with the none-too-subtle *TONY! The Blair Musical*, and graduated in 2007 fully convinced I was skyrocketing towards a glittering career. Then nothing happened for about five years.

Actually, that's not quite true. I was writing lots, and continually sending scripts off into the void (occasionally trying to stage them myself, which was never the best idea), while working whatever minimum-wage/zero-hour/low-commitment jobs would pay my rent. Towards the end of 2012 I received a year-long attachment to the Crucible through the Pearson Playwrights' Scheme (now the Peggy Ramsay/Film4 Awards), and a two-month residency at the National Theatre Studio. It was while on attachment in Sheffield that I was commissioned to write my first piece of large-scale community theatre (*The Sheffield Mysteries* in 2014, directed by Daniel Evans), something that has formed a huge part of my practice over the last decade. It's complete madness that big community plays are often entrusted to less-experienced, emerging writers, seeing as they're just about the most technically challenging work there is, but I'm not complaining. These vast logistical undertakings taught me a huge amount about storytelling and practical theatre-making, as well as about community and purpose and audiences and collective ownership of work, and this grounding has informed just about everything I've written since.

So, by the time we reach *Steel*, the first play in this volume, I'd been writing theatre on and off for eighteen years. I think this is worth mentioning as a useful counter-narrative to all the overnight successes who get their debuts staged at the Royal Court before they can legally drink, and fame and fortune seems to follow immediately. 2018 was a real breakthrough year for me, and felt like it had been a long time coming. I made *The Changing Room* for National Theatre Connections, *The Assassination of Katie Hopkins* for Theatr Clwyd, my adaptation of *Pericles* in the Olivier (my first NT Public Acts project), and *Steel* for the Crucible Theatre Studio (now the Tanya Moiseiwitsch Playhouse). By this point I'd written three large-scale community shows for the Crucible, and was looking for a new challenge. Somehow, I managed to corner incoming Artistic Director Robert Hastie within his first couple of weeks on the job, and pitched him an ambitious political epic spanning several decades. He agreed to commission it just so long as I could make it work with two actors, and *Steel* was the result. I knew Rebecca Frecknall from some shared time together at the National Theatre Studio, and was delighted when she agreed to direct. Having made so many big and complex shows in the run-up to *Steel*, I found the whole process a joy, and a fairly straightforward prospect, although I remember at the time Rebecca saying it was the most stressful thing she'd ever done. In a two-hander there really is nowhere to hide, no bells and whistles or theatrical dazzle camouflage to distract an audience from anything that doesn't quite work. Fortunately we were blessed with a superb cast and phenomenal team, and of course now everybody knows what a genius Frecks is. The themes contained within – those of power, female agency, northern identity, a sense of place and belonging, and good people fighting a flawed system – can be found throughout much of my work.

2019 was another full year, with the inaugural production of *Standing at the Sky's Edge* in Sheffield and *The Last Noël* for Attic Theatre. I was also busy working on a string of other projects, including *Faustus: That Damned Woman* for Headlong, which was commissioned in late 2018. I had been wanting to put my own spin on the Faust myth for years, but initially struggled to get going. I got it into my head that I wasn't just writing a play this time, but proper *literature* – this was to be big, serious, grown-up work for an internationally renowned company, and it had to be just right. The self-imposed pressure to create something great – or even worse, *important* – is a terrible thing for a first draft. But I persevered, first developing the script with the brilliant Amy Hodge, and later with Caroline Byrne once she was attached to direct. We opened at the Lyric Hammersmith in January 2020, before embarking on a small UK tour. Far beyond anything else I'd written, I was convinced this was the show that would make my career.

Then the world fell apart.

Faustus was playing at the Bristol Old Vic in March 2020 when theatres across the country closed. By chance, I ended up catching what would be the penultimate performance of the run, and I'm so glad I did. *Faustus* wasn't an easy make and took some critical flak along the way, never quite making the splash in London that I'd hoped for. Still, by this point in the tour it felt like it had really found its feet. Jodie McNee and Danny Lee Wynter were firing on all cylinders, and the whole production had gained the confidence and propulsion it always needed. The Bristol Old Vic is an exceptionally beautiful theatre, which wears the scars of its history for all to see. Sometimes plays reveal their true nature to you very late in the day. My *Faustus* is about morality, religion, patriarchy, ambition, gender, vengeance, and many other things besides, but sitting in that ancient auditorium that afternoon, it fully struck me how much the piece is about disease – not just the great plague of 1665 in which the action starts, but sickness and medicine and mortality are at its core. Because theatre is a live art form, our understanding of a text will always be influenced by the circumstances under which we experience it. At a recent student revival I attended, themes of AI and technology felt particularly prevalent. In future productions, should I be fortunate enough to have them, who knows what will leap to the fore? Still, on that strange day in March, this was a show about plague. On the train back to London I got a call from one of the producers – the theatres were closing, but this was just a temporary measure. With a bit of luck we'd be off for no longer than a fortnight, and able to finish the run in Leeds as planned. It turns out everything took a little longer.

I'm not sure I've made a 'normal' show since Covid, by which I mean a show not in some way impacted, curtailed, postponed, reimagined or somehow interfered with as a result of the pandemic. Maybe that just is what 'normal' looks like now. In October 2020, while everything was still extraordinarily uncertain, I got a call from

Rebecca Frecknall to make a show with her for the Almeida. A week later we met actors, and a week after that we were in rehearsals for what became *Nine Lessons and Carols: Stories for a Long Winter*. The idea wasn't to make a show about the pandemic as such, but to make something of a response piece to the year we'd all been through, fully aware of the fact that we were still in the eye of the storm, with no clear end in sight. Everyone involved had experienced their own unique lockdown, but common themes soon emerged. We wanted something that touched on ideas of isolation and loneliness, of loss and resilience, of gathering together in the darkest part of the winter in some sort of collective act of defiance, at a time when any collective act felt nigh-on impossible. It is the most truly collaborative piece in this collection. While the words are mine, they came from conversation, reflection, improvisation, devising exercises and writing prompts with our brilliant and brave company (augmented with the beautiful songs of Maimuna Memon). We ran a socially distanced rehearsal room, where infrared scanners checked our temperatures on the door and health professionals regularly visited to stick swabs up our noses (this was before the days of self-testing). We were all, I think, immensely grateful to be given the chance to make anything, but it was a deeply surreal process. The resulting piece was strange and fragmentary, funny, sad, dreamlike, born of courage and vulnerability and holding our nerves through eleventh-hour rewrites and ever-changing government policy. What we ended up with was remarkable, and contains some of my very favourite writing. After a monumental effort, we were closed the day after press night, when London was bumped up into a different tier and all the theatres shut again. It was an immense privilege to be able to make it, and in a strange way, and despite everything, one of my happiest rehearsal-room experiences.

Of all the plays here, *Hungry* had the longest journey to the stage. I wrote a very different version of the show back in 2013 while still on attachment in Sheffield; another big, sprawling piece that played out over the course of a single day but raced through a range of settings, characters and food hierarchies. It was entirely reconceived as a two-hander when Katie Posner and Charlotte Bennett asked me to write something for Paines Plough's Roundabout venue, but retained its core themes of food, class and grief, and the queer relationship at its heart. *Hungry* was due to open in 2020 as part of Katie and Charlotte's first season as Artistic Directors, but naturally that production was delayed. The Roundabout got back up and touring in 2021, with *Hungry* returning for a longer run at Soho

Theatre and the Edinburgh Fringe in 2022. Katie's production of *Hungry* is one of those very rare, very happy occasions where everything just seemed to click, and I genuinely wouldn't change a thing about it. In retrospect, I think it also helped that the germ of the idea for the piece had been rattling around my head for so long. As much as I always want everything to happen straight away, the chance to sit with these characters for the best part of a decade, and then to further refine and redraft every element due to production delays, really enabled the script to be the best it could be.

The final text in this collection, *~~Not~~ the End of the World*, has yet to be performed in English, but opened as *~~Kein~~ Weltuntergang* at the Schaubühne in Berlin in 2021, directed by Katie Mitchell and translated by the wonderful Gerhild Steinbuch. I first met Katie in early 2020, and we talked at length about how to make meaningful work about the climate crisis. As we hurtled into lockdown our ideas started to shift. At one point, what eventually became *~~Kein~~ Weltuntergang* was going to be a multi-part, mixed-media project, consisting of a series of short films shot remotely and a live stage show acting as a companion piece. Our plans simplified over time, although what remains is still one of the most formally ambitious scripts I've attempted.[1] As it transpires, making a production entirely remotely from a different country in a language you don't speak during a global pandemic isn't the most straightforward prospect, but we more or less got there. I loved the chance to do something unapologetically strange which could couple complex science and dense imagery with a really bold sense of theatricality. I still very much hope I'll get to make an English-language version of it some time soon.

I've had a remarkably productive few years, and am well aware that I'm incredibly fortunate to be in the position I am today. I write theatre for a living, which is something very few people are able to say. I take on a lot of work because I genuinely love what I do, but also because I live with the constant fear that if I turn any project down, I'll never work again. Perhaps one day I'll find a somewhat healthier life/work balance, but realistically that's not happening any time soon. As long as people keep offering me opportunities, I'll keep finding stories to tell, so I hope this volume might ultimately prove to be the first of many.

Of course, a script is all but useless without the people who bring it to life. While I hope there's still merit to encountering these plays on

1. 'Don't worry, the Germans like weird,' Katie would often tell me.

the page, I'm a fundamental believer that playtexts are not art by themselves, but rather the instruction manuals (or perhaps recipe books) from which the art gets made. Looking back at this selection, I'm struck by just how spoilt I've been with my directors – Katie Mitchell, Katie Posner, Caroline Byrne and a Rebecca Frecknall double-bill – it simply doesn't get any better than that.[2] In each of these extraordinary women I found true visionaries, brilliant minds, creative problem-solvers, and above all else, generous and open collaborators. A good director will give you the version of the play that you had in your head from the start, but a great director will give you something better. If making theatre was a simple act of assembly – take what's written, and put it on its feet – you might as well do it yourself, but that way madness (and egomania) lies. Surround yourself with excellence, and you will be constantly surprised and delighted by the different angles, nuances and additional dimensions other artists will find in your work. If I could offer one piece of rock-solid advice to an emerging writer, it would be to find fellow creatives who you trust and admire, and to put your faith in them. As long as you're all fundamentally trying to make the same show (not always a given!), it's critical that you can hold your nerve and give them the breathing space they require to excel. This doesn't mean you hand over your work carte blanche – I think it's equally important to stay present and approachable throughout the rehearsal process, checking in, making changes, learning the things you'll only learn once the work is on its feet – but a truly great piece of theatre is born of a shared vision, not just a bunch of hired hands trying to deliver yours. This is why I have little patience for 'auteurs' in the theatre industry who want to do everything themselves (and why 95% of writer-directors are sociopaths). A plurality of voices always have more to say than a singular one. Let good people make your work better. Anyway, all this is to say I'm incredibly fortunate to have worked with a string of wonderful people, and hope I never take their contributions for granted. As well as the directors listed above, I'm hugely grateful to the plethora of actors, designers, composers, creatives, producers, stage management, and anyone else who has ever helped my words find a third dimension. Huge thanks too to Matt and Alex, my fantastic agents, and the brilliant team at Nick Hern Books for allowing this volume to exist at all.

Telling stories for a living can feel like a very silly thing to do, especially when it also feels like the world is ending. The urge to

2. It also feels remiss not to mention two of my most frequent collaborators here, not represented in this volume for purely logistical reasons. Rob Hastie, I wouldn't have this career without you, you are a glorious leader, a wonderful human and a brilliant friend. Emily Lim, you are the very best of us.

retrain as a doctor or climatologist or human-rights lawyer can be strong, but there's one thing (or two things, if you count my complete absence of transferable skills) that keeps me going. I do think that stories matter. In fact, I think that stories are extraordinarily important. We tell stories to be understood and to understand others, to explain the place we've come from and to imagine where we might go next. The right story, told well, can change the world, because a story is the very best tool we have to change someone's mind. This book is full of stories, waiting to be brought to life. I hope you enjoy them.

Chris Bush
January 2024

STEEL

Steel was first performed at the Crucible Theatre Studio, Sheffield, on 13 September 2018. The cast was as follows:

IAN/DAI	Nigel Betts
VANESSA/JOSIE	Rebecca Scroggs
Director	Rebecca Frecknall
Designer	Madeleine Girling
Lighting Designer	Jack Knowles
Sound Designer	James Frewer
Casting Director	Anna Cooper CDG
Dialect Coach	Michaela Kennen

Characters

1988

DAI GRIFFITHS, *fifties/sixties. Welsh. Seasoned Labour councillor. Member of cabinet for Business and Economy.*

JOSIE KIRKWOOD, *thirties. Local. Junior engineer at a local steelworks and Women's Officer for her union.*

2018

VANESSA GALLACHER, *thirties. Labour candidate for Metro Mayor. Born here, but has mostly lived in London. A former MP who lost her seat in 2017. Southern accent.*

IAN DARWENT, *fifties/sixties. Local. Deputy Leader of the Council. Vanessa's election officer.*

Actor playing Dai and Ian is white. Actor playing Josie and Vanessa is Black.

Note on Text

A forward slash (/) indicates an overlap in dialogue where the next character starts speaking.

Author's Note

The piece takes place in a city unquestionably modelled on Sheffield, and references various real-world events, but the story is entirely fictional. No characters are based on any specific individuals.

ACT ONE

Scene One

2018. Outside the local Labour Party headquarters. IAN *waits.* VANESSA *enters. There's a certain forced joviality on both parts.*

IAN. Vanessa!

VANESSA. Ian – hi!

IAN *extends a hand, but* VANESSA *is going for the hug. A shuffling moment of awkwardness.*

Hah. Okay.

IAN. Sorry.

VANESSA. How about – ?

She goes for a kiss on the cheek instead. That's fine. IAN *doesn't anticipate the second.*

Well. Um.

IAN. Very continental.

VANESSA. Thank God that's over.

IAN. You found us alright?

VANESSA (*a little surprised by the question*). I've been here before.

IAN. You have?

VANESSA. Of course I have.

IAN. Right.

VANESSA. Must've been, I don't know, half a dozen times in the last –

IAN. I wasn't suggesting –

VANESSA. You know it's actually not far from… I used to do Woodcraft Folk, just round the corner, well, just down the –

IAN. Oh.

VANESSA. Back in the day.

IAN. Woodcraft Folk?

VANESSA. Yes.

IAN. That the one that's like hippy Scouts?

VANESSA. Something like that.

IAN. Very good.

VANESSA. Never really my… A bit too Kumbaya for my liking, but…

IAN. And you're well? You look well. Very –

VANESSA. Thanks.

IAN. Nice to see some people still make an effort.

VANESSA. Um. Thank you. I wasn't really… I just –

IAN. Nervous?

VANESSA (*surprised*). Nervous?

IAN. Don't be.

VANESSA. Oh, I'm not.

IAN. Right. Good.

VANESSA. I mean this is –

IAN. Yes.

VANESSA. Isn't it?

IAN. Hmm?

VANESSA. This is all… Look, I don't want to imply this is a foregone conclusion, I don't want to be presumptive, but I am… I have been the, um, the presumptive candidate, in fact, for a while, if we used that term, haven't I? So –

IAN. Indeed.

VANESSA. And nothing's happened to…? Do you know something?

IAN. Rarely.

VANESSA. Right. (*Beat.*) But just to be clear, the situation hasn't…? You're not expecting any nasty surprises?

IAN. Not at all.

VANESSA. So why should I be nervous?

IAN. Sometimes people just get nervous.

VANESSA. Right.

IAN. But I can see you're not.

VANESSA. I wasn't.

IAN. My apologies.

VANESSA. It's fine. I'm fine. Sorry. You just gave me a little… Because I don't want to sound dismissive. Obviously the other candidates are both –

IAN. Obviously.

VANESSA. So I'm not –

IAN. Don't want to insult your sisters.

VANESSA (*forcing a laugh*). Hah. No.

IAN. And the sisters are particularly good at getting insulted. Carol practically makes a living from it.

VANESSA (*biting her tongue*). Hmm.

IAN. Sure everything's alright?

VANESSA. Yes. Yes, everything's… Actually no, sorry. Sorry, can I be an arsehole?

IAN. Uh…

VANESSSA. Sorry, but… No, actually, I'm not sorry and I'm not being an arsehole, this is actually a very… And I know you're one of the good guys –

IAN. Right.

VANESSA. But if you could not… That word. Can you not use that word, please?

IAN. Beg pardon?

VANESSA. The S word.

IAN. I'm not –

VANESSA. 'Sisters' – with that inflection, and that general… Because look, it's bad enough when a woman says 'sisters' about a group who aren't actually… I genuinely feel my ovaries cringe every time I hear it, but when a man – and I know you're not a…

and look, hashtag-not-all-men and so on, but when you refer to me and my fellow democratically selected candidates as 'the sisters' it sort of makes me want to put my fist through something.

IAN. Right.

VANESSA. Sorry.

IAN. Don't be.

VANESSA. No. Right. I'm not.

IAN. I'm sorry to –

VANESSA. As you should be. (*Beat.*) Joking – that was joking. Only not really –

IAN. Understood.

VANESSA. Because we are… We're not a sorority, we're serious political operatives, and it is a big deal, actually – to have an all… And not an 'All-Women Shortlist' by design, not because it was enforced, but a shortlist which happens to be only –

IAN. Yes.

VANESSA. Because the best three candidates just happened to be –

IAN. Absolutely.

VANESSA. Which is what happened.

IAN. No argument from me.

VANESSA. Each of us here on merit, each with our own… Carol can moan, but her business record is exemplary, and Deborah, well, Debbie is… the heart of the community, isn't she? The backbone of… Salt of the earth –

IAN. Both got a lot going for them.

VANESSA. And when I heard… I think we were all thrilled, weren't we? All so excited, because –

IAN. You knew you could beat them?

VANESSA. No! (*Beat.*) Well yes, but –

IAN *laughs.*

But not only because of that, because it represented a real… It shouldn't be remarkable, it shouldn't be remotely surprising, but these are milestones, they are, and they need to be celebrated, not derided, not treated with suspicion, or undermined by… I get enough of that from elsewhere.

IAN. Won't happen again.

VANESSA. Thanks. Thank you. (*Breathing, calming slightly.*) Look, let's just get through tonight, let's just… And it will be easier then, won't it?

IAN. How do you mean?

VANESSA. Once I'm… Presuming I'm… Once they're stuck with me. Because I can win over the public – I know how to do that, but it's you bastards who're the real… Sorry.

IAN. That's alright.

VANESSA. And I'm all for healthy debate, I am, and a rigorous, forthright… But it's exhausting – this has all just been very draining, actually, day after day, the three of us continually having to justify our collective existence, so after this evening I would really like to just be able to say, 'Look, this is who you've got, so fall in line.'

IAN. And I think people will. I think yes, to an extent…

VANESSA. Good. And I know – I do realise with all the… Tonight might not feel exactly like a coronation. I'm prepared for that.

IAN. You saw the email then?

VANESSA. What email?

IAN. The… Never mind.

VANESSA. What email?

IAN. Not important – we can talk about it later.

VANESSA. Ian –

IAN. It's nothing, it's… It's just a new email chain with a few idiots blowing off some steam.

VANESSA. Right.

IAN. Honestly –

VANESSA. Can I see it?

IAN. I'll show you after.

VANESSA. That bad?

IAN. No! (*Beat.*) Fine. Hang on.

IAN *starts trying to find the email on his phone.*

VANESSA. Because this is exactly the… It's embarrassing – I'm actually just embarrassed by all of it – the pettiness, the squabbling, the continual –

IAN. Now just bear in mind –

VANESSA. I'm a big girl – please.

IAN (*passing his phone to* VANESSA). Alright.

VANESSA. Alright then. (*Scrolling through.*) '…high-handed interference from the NEC, forcing upon us…' well, naturally – 'a sordid selection process swaddled in scandal, secrecy and scurrilous self-interest…' You know that's Brian, he's the one who writes his own poetry.

IAN. Christ, don't remind me.

VANESSA. Oh, and here it is: 'instead of representing the true interests and values of the local party, we have become a Petri dish for political correctness and social engineering.' Jesus. It's not a dog whistle, it's an air-raid siren.

IAN. You've got to remember this is just a vocal minority.

VANESSA (*passing the phone back*). Who are these people? How do they think this is helping?

IAN. They're just a little stuck in their ways.

VANESSA. Unbelievable. Infants. That they're so threatened by… They need me. Do you have any idea how much they need me up here?

IAN. Everyone appreciates –

VANESSA. They don't! Ungrateful fuckers. They don't make it easy.

IAN. Alright, let's try not to –

VANESSA. Yes, yes, you're right. Okay then – let's get this shit-show over with.

VANESSA *leaves and* IAN *follows. We hear* (*but needn't see*) *the returning Officer announcing the results of the candidate vote.*

OFFICER. The total number of votes cast was four thousand, five hundred and eighty-five, representing a sixty-four-point-three-per-cent turnout. Two hundred and twenty-one votes were found to be invalid or spoilt, bringing the total number of eligible votes to four thousand, three hundred and sixty-four. They were cast as follows: In the first round, Gallacher, Vanessa: one thousand, nine hundred and thirty-three votes. Henshaw, Carol: one thousand, five hundred and forty-two votes. Lister, Deborah: eight hundred and eighty-nine votes. As there is no overall winner, Debbie's votes went to second preference. Four hundred and seventy-four of those went to Vanessa Gallacher, bringing her total to two thousand, four hundred and seven, and four hundred and fifteen to Carol Henshaw, coming to one thousand, nine hundred and fifty-seven. Therefore Vanessa Gallacher is duly elected as the Labour candidate for Metro Mayor.

The sound of applause, perhaps not exactly deafening. Scene ends.

Scene Two

1988. We're now inside a small meeting hall, where a CLP meeting has just finished. DAI, *a seasoned councillor, is with* JOSIE, *the evening's guest speaker.*

DAI. Can I just stop you there?

JOSIE. I didn't say anything.

DAI. But before you do –

JOSIE. I should… My bus is…

DAI. Can I just explain what I think happened?

JOSIE. Um…

DAI. Just to… Just because –

JOSIE. I was there, so –

DAI. Yes. No. Absolutely. But what I think is, I think you may have misinterpreted the, uh, the intent of –

JOSIE. It's fine.

DAI. You're upset.

JOSIE. I'm not.

DAI. It's fine to be upset, but I think if I just explained –

JOSIE. I'm really not.

DAI. Because it was a joke.

JOSIE. I know.

DAI. But I'm not sure you understood the… the… If I could just take a moment – please – if you'd indulge me?

JOSIE (*still somewhat reluctantly*). Of course.

DAI. Good. Excellent. Thank you. So the first thing to say is that we don't even have a tea lady.

JOSIE. Right.

DAI. We… So there could be no, no one was genuinely mistaking you for – nobody thought you were actually –

JOSIE. No.

DAI. Because we just sort ourselves out, you see? There isn't a… We have a biscuit rota. Sometimes one of the women bakes. (*Then immediately worried.*) And that isn't to say – not that… I do believe it is only the women who bake – in my experience of these particular meetings – but that isn't a… a… that's not a matter of policy. There's no expectation.

JOSIE. Of course.

DAI. Always very welcome, but –

JOSIE. Got it.

DAI. But – but yes – but my point is everyone did know who you were. You were on the agenda. Josie Kirkwood: British Steel.

JOSIE. I saw.

DAI. So. So. And here's where I think things got… The joke, as I understand it – and it was a joke – was look, here you are, guest speaker at your first constituency meeting, brilliant, um, brilliant mind, young blood, sister in solidarity and all that, and then, 'Oh no, what's this? Everyone thinks I'm the tea lady!'

JOSIE. Right.

DAI. Which is, yes, in itself isn't funny – unkind, maybe – but then, then it would become clear that was all just ribbing, just pulling your leg, and that would, you see, would put you at ease, funny because it's so ridiculous, the idea that any of us would… Shows we're all on the same side.

JOSIE. I see.

DAI. You do?

JOSIE. I do. I did. Honestly.

DAI. So it really was all just a… It is, I believe, it's just how they show their affection around here – it took me a while to get used to it.

JOSIE. Oh, I know. We give as good as we get.

DAI. Yes. Yes of course, and when I said… Yes, of course you're the local, not me – I didn't want to imply anything otherwise.

JOSIE. It's really fine.

DAI. Good. That's good. I'm glad.

JOSIE. You can't be a woman in steel without developing something of a thick skin.

DAI. I can imagine.

JOSIE. But I should probably –

DAI. I would just really hate to think of you leaving with the wrong impression.

JOSIE. Mr Griffiths –

DAI. Dai, please.

JOSIE. Dai – can I tell you what they said to me – what the foreman said to me on my very first day at the steelworks?

DAI. Please.

JOSIE. He said, 'Steel? Face that colour, I thought you'd come straight out of the mines.'

DAI. Oh. Oh, I…

JOSIE. So as first impressions go –

DAI. And that is… Believe me, I would never –

JOSIE. I'm saying it's fine. I'm saying jokes about being the tea lady pale in comparison.

DAI. Right.

JOSIE. No pun intended.

DAI. Hmm?

JOSIE. 'Pale', because… Doesn't matter.

DAI. Ah.

Pause.

Anyway… Anyway your talk was very… Truly powerful. Challenging but powerful. It was just what we needed.

JOSIE (*very much summing up*). My pleasure.

DAI. No, all mine, really. (*Beat.*) Sorry, there was just… There is one other thing, if you have the time.

JOSIE. Um –

DAI. It won't take a minute.

JOSIE. Sure.

DAI. Excellent. Yes, so again, tonight was really… A very different, a very exciting energy, I thought, in the room. And we are always looking for… young blood, fresh perspectives. I don't know if you heard, but there is an opening coming up here, shortly – locally.

JOSIE. An opening?

DAI. You do live in this ward, don't you? I know your father, his shop is –

JOSIE. Yes.

DAI. Is it something you'd given any thought to?

JOSIE. I'm sorry, is what something?

DAI. Standing – when Bill retires.

JOSIE. For the council?

DAI. And of course my seat's here too, so I'd be happy to talk you through any of the… the… I'd be in your corner.

JOSIE. Um… Right. Er…

DAI. You hadn't considered – ?

JOSIE. No. No, I genuinely… Not for a second.

DAI. But you are a Party member – and you're active in your union?

JOSIE. Yeah.

DAI. You have things to say, obviously.

JOSIE. I suppose, but… Yeah, on certain… But I'm not sure this is my natural –

DAI. How would you know?

JOSIE. Because I… Um, I guess I don't, really, but the impression I get is… I want to say this carefully because I don't want to cause offence and I'm sure – I know – what you do here is, is… it does matter, it does have some impact –

DAI. But?

JOSIE. But… Yeah, I guess the 'but' is just whether this environment is… uh…

DAI. Not quite your scene?

JOSIE. I'm very flattered.

DAI. It's alright.

JOSIE. But is this somewhere where I – where someone like me…?

DAI. Yes. I'm afraid we are a little… pale, male and stale, I believe the phrase is.

JOSIE. I didn't mean that.

DAI. No, I understand. Well, I thought at least I'd… Worth a shot, anyway.

JOSIE. But it's so nice that you'd… Thank you, honestly.

DAI. Not at all. (*Beat.*) Who knows how we change that though.

JOSIE. Sorry?

DAI. Sorry – you needed to get off.

JOSIE. Yeah, I… (*Checking watch.*) Doesn't matter, it's not far to walk.

DAI. Oh no, have I – ?

JOSIE. It's fine, really.

DAI. I do go on.

JOSIE. But you were saying? Change what?

DAI. Oh, it's… Yes, well it's the problem I've been struggling with – that a number of us – of the more enlightened… How do you make this a more appealing environment to begin with for those people who will, ultimately through their very presence, make the environment more appealing? And, and yes, there is a school of thought that says decisions are made by the people who show up, and we shouldn't be going out of our way to… If they're not interested, that's their loss. But I don't think that's fair. I don't think it's accurate. I don't think they're uninterested, I think they're put off by, by, by the very design of places like this – the smoke-filled backrooms and sticky floors. And that will change – it will change as our make-up changes – but the question, the challenge, is how can we coax those first few people through the doors?

Beat.

JOSIE. Right.

DAI. Anyway. Not to worry.

JOSIE. Sure.

DAI. I have my car – can I drop you somewhere? Where are you heading?

JOSIE. What would I need to do?

DAI. I'm not… I don't want petrol money or anything.

JOSIE. To stand – if I was interested in standing?

DAI. Oh.

JOSIE. Not saying that I am.

DAI. Right.

JOSIE. Not necessarily. But just out of –

DAI. Right. Right, yes. Well it's all very straightforward, very simple. There's a form – I can talk you through it – then a little chat – just to make sure you don't have any particularly ghastly skeletons in your closet. All very informal. In fact I recommend not taking any of it too seriously. Not *un*seriously, but just to keep it all quite light, actually, show them you can have a laugh – you have a sense of humour –

JOSIE. That I can take a joke?

DAI. I… Yes. And again I will apologise about earlier if you did feel –

JOSIE. Please don't.

DAI. But yes, people respond to… If you show you can play nicely with others –

JOSIE. Got it. I can do that. And I can be funny. I can do jokes.

DAI. Great stuff.

JOSIE. I can… Not that I'm committing – but I will have a think – I will give it some serious thought, and – not *too* serious, mind, but I will… Yeah. I've got a lot to – it's a lot to process, but… Yeah. No. Good. That's all good.

DAI. Smashing.

JOSIE. But right now I should –

DAI. Of course. Sure you don't want a lift somewhere?

JOSIE. No, I'll be fine, thank you. I think some air would…

DAI. As you wish. Well then. (*Offers his hand, slightly awkwardly.*) Miss Kirkwood, welcome to the council.

Scene ends.

Scene Three

2018. IAN *greets* VANESSA. *She has with her a large refillable coffee cup.*

IAN. Madam Mayor!

VANESSA. Alright, let's not get… One step at a time.

IAN. Absolutely. Still, got what we needed – and all without too much unpleasantness.

VANESSA. And only two hundred spoilt ballots.

IAN. Don't worry about that. Onwards and upwards.

VANESSA. Exactly. Next step – top of the agenda – crush the saboteurs.

Beat.

IAN. Right.

VANESSA. I'm joking – Jesus!

IAN. Alright.

VANESSA. Your face.

IAN. I just think… even in private we should avoid drawing any comparison between –

VANESSA. Oh really?

IAN. I just –

VANESSA. That wouldn't be a vote-winner?

IAN. Maybe not.

VANESSA. And that's a comparison a lot of people have been drawing, is it?

IAN. I didn't say that.

VANESSA. I mean I do still intend to crush them – if they're not suitably crushed already.

IAN. Let's not get –

VANESSA. Because seriously, the constant infighting within the various enclaves of the Judean People's Front that is the Labour Party does make me want to open up a vein, but now I've actually won, I say let's nail the fuckers.

IAN. Right.

VANESSA. That's a Monty Python reference, just for the record, not antisemitism.

IAN. Yes.

VANESSA. Because you can't be too careful these days, can you?

IAN (*gesturing to the coffee*). Not your first of the morning?

VANESSA. Hmm? No, no. No, I'm full of beans. I've got one of the, the little – the pod machines, y'know? The capsules – the automatic – godsend. Because I'm not being funny, but half the places you go into here, you ask for a soya latte and they look at you like you've pissed on their parkin, so…

IAN. Right.

VANESSA. You know what I mean?

IAN. I'm more of a Yorkshire Tea man myself.

VANESSA. Ah yes, of course, very on-brand.

IAN. Anyway –

VANESSA. Sorry, that was really obnoxious.

IAN. No –

VANESSA. No, it was, and here's the thing – let London have its wanky coffee. I want the tea. I want the pies. I want the chips cooked in dripping. That's who I really am – that's what I was brought up on.

IAN. Yes.

VANESSA. That is… You should be writing that down actually, because that's my narrative. This is my homecoming.

IAN. Yes. (*Beat.*) Only the issue is –

VANESSA. Perception. It's about perception, that's all. And this is where we – where *I* – we've all failed to… They don't realise I'm one of them.

IAN. Now there's a little truth in… But you are, to be fair, a relatively new addition to, to the landscape –

VANESSA. I was born here.

IAN. The *political* landscape.

VANESSA. Just because my parents were dirty southerners, that doesn't mean –

IAN. No.

VANESSA. Or are you getting at something else?

IAN. All I mean is –

VANESSA. Jerry Allen turned his back on me when they announced the vote. He literally turned his back.

IAN. Most I've seen him move in years.

VANESSA. A former Party Treasurer.

IAN. It's… Yes. Disappointing.

VANESSA. One word for it.

IAN. Jerry is… passionate. A bit of a hothead, but his commitment –

VANESSA. Jerry Allen is a crybaby and a bully who doesn't like being told no.

IAN. He only wants what's best – what he considers to be best for the party.

VANESSA (*reading from her phone*). '@Vanessa4MetroMayor needs to get back to where she came from.'

IAN. Jerry's not – ?

VANESSA. No. (*Checks.*) 'EricTheRed66'. Anonymous Twitter troll. Actually far more polite than most.

IAN. And that is unacceptable, and we will –

VANESSA. Where do you think they mean, exactly?

IAN. I'm sorry?

VANESSA. That I should be getting back to? I mean are we just talking Islington, or are they going full Bongo-Bongo Land?

IAN. It sickens me, it does, and anything I can do to –

VANESSA. You can challenge the narrative.

IAN. Right.

VANESSA. That I don't belong here. That this isn't home.

IAN. Yes, I do see that, only –

VANESSA. That this can't be home for people like me.

IAN. No, and it isn't… I honestly don't think it's a race thing, not for the vast majority of… I think entirely separately, some people have qualms about your, your route here –

VANESSA. Qualms?

IAN. And I'm not saying they're justified –

VANESSA. I wasn't dropped in. This isn't parachuting.

IAN. No.

VANESSA. I am a prodigal daughter. Yes, I moved away. In order to, to… to gain experience, to seek my fortune in the big city, and that is why, actually – that's why I beat Carol, who's never set foot inside Westminster, and Debbie, bless her, who's never been south of Derby. That's critical.

IAN. I agree.

VANESSA. And actually, actually losing my seat in the Commons last year, that was – it was tough, yes, it was character-building, it was a learning experience – but it was in truth the best thing that could've happened to me, because it meant I got to come back here – I got to do this – I got to come *home.*

IAN. Right.

VANESSA. Because this is where I need to be. It's not a back-up plan, it's not my consolation prize, it's bigger than any… The Metro Mayors are a fundamental shift in the power dynamic. This is a grassroots revolution in local governance.

IAN. Yes, I think I got that memo too.

VANESSA. I mean it. And I've got plans – big plans for this city – plans like you wouldn't believe. When I'm Mayor –

IAN. Now who's getting carried away?

VANESSA. Okay, okay, but I am the Labour Party candidate and look at where we are, so hello! I am the Labour Party candidate whether Jerry Allen and all his little gammon-faced, pin-dick friends like it or not.

IAN. And seeing as you are, perhaps you could extend an olive branch to –

VANESSA. And seeing as I am, perhaps they could form an orderly queue to kiss my arse.

IAN. Have you given much thought to decaf?

VANESSA. I am the Labour Party candidate. Now ask me why.

IAN. Why?

VANESSA. Because I am the best damn person for the job. Now ask me why again.

IAN. Why?

VANESSA. Because I belong here.

IAN. Right.

VANESSA. I belong here, and we are going to make sure everybody knows it. No one's going to make me look like an idiot.

Scene ends.

Scene Four

1988. JOSIE *has just come from her selection interview. For some reason she wears an apron and hairnet akin to Mrs Overall from* Acorn Antiques *and holds a tea tray. She is clearly upset, and* DAI *is trying to calm her.*

DAI. So. So okay. So that was… I'm not entirely sure what that was, but –

JOSIE. Don't.

DAI. But a very spirited, uh –

JOSIE. Your idea.

DAI. I'm sorry?

JOSIE. This – all this – this was your –

DAI. Uh –

JOSIE. Show them you're a laugh. Show a sense of humour.

DAI. I'm not sure I followed –

She rattles the tray, impersonating Julie Walters.

JOSIE. 'Two soups!'

DAI. Who is it again?

JOSIE. Mrs Overall!

DAI (*still blank*). Right.

JOSIE. Julie Walters!

DAI. Okay.

JOSIE. Tea lady. She's a funny tea lady, that's her thing, so after the whole… I was referencing – I was playing on their… I was being in on the joke.

DAI. I see.

JOSIE. Like you told me.

DAI. You did make quite a mess.

JOSIE. That's what she does!

DAI. Right.

JOSIE. That's why it's funny!

DAI. Understood.

JOSIE. She does this walk with the… She… She has this tray, and…

DAI. And she's on the television, is she?

JOSIE *lets out a moan.*

I'm just trying to –

JOSIE. Yes! Yes, she's a funny tea lady off the telly, so I thought – I thought it would be a nice idea to… I had a speech and everything, I'd planned a… After I'd, I'd broken the ice, I'd won them over –

DAI. Right.

JOSIE. I was going to talk about tea – about how tea is the most quintessentially English thing you can imagine, right? Except it isn't – it's from China, it's from India, it's from the Orient, it's fuelled empires and trade wars and sparked revolution, and, and… but it is, it still is the most quintessentially English thing, because we made it ours. Because we – we British are at our best not as colonisers but as magpies – this tiny island that takes the best the world has to offer and finds a new home for it – makes it our own. And that is what we must keep doing, because that is what we've always done – that's how we got here. A cup of tea was at one point the most unusual, most exotic, the most foreign thing I could've shown you, and now it's the very emblem of our nation – something we cannot live without. So I am proud to be your tea lady, because tea ladies are the harbingers of the revolution!

DAI. Right. Golly. Well that's –

JOSIE. In closing – in closing, gentlemen, I'd say – I'd like to quote Eleanor Roosevelt. Eleanor Roosevelt said 'A woman is like a tea bag: you can't tell how strong she is until you put her in hot water.' Well, I'm more than used to a bit of heat, and I'm confident I'm strong enough for anything this role can throw at me.

Pause.

You hate it.

DAI. No! No, I imagine if you'd said any of that it would've gone down rather well.

JOSIE. Ugh!

DAI. It's alright.

JOSIE. No it isn't.

DAI. I don't think it was as bad as you think it was.

JOSIE. Forget it. No – you're right – we should forget all about it.

DAI. I didn't say that.

JOSIE. I never wanted this anyway – this was your idea. And I told you, I told you it wasn't for me, but you pushed and you pushed and –

DAI. Josie –

JOSIE. And you got in my head –

DAI. Please –

JOSIE. And you told me it would be straightforward.

DAI. And – yes, and just to… In my defence I do believe you might've overcomplicated things.

JOSIE. I like to plan ahead.

DAI. Yes.

JOSIE. I put a lot of thought into this.

DAI. I can tell.

JOSIE. Please don't make fun of me.

DAI. I'm not – I promise I'm not. I see how all this was… I see the effort that you've… (*Beat.*) Can I ask you one thing?

JOSIE. What?

DAI. Why is a tea lady carrying soup?

A pause. JOSIE *realises he's right. She lets out an audible groan. She might cry. She is exhausted.*

Sorry.

JOSIE. Oh God.

DAI. I shouldn't have said anything.

JOSIE. She isn't… Two Soups is a waitress, Mrs Overall is a different…

DAI. So perhaps –

JOSIE. Stupid. I'm stupid. They all must think I'm so stupid.

DAI. Nobody thinks that.

JOSIE. Well they should.

DAI. Spirited. Memorable –

JOSIE. Look at me! (*Looks down at herself.*) Why am I still wearing this? (*Tears off the apron.*) Like a… Like a joke, like I think it's all some big… And I don't. I want this – I really want it.

DAI. I know.

JOSIE. I didn't before, but now… I do this, I get inside my head, I fixate, I overthink and I lose sight of –

DAI. It's okay.

JOSIE. How is this okay? I had one chance – one opportunity to show I was competent and professional or at least not mentally deranged and instead I turn up looking like this and I throw cream of leek all over them –

DAI. I think… it was a smattering at most.

JOSIE. It isn't funny! It isn't to me!

DAI. It's fine.

JOSIE. No it isn't. (*Beat.*) I need to go back in – can I go back in? Can I talk to them, or write to them to apologise? I need to –

DAI. There's no need, I assure you.

JOSIE. You don't understand. People like me only get one chance.

DAI. Josie, please – please just let me… Can you listen, just for a moment?

JOSIE *looks up at him.*

These chats, these 'interviews', what we're checking for is… Are you a murderer, a child molester or a Conservative? That's pretty much it – that's the grounds for dismissal.

JOSIE (*sniffs*). What're you saying?

DAI. And you're not, are you?

JOSIE. No.

DAI. Didn't think so. You are a Party member, a union officer, you work in steel. Your family are good, honest people.

JOSIE. I'll tell Dad that.

DAI. Of course being a grocer's daughter, that does count against you in today's political climate.

JOSIE (*laughs*). Right.

DAI. Furthermore, you are an intelligent, passionate, colourful woman, who – not *colourful*, but… characterful – a woman of great character who would make a very fine council candidate indeed.

JOSIE. So you mean…?

DAI. So I mean you're not getting out of this that easy. You're one of us, anyone can see that. You'll go on our roster, then there's another shortlisting meeting before the member vote, but that should all be a formality.

JOSIE. Honestly?

DAI. Scout's honour. Councillor Two Soups, here we come.

Scene ends.

Scene Five

2018. VANESSA *and* IAN. VANESSA *is furious.*

VANESSA. Bastard.

IAN. Alright.

VANESSA. Pathetic, infantile –

IAN. Let's try to –

VANESSA. I mean this is, isn't it, this is just flinging toys out of the pram?

IAN. We all knew he was unhappy.

VANESSA. Unhappy? Yes, unhappy is… But can you believe the nerve of him?

IAN. I didn't think he'd go through with it, no.

VANESSA. But you knew what he was thinking?

IAN. He'd been running his mouth, but –

VANESSA. And it never crossed your mind to…? Because a little heads-up might've been, y'know, exactly within the remit of your job, actually, Ian.

IAN. And I apologise if –

VANESSA. That makes it all better then.

IAN. If I failed to take seriously –

VANESSA. Because actually what is the point of you, if not to keep the local wildlife under control?

IAN. Now I know it's not really me you're angry at, so –

VANESSA. I can be angry on multiple fronts. I can multitask.

IAN. Very good.

VANESSA. And you might hope that once – just once – that the Labour Party could be presented with an open goal and do something other than turn around and headbutt the referee.

IAN. 'Twas ever thus.

VANESSA. And people wonder why… (*Distracts herself.*) Oh, and just so you know, I am mad as all hell, but that was still a solid football analogy, so anyone who says I can't connect with the average male voter can go swivel.

IAN. Noted.

VANESSA. But seriously – Jerry Allen – former, yes, Party Treasurer – what else? Exec committee member, donor, fundraiser, union liaison. Now Jerry Allen wants to be Mayor? As an *independent*?! Can you believe him?

IAN. He has a lot of –

VANESSA. He was never… His name never came within a million miles of a shortlist, right? He was never in contention?

IAN. No.

VANESSA. He never even put himself forward?

IAN. Not that I'm aware of.

VANESSA. And now he pulls a stunt like this?

IAN. He… Jerry has been around forever. He has a very clear idea of how things should be done.

VANESSA. No women, no Blacks, no Irish?

IAN. No – no I don't think that's fair –

VANESSA. He's a dinosaur.

IAN. He –

VANESSA. And he knows I'm the motherfucking asteroid.

IAN. He might be old-fashioned, but…

VANESSA (*reading*). 'In light of recent events we must concede that the Labour Party is no longer interested in representing the best interests of the working man. Therefore it is with a heavy heart – '

IAN. I've read it.

VANESSA. 'Heavy heart.' Three months from a cardiac arrest, more like.

IAN. Let's all take a breath –

VANESSA. I mean it. Slice him down the middle he bleeds coal tar and reconstituted pork.

IAN. Jerry has a base. He is known. He has something of a following.

VANESSA. Probably just caught in his gravitational pull, the fat fuck.

IAN. You need to take this a little seriously.

VANESSA. Do I look like I'm having fun?

IAN. He speaks to a certain type of demographically significant…

VANESSA. Professional Yorkshireman?

IAN. Man of the people. Business leader.

VANESSA. Leader?

IAN. Well respected as a –

VANESSA. He took his daddy's firm and he's running it into the ground. He's not some… some…

IAN. But the perception –

VANESSA. Right.

IAN. Close your eyes and picture the face of Labour in the Industrial North, you see Jerry Allen.

VANESSA. I try to close my eyes whenever I see Jerry Allen. I find it helps.

IAN. Seriously.

VANESSA. Right. Okay, right. Except he's screwed himself then, hasn't he? Because he's stabbing the Party in the back – he's tossed all that aside. Don't they have a word for that up here? A scab is what he is.

IAN. He wouldn't do this lightly.

VANESSA. But he has.

IAN. Exactly. Which is what scares me.

VANESSA. Yeah? Well I'm not afraid of him.

IAN. Scared because… You're right, this is a, a betrayal, if you like, a massive… And men like Jerry, whatever their faults, loyalty does matter to them. Labour men. Union men. Dyed-in-the-wool. So this is a big deal. It takes a lot to push a man like him that far.

VANESSA. And I'm really just that awful?

IAN. I don't want this to feel personal. But if he's a bellwether – if he's indicative of a larger problem – we have to take that on board.

VANESSA. Why doesn't he have to get on board with me?

IAN. Vanessa –

VANESSA. I mean it. I won! So why doesn't it feel like it?

IAN. You've not won anything yet.

VANESSA. That isn't true.

IAN. We're not home and dry. And my job, as your election officer, is to make sure we can finish what we started. You do understand that?

VANESSA. Yes. Yes, of course I do. (*Sighs, recomposes.*) Fine. So what does he want? Should I be sitting down with him? If I make him feel heard will he maybe shut up and go away?

IAN. No, no I think for now let's just… I think that could further antagonise… Sit tight. Leave it with me. I'll figure something out.

VANESSA. Right. Okay. Thank you.

Scene ends.

Scene Six

1988. DAI *and* JOSIE *are at a branch party meeting house.*

JOSIE. So… That just happened.

DAI. How do you feel?

JOSIE. Good. Yeah, I think good. Just…

DAI. A little anticlimactic?

JOSIE. No –

DAI. I'm afraid we don't really do tickertape parades up here, but…

JOSIE. Just quick – in and out before… Didn't get the chance to use my sock puppets or anything.

DAI (*laughs*). Good to hold something back. It's a big step, anyway – an important step. So – congratulations.

JOSIE. I haven't won anything yet.

DAI. *Au contraire.* You have secured your Party's nomination – that's the biggest hurdle around here. The rosette will do a lot of the heavy lifting now.

JOSIE. I'm not going to –

DAI. I know.

JOSIE. I'm doing this so I can do something, you know?

DAI. Absolutely – and you will. Without sock puppets – without soup – just you. I don't think they knew what'd hit them in there.

JOSIE. How do you mean?

DAI. I mean you… It's a good thing! You have a presence – an energy.

JOSIE. Yeah?

DAI. They'd never seen anything like you.

JOSIE. Yeah, well, maybe not.

DAI. Not like… I think people were excited – excited by the idea of you.

JOSIE. They didn't all look thrilled.

DAI. But they were all paying attention.

JOSIE. Maybe.

DAI. I should call Kenny at the… Have you met Kenny? And his wife Helen, who you'll love. Both just… Big movers and shakers – great people. She's a force of nature. Three kids, all terrific, never stops for breath.

JOSIE. Right.

DAI. Anyway, I'd love to introduce you.

JOSIE. Yeah, great – absolutely.

DAI. Because she – one of the things I thought you might… Helen's a housing officer by day, but actually her big thing is childcare provision.

JOSIE. Right.

DAI. Which is something none of us are taking seriously enough, actually – and I did think of you, because it's a real area where… If we want to create a family-friendly, a woman-friendly environment, then we have to ensure…

JOSIE. Uh-huh.

DAI. And she's just smashing – I think you'd have a lot to talk about.

JOSIE. Yeah. No, definitely. I mean I'm all for anyone who –

DAI. It's a good fit for you.

JOSIE. Yeah. (*Beat.*) But I mean you do know I don't?

DAI. Hmm?

JOSIE. Kids you know I don't have any?

DAI. Right. Yes.

JOSIE. So I've no experience with –

DAI. And is that because of a lack of appropriate childcare provision in the workplace?

JOSIE. Um, I think it's more to do with not having a boyfriend, but –

DAI. Hah. Okay. Alright, and I didn't mean to… I'm not suggesting that just because you're a woman, but I think because you *are* a woman, I think you'll have certain insights, certain knowledge, certain areas –

JOSIE. Not really.

DAI. You'll campaign on a range of issues, naturally, but it's good to have a key… a focus – something you're known for.

JOSIE. Yeah. No, of course. I guess… I just sort of presumed it'd be steel.

DAI (*slightly surprised*). Steel?

JOSIE. Yeah. Maybe manufacturing in general, but –

DAI. Right.

JOSIE. It's what I do. It's what I know.

DAI. Yes. No of course.

JOSIE. Not… I mean I am only a junior, a very junior engineer, but in terms of expertise –

DAI. Yes. Now absolutely, now that is… All I would say is, when it comes to steel, I would tread a little carefully.

JOSIE. Why?

DAI. I would… Steel can… Steel has the potential to become a bit of an albatross, if I'm honest.

JOSIE. Right.

DAI. A bit of a dangerous thing to hitch your wagon to. I'm no expert, not like you, but I do sit in various rooms. I'm meant to give a talk, actually, to some business leaders next week on the future of industry beyond denationalisation. Do you want to hear what I've got so far?

JOSIE. Um, sure.

DAI (*clears throat*). 'There isn't one.'

JOSIE. Ah.

DAI. In layman's terms. Do you see what I'm saying?

JOSIE. Not really.

DAI. I'm saying don't shackle yourself to –

JOSIE. Because I don't – I don't accept that… There are challenges, yes, but opportunities too. It isn't hopeless.

DAI. Well, I am glad to hear that.

JOSIE. I mean it.

DAI. Good. In fact if you could elaborate on that for me before next Tuesday I'd be very grateful.

JOSIE. Sure. Yeah, definitely I can… Do you want to hear about this right now?

DAI. Please.

JOSIE. Right. No, it isn't all sunshine and roses, but… Okay. So first off, the technology – from an engineering side it's… The processes we're developing, they're safer, cleaner, more efficient, and that is –

DAI. Wonderful.

JOSIE. Yeah. Yes, it's great. So exciting. And also awful, but –

DAI. I'm sorry?

JOSIE. Great because it's impressive, it's a testament to everyone involved. And awful because right now progress means efficiency and that means man hours per tonne of steel produced, and, and yeah, as a mathematician – as an engineer – there's only one way those numbers are meant to go. And those numbers are better now. Business is numbers. Science is numbers. I can give you numbers to pass on to people in suits that will show them we are in rude health.

DAI. I see.

JOSIE. But there are people too. There are people behind the numbers, and the more efficient, the more innovative, the better I do my job, the fewer people we get to employ. So I don't like to call that progress – not the progress we need.

DAI. Of course.

JOSIE. So what I would tell them – not to put words in your mouth, but if I was there – I'd tell them we can do better – think bigger, aim higher. I'd tell them we're not out of options. I'd tell them that progress doesn't look like just one thing.

DAI. Right. Thank you.

JOSIE. And let me… I will write you down some numbers, if that'd help.

DAI. That would be marvellous.

JOSIE. And I don't have to campaign on it – whatever's best politically, I'm not… But that is a battle I'll always be fighting, regardless of any… It's who we are – and numbers won't always tell you that. Men and women of steel. That's always going to mean something.

Scene ends.

Scene Seven

2018. VANESSA *and* IAN. *They are discussing a document* IAN *has prepared.*

VANESSA. Steel?

IAN. Trust me.

VANESSA. Seriously?

IAN. Still means quite a lot up here.

VANESSA. Yes, I am aware, but –

IAN. Steel is a vote-winner.

VANESSA. Now look – industry, yes – commitment to industry, manufacturing, advanced technologies, all kinds of –

IAN. Isn't enough.

VANESSA. I am proposing radical investment in infrastructure, retraining schemes, in high-tech, ecologically sound… But this? (*Quoting from a document.*) 'To plot our brightest future we must look back to our greatest triumphs.'

IAN. Objections?

VANESSA. If your greatest triumph was during the Industrial Revolution you might need to move on.

IAN. Steel isn't just a trade, it's an identity.

VANESSA. Tell me about it.

IAN. And it's one you need.

VANESSA. I'm not going to pledge millions to prop up a dying industry because it makes people feel warm and fuzzy inside.

IAN. Steel is what gets Jerry Allen off our backs.

VANESSA. He's not a serious –

IAN. He is. He is your only serious competition. And his main line – the *only* line of attack he needs – is that you're out of touch, an outsider. You don't know what matters to us up here.

VANESSA. Wouldn't it be cheaper just to do a photo-op with a Yorkshire pudding or something?

IAN. It wouldn't have worked against Debbie – she's as local as they come. Even Carol it wouldn't have stuck on, because she's got the business background. This is where you're vulnerable.

VANESSA. But steel isn't… Trust me on this – I do actually know what I'm talking about – steel, without getting too technical, actually just sucks.

IAN. It sucks?

VANESSA. It honestly does. Against all environmental, socio-economic and human-centric metrics, the steel industry as it exists today sucks balls. Didn't always, but does now. It doesn't need another rescue package, it needs putting out of its misery.

IAN. And this is why we have a problem.

VANESSA. On emissions, on working conditions, on financial viability, there are so many better… Why are we even pursuing this?

IAN. And until you can answer that you'll never win here.

VANESSA. Are you a cat person?

IAN. Excuse me?

VANESSA. Or a pet person in general? I doubt it – people with pets really like to tell you about their pets, so… Anyway, the problem with pet-people is they get attached, they form these emotional bonds completely disproportionate to the reality of the situation – are you with me?

IAN. Not entirely.

VANESSA. My mum – she was a cat person, big time – before she got sick. Now she can't really… She adopted this mangy old stray after I moved out – knackered from day one – and then he got some… I don't know, some growth, needed operating, and it was going to cost her five grand. Five thousand pounds! And that isn't – that's not money they just had lying around. Five grand for what was going to extend his life by another six months – a year, tops. But she insisted, so Dad forked out for it.

IAN. And you would've drowned it in the canal?

VANESSA. I very sensitively, very humanely I suggested –

IAN. Classic sign of a psychopath, that.

VANESSA. I wasn't volunteering to do it myself!

IAN. Are you sure you're not a Tory?

VANESSA. My point is the logical thing – any rational person would conclude –

IAN. Just get another cat?

VANESSA. Yes! Exactly! Get another cat, or a goldfish, or a hobby. Cut your losses – move on.

IAN. Easy as that.

VANESSA. No, it's not easy – it's hard, and it's heartbreaking. She really loved that cat, even when its fur was falling out and it started pissing on the carpets. But it wasn't healthy – sometimes only an outsider can see that.

IAN. We are not in a toxic relationship with steel.

VANESSA. You're not even in the relationship any more. They're gone! You need to put yourself back out there! And that's scary – it is – it's terrifying – but you deserve better. The people aren't crying out for steel jobs, they're just crying out for *something*, and this – (*Waving document.*) This is unworthy of them. This is Jerry Allen, promising more of the shitty same because he lacks the imagination to offer anything new. Screw that. This isn't a pit town. It's not some little hamlet in the arse-end of nowhere with one road in and one road out. There are options. And we need more options and better options, yes, but that's what we should be investing our energy in. The truth that dare not speak its name isn't that the steel industry is doomed, it's that it's actually fine that it is.

IAN. Do you actually want to win this?

VANESSA. We are going to win.

IAN. Not if you ever say anything like that again.

VANESSA. Ian, come on –

IAN. No. No, you will hear me. I'm not here to tell you what to do once you're in office, I'm just trying to drag you over the finish line. You need this. You need something, because we are taking on water fast and this is the best way I know how to bail you out. Please. Listen to me.

VANESSA. Wow. Now you're actually scaring me a little.

IAN. Good. Get scared, learn the numbers, sell it hard. Don't blow it.

Scene ends.

Scene Eight

A split timeline. DAI, *in 1988, and* VANESSA, *in 2018, are both making speeches at Cutler's Hall.*

DAI. Master Cutler –

VANESSA. Ladies and gentlemen –

DAI. Distinguished guests –

VANESSA. Friends –

DAI. Brothers –

VANESSA. Comrades.

DAI. These are uncertain times.

VANESSA. This is an age of innovation.

DAI. There are worries. There are fears.

VANESSA. There are challenges, yes, but opportunities as well.

DAI. There is the suggestion in some parts that what we do – who we are – the very essence of our being is under threat. That perhaps we are already far too late – the damage has been done – that there is no way back from here.

VANESSA. The Labour Party has a plan – a plan that will leave no citizen behind.

DAI. But if there is no way back, then let there be no doubt that we shall be offering an alternative way forward.

VANESSA. And we in Labour are continuing to do what we have always done. To defend the rights of the many. To strengthen communities. To provide opportunity – opportunity for all – opportunity for anyone who will grasp it. Master Cutler, I say to you that the purpose of government – the purpose of the Labour Party – is to make spoons. We make spoons for the simple reason that people need to eat, and we must ensure everyone has the means to. Conservative governments see things differently. They say, 'Well, everyone I know has a spoon already – they've got drawers full of them. This fellow here, he was actually *born* with a very nice spoon just sitting there right in his mouth. Why should I spend my money making something that all of *my* friends have already?' They will tell you that the people are not really hungry, they are simply lazy. They will look to their full plates and not believe anybody's cupboards could be bare.

But I'm not talking about free lunches. The Labour Party doesn't want – has never been in the business of handouts. All we want to do is make sure everybody has a spoon – we want to make sure everybody has the tools they need to feed themselves. Making spoons – that's what I got into government for. And not silver spoons – spoons of solid steel! As your Metro Mayor I'm going to make sure we're right back in the business of making things, and that there is a spine of steel in everything we do.

DAI*'s closing speech is altogether a bit more rousing and successful than* VANESSA*'s.*

DAI. Now this, my friends, is what I call on you to do. I call on you to be brave. I call on you to be resolute. I call on you to hold your nerve, and honour all of those who came before us. To look to the example they set. To build upon their legacy. At times like this it falls upon us all to be Men of Steel. For we are stronger than we know. For our faith shall be unwavering. For that steel is not just something we make – that our fathers made, and their fathers before them – it is something inside of us. Something at our core. We are – yes, we are – those things we forged. We poured our molten selves into each mould, tempered the metal with the sweat from our brows, kept the furnace blazing with our very breath – but our lives do not begin and end at the factory gates. We are not defined by this, and this alone. And we'll fight – we shall fight – to keep those jobs – to keep those gates open – to keep making those things of strength and beauty that have made us the envy of the world. But whatever happens, whatever fate our future holds, we shall always be Men of Steel. That can never be taken from us. That can never be cast into doubt. Men of Steel, who shall not be downtrodden. Men of Steel, who shall not be overlooked, or cast aside. Men of Steel, who cannot be forgotten, forsaken, humbled or humiliated, because we were made too well for that. We are Men of Steel, and we shall never lose our shine!

End of Act One.

ACT TWO

Scene One

Split scene. DAI *and* VANESSA *are both reading newspaper accounts of their recent speeches.* DAI *holds an actual newspaper,* VANESSA *perhaps consults a tablet.*

DAI. 'All hail the Steel Caesar'.

VANESSA. 'Make way for the Steel Lady'.

DAI (*calling over his shoulder, off stage*). You read this?

VANESSA (*to herself*). Jesus Christ.

DAI (*continues reading*). 'The city's very own Welsh Windbag, councillor Dai Griffiths, made a barnstorming speech to Party faithful last night, but anyone hoping the council would be adopting a less severe – or even less insane – stance were bound to be disappointed.'

He chuckles.

VANESSA. 'Miss Gallacher, with her cropped curls and plunging silk blouse cut an…' Oh, for crying out… 'cut an *exotic* figure at Cutler's Hall…'

DAI (*still calling off*). Excelled themselves this time.

VANESSA. 'The outfit said "Hello Boys", and she intended to seduce. "I'm one of you," she pleaded, though many will still need convincing.'

DAI. 'Perhaps the hills are to blame (seven, just like Rome, the locals never tire of telling you); the thinner air causing Mr Griffiths to lose all his senses…'

VANESSA. 'For all the predictable Tory-bashing and lip service to local industry, this was not a typical call to arms. But then Miss Gallacher is not your typical Labour candidate. With her…' Christ Almighty. 'Her lavish praise of public-private partnerships and a stern pledge to help people help themselves, the tone was more Mrs T than TUC.'

DAI. 'Whatever the source of his lunacy, this Steel Caesar of the People's Republic took great pleasure in laying out his stall.'

VANESSA (*calling off*). Can you believe them?

DAI (*also calling off*). You getting all this?

1988. A shift in light, as VANESSA *now becomes* JOSIE, *jumping into* DAI*'s timeline.*

JOSIE. How're you feeling?

DAI. I've been called some pretty spectacular things before, but –

JOSIE. Yeah. Although –

DAI. Your handiwork, is this.

JOSIE. I only –

DAI. Your masterpiece.

JOSIE. I… You did ask for… Not that I'm, I didn't, I wasn't –

DAI. Relax.

JOSIE. I didn't realise you were going to use quite so much of what I gave you, if I'm honest.

DAI. Why wouldn't I? It was all magnificent. (*Chuckles.*) The Steel Caesar!

JOSIE. So you're… you're happy with – ?

DAI. Don't you think I'm suitably imperial?

JOSIE. No, of course. I just –

DAI. I mean Caesar is… He's one of the greats, isn't he? The greatest, arguably. Not one of the… like the… the horse one?

JOSIE. The horse one?

DAI. The mad one. Y'know – horses – violins.

JOSIE. Violins? Oh… Nero? Fiddled while –

DAI. Right. Yes. Fiddled with horses while Rome burned.

JOSIE *giggles.*

But seriously – seriously though – schoolboy error. Who uses Caesar as an insult? Who thinks being Caesar is a bad thing?

JOSIE. Brutus?

DAI. Alright, smart alec, but – but the point is – they're calling me an emperor. They're giving me power – status – this shows I'm under their skin.

JOSIE. Right.

DAI. Nicest thing they've ever said about me. Steel Caesar, it just sounds… Trips off the… It isn't… I don't know – Pig Iron Napoleon –

JOSIE (*laughs*). Sure.

DAI. Or… Mineshaft Mussolini.

JOSIE. Flat-cap Castro?

DAI. Oh, I don't know – I quite like that actually.

JOSIE. Because on the… I did worry 'Men of Steel' could sound a little – read as Stalinist, but –

DAI. Superman, isn't it?

JOSIE. Which is why I suggested… 'men and women of steel' – it's a bit softer, more inclusive, not as –

DAI. Yes. I mean yes, but it hardly scans.

JOSIE. Right.

DAI. As a piece of oratory.

JOSIE. Hmm.

DAI. And 'men' isn't… Just universal, isn't it? 'Friends, Romans, countrymen.' As in 'mankind' – not excluding –

JOSIE. No.

DAI (*still grinning*). No, it was perfect – pretty perfect, I'd say. I do feel bad for you, actually, but we'll find you something else.

JOSIE. Sorry?

DAI. Other than steel – for you to campaign on. We really must now. A bit of steel, certainly, because they're lapping this up, but you need your own voice, not just parroting…

JOSIE. Right.

DAI. And that sounds horribly unfair, I know, but you understand?

JOSIE. I… Yeah. I mean we're all on the same team, aren't we?

DAI. Absolutely. Yes, absolutely that. 'Steel Caesar'! Hah. Can't get over it. Get them to call you steel anything up here and it's a home run.

Lights shift and we're in 2018, JOSIE *and* DAI *immediately becoming* VANESSA *and* IAN. *The article is still being discussed.*

VANESSA. 'The Steel Lady'?

IAN. Try not to –

VANESSA. 'Close your eyes and you'd swear the city had found its own self-styled Steel Lady.'

IAN. Ignore it. Don't rise to it.

VANESSA. Ignore it?

IAN. It's trash. It's a gossip blog.

VANESSA. 'Self-styled', as if I've intentionally, actively modelled myself on… I feel sick – actually physically sick –

IAN. If you look at it from a… 'Steel Lady' – 'Woman of Steel' – same thing –

VANESSA. They are not the same thing!

IAN. In so many words –

VANESSA. 'Woman of Steel' gets a statue – 'Steel Lady' gets an… an effigy.

IAN. It's what we wanted. Steel is good. Steel ticks boxes.

VANESSA. Come on!

IAN. Strong, tough, local – everything we planned –

VANESSA. And that's honestly what you think they're implying, is it?

IAN. Doesn't matter. We lean into it – take ownership of –

VANESSA. Uh-huh. And I don't look like an idiot at all in that scenario, do I?

IAN. I'm not sure I follow.

VANESSA. 'Oh, Steel Lady – thank you very much. You love a bit of steel up here, don't you? How welcoming! What an honour!' Entirely oblivious to any of the… No, because I'm just another airhead millennial with no sense of history – file Thatcher alongside the Spice Girls under hashtag-feminism hashtag-boss-bitch culturally tone-deaf bullshit –

IAN. Yes, alright. Fair point.

VANESSA. Too stupid to even know when I'm being insulted. No, must be a compliment – couldn't possibly still be upset about Maggie round here, could they? Not after all this time. Well tell me, Ian – do you reckon there might be one or two who still hold a grudge?

IAN. I dare say.

VANESSA. So if we could try really quite hard to avoid 'leaning in' to any comparison between… (*Glancing down at the article.*) I mean, for fuck's sake – they even gave me her hair – they photoshopped it.

IAN. Didn't see that.

VANESSA. That's 'self-styled', is it? It's slander – I should sue for defamation.

IAN. Alright, just –

VANESSA. But then I can't – I can't actually call them out on it either, can I? I can't say 'Steel Lady – how dare you?' Because then I'm insulting steel – I'm too good for steel. Like I've told them to go shove their Bessemer converter where the sun don't shine.

IAN. Bessemer converter?

VANESSA. I told you I know my stuff.

IAN. I'm impressed.

VANESSA. I told you I didn't want to get drawn into… Well screw them. It's pathetic, it's cheap, it's beneath me, and you know what, I won't engage with it. We don't give them the satisfaction. No comment. How's that for steel?

Scene ends.

Scene Two

1988. DAI *is visiting* JOSIE. *She isn't well.*

DAI. I brought you soup.

JOSIE. Dai –

DAI. Don't worry, Margie made it, not me.

JOSIE. She didn't have to.

DAI. I did suggest it might trigger a flashback, but she insisted. Chicken and leek – highly restorative.

JOSIE. I'm fine.

DAI. You're not.

JOSIE. Honestly –

DAI. She's on quite the health kick. I bear the brunt of it. She said to me, she said, 'Dai, if you are going to insist on calling yourself Caesar you might try a salad once in a while.'

JOSIE *smiles.*

That's better. Now, I've also come for a serious word in your ear.

JOSIE. What? What's happened?

DAI. Consider this your official cease and desist order.

JOSIE. I'm not –

DAI. You're meant to be on bed rest.

JOSIE. I am.

DAI. I have it on good authority that in the past twenty-four hours you've called Andy Yates at Highways and Byways, Roger at the NUM, Gareth in Town Planning said you'd phoned three times –

JOSIE. And I phoned them all from my bed.

DAI. You don't need to be doing any of this. You're running a fever and you're still campaigning twice as hard as any councillor in the city – ten times harder than most. You can slow down a little.

JOSIE. It's just a bit of cold.

DAI. Bill held this seat for twenty years and I never saw him do so much as give out a flyer.

JOSIE. I'm not Bill.

DAI. Which is only a good thing, as far as I'm concerned.

JOSIE. And you're not everyone.

DAI. Can you not…? I know you're a worrier, but please believe me when I say you are every inch the attractive candidate. Not right this moment, I'll concede – I prefer you without the phlegm.

JOSIE. You don't see what I see – you don't notice it.

DAI. Josie –

JOSIE. I can't take anything for granted.

DAI. Speaking from experience –

JOSIE. You don't have experience of this. You don't have to fight like I do. Please.

DAI. And if you collapse with nervous exhaustion before election night, what was the point of any of this?

JOSIE. I told you I'm fine.

DAI. Then at least try to… Preserve your energy. Focus your approach. Helen said you had a good chat about childcare.

JOSIE. Yeah. You're right – she's brilliant.

DAI. I knew you'd hit it off. And that's enough – more than enough for now.

JOSIE. But I still don't know anything about it. I'm not –

DAI. You're a fast learner – you'll be an expert in no time.

JOSIE. Yeah, but –

DAI. No buts. Now, I've been given reheating instructions that even I can follow, so – point me towards your kitchen please.

JOSIE. Okay. It's this way.

Scene ends. Snap to:

Scene Three

2018. VANESSA *and* IAN. IAN *is reading from a document.*

IAN. 'The industry must face certain harsh realities – '

VANESSA. I know what it says.

IAN. 'We believe there is no long-term, financially viable future in – '

VANESSA. I know because I wrote it.

IAN. Quite.

VANESSA. Not… Not all of it, but –

IAN. But enough.

VANESSA. I told you I'd done my research.

IAN. You didn't tell me about this.

VANESSA. These aren't personal opinions. These are the objective findings and recommendations of a politically neutral working group looking into the long-term future of manufacturing.

IAN. Which state the steel industry should be quietly left to die.

VANESSA. Which suggest there are better options –

IAN. Like your mum's mangy old cat.

VANESSA. If you like, yes.

IAN. Do you realise what a complete fucking disaster this is?

VANESSA. I've got some idea, yeah.

IAN. It's not just the… It isn't just this – I mean this is bad enough – this is really pretty bad just by itself –

VANESSA. It isn't –

IAN. But – and just let me… But it's the… You can't write a paper – co-author a paper saying close the factory gates and then turn around and declare yourself the Steel Lady. You just can't!

VANESSA. Which is what I told you! I told you I didn't want to get into steel. I told you there was no future in it. My views haven't changed.

IAN. You stood up, you laid out, you… you and your spoons –

VANESSA. You made me!

IAN. Oh please.

VANESSA. Oh please what?

IAN. Since when has anyone been capable of making Vanessa Gallacher do or say anything she didn't want to?

VANESSA. You insisted, you… I was explicit, I was clear, I was consistent. Industry yes, investment yes, but don't… And you, you said that wasn't good enough. You said just tell them what they want to hear. I warned you –

IAN (*waving the document*). And I didn't know this was out there!

VANESSA. Sure. Except it's kind of your job to know, isn't it?

IAN. If a candidate won't divulge, deliberately conceals –

VANESSA. I never –

IAN. I'm not taking the fall for this. I've been putting out fires for you since day one, but *this*.

VANESSA. If people actually read it – the detail of it – they'd understand… We make a series of recommendations, none of which are –

IAN. 'Labour Mayor declares war on steel.'

VANESSA. That isn't true – it doesn't say –

IAN. This is the… It epitomises the flip-flopping, the opportunism, the hypocrisy of… And why it's perfect, why it's so deadly – is it's the scandal everyone *wants* to believe. Like the pig-fucking – you could just picture it. They look at you, Vanessa, and they think, 'Yeah, yeah, that's her down to a tee. We knew she was never one of us.'

VANESSA. Don't say that.

IAN. Jerry's lot are going to have a field day: Titan of Industry versus the woman who'd sell us for scrap.

VANESSA. So what do we do?

IAN. Now she's asking.

VANESSA. I'm asking for your help, yes.

IAN. Is there more to come?

VANESSA. Sorry?

IAN. Is there any more to…? Have you drowned any puppies lately? Are you carrying Michael Gove's love child?

VANESSA. I… There is nothing else pertinent that I'm aware of, no.

IAN. Right, well let's hope not.

VANESSA. This isn't… I mean, no one's died.

IAN. Not yet.

VANESSA. I haven't done anything wrong. All I did was… This is going to be fine. Ian? This is going to be fine, isn't it?

He doesn't immediately answer. Scene ends.

Scene Four

1988. DAI *waits in a long overcoat and scarf, holding a bundle of flyers.* JOSIE *enters, in a rush. She's a bit shaky and trying to hide it.*

JOSIE. Sorry, sorry.

DAI. Don't worry.

JOSIE. You must be frozen.

DAI. I'm layered up. And you – are you okay to be out?

JOSIE. Yeah, I'm good. Much better.

They start talking together.

DAI. / So I thought we could –

JOSIE. It's just my parents, they had a –

DAI. Sorry.

JOSIE. No, sorry, go on.

DAI. Your parents?

JOSIE. Doesn't matter. We can just get going.

DAI. Are they alright?

JOSIE. Yeah. Yeah, I just… I had to go over this morning. But they're fine – they're both fine.

DAI. Good.

JOSIE. Yeah. Honestly.

DAI. Are you sure?

JOSIE. They had a… No, they are, but… Sorry. It's nothing. Someone smashed one of the shop windows last night.

DAI. Oh.

JOSIE. Yeah.

DAI. Right.

JOSIE. And, y'know, because they live above… Because their flat is –

DAI. But they're…? They weren't – ?

JOSIE. No, they're both okay. Mum slept through it, so –

DAI. And did they take much?

JOSIE. No. No, they didn't take anything, I don't think.

DAI. Oh. (*Beat.*) Well good. That's good, isn't it?

JOSIE. Um, yeah.

DAI. I wonder why? Do you think they were scared off, or – ?

JOSIE. Um, no. No, I don't think they wanted to… They put a brick, uh, through the window. They weren't trying to break in, they just wanted to… to…

DAI. Ah.

JOSIE. To do whatever these people want to do when they… Shit. Sorry.

DAI. I see. (*Beat.*) And you think, you think this was a…?

JOSIE. 'Go Home.' There was a note, um, tied to the brick. Said 'Go home'.

DAI. Right.

JOSIE. Fairly unambiguous, really.

DAI. Jesus.

JOSIE. Not really a lot of… of…

DAI. Are you okay? What can I – ?

JOSIE. And what I kept on thinking, I mean beyond the, the, the shaking rage and the general… They live there. Mum and Dad – they literally live above the shop.

DAI. Must have been terrifying.

JOSIE. No, but I mean… They're right there. And you're saying 'go home' – they were home. He was in bed. So what you've made him do, what you've done is you've got him up, you've marched him downstairs to, to, to pick up broken glass on his hands and knees and then find this note, this scrawled, stupid, childish… He was home.

DAI. I don't have words, honestly.

JOSIE. No.

DAI. Have they spoken to the police?

JOSIE. Yeah. They came while I was there. They were fine – nice – took it as seriously as you'd hope.

DAI. Good.

JOSIE. But they're not… Most likely just an isolated incident, they said. They did have one other, but that was – I was still in school – must've been twenty years ago.

DAI. One other…?

JOSIE. Another window put out, yeah.

DAI. Right.

JOSIE. But y'know, two in twenty years, I mean that's… Not too bad going, is it?

DAI. I would say once is far too much.

JOSIE. Yeah. Of course yeah, but –

DAI. But they're not being targeted.

JOSIE. No. My dad, he's… Well, you've met him. Difficult man to dislike.

DAI. Yes.

JOSIE. And we always say he worries too much about getting people to like him, but… The officer – one of the officers – he asked to see the note – the 'go home' note – and Dad went dead funny. Said he didn't see why they needed it, then he doesn't know where it is, then he thinks he threw it away, and we can all tell he's lying, so I say, 'Dad, what's the matter? What's going on?' and the police, they're nice, but they're insistent, and they're starting to get suspicious now, and eventually, eventually he throws his hands up and he says, 'Alright, fine, fine, just don't overreact,' and he fetches it, and I understand now, because it's not just any scrap of paper, it's written on one of these. (*Pulls out a crumpled flyer.*) 'Josie Kirkwood: Your New Councillor.'

Pause.

'Josie Kirkwood: Go Home.'

DAI. Oh. That is… That is just…

JOSIE. So you're right – no one's targeting them. No, it's me.

DAI. Josie –

JOSIE. And all they ever wanted for me – a good man, couple of kids, a quiet, respectable… Couldn't give them any of that – only this.

DAI. This isn't your doing.

JOSIE. That's my face.

DAI. You cannot be / held –

JOSIE. Which I never wanted printed on anything, but…

DAI. The police, they, they… They're going to find whoever… And I won't allow… I will do everything I can to make sure –

JOSIE. Is this just…? Is this how it's going to be now?

DAI. Of course not.

JOSIE. Because I thought… And no disrespect, but who cares this much about the council? This isn't high profile – it's not drinks with the ambassador and a cover spread for *Smash Hits*, it's boring, behind-the-scenes anonymity.

DAI. Generally speaking, yes.

JOSIE. It isn't painting a target on your back. It isn't bricks through my parents' windows. I didn't sign up for that.

DAI. No.

JOSIE. If that's what comes with the job then…

DAI. It isn't. I promise you, this isn't… (*Gesturing to the wodge of flyers he's still holding.*) Look, we will resolve it, but let's forget about this for today. Let me buy you breakfast.

JOSIE. I'll be okay.

DAI. I know you will. Come on – cup of tea, at least – fuel of empires.

JOSIE. I'll be… I just…

DAI. Something warm and you'll be right as rain. But what I won't – what I can't allow – we will not be intimidated. We will not be ruled by fear, or dictated to by the pea-brained troglodytes who represent the lowest – the absolute dregs of our society. The actions of imbeciles shall not keep the world from knowing Josie Kirkwood.

JOSIE. Why're you so nice to me?

DAI. Because you are the future, and I'd like to stay on the right side of you. Come on.

JOSIE. No.

DAI. Excuse me?

JOSIE. We give out half of these, then we stop for tea.

DAI. Josie –

JOSIE. We plough on. I'm not going to hide behind the rosette. If I'm asking for their vote they should know who I am.

DAI. If you're sure.

JOSIE. I'm sure. We're on the home stretch. Josie Kirkwood's coming home.

Scene ends.

Scene Five

2018. VANESSA *is just finishing a campaign speech.*

VANESSA. Because we deserve better. Better than we've been given, better than we've been promised, better than we've grown accustomed to. I don't just want to build houses, I want castles. We won't just bring jobs, but vocations. I won't just be your mayor, I will be a citizen, working beside you day after day to bring you the future you truly deserve. Thank you.

Slightly lukewarm applause. As VANESSA *steps off,* IAN *is waiting. Their opening exchanges are a bit stilted, like they're still slightly tiptoeing around each other.*

Okay?

IAN. Oh. Yes, yes, very…

VANESSA. Nice crowd – good turnout – thanks for that.

IAN. I do my best.

VANESSA. I'm not sure about 'castles' – bit grandiose, maybe? A bit Marie Antoinette.

IAN. Oh?

VANESSA. Yeah, a bit… 'The peasants have no affordable housing' – 'Then let them live in castles!'

IAN. I see. (*Beat.*) I'm not sure it's a reference many will be leaping to, but…

VANESSA. No.

IAN. But we can –

VANESSA. I'm probably just second-guessing myself.

IAN. Tweak it if you want to.

VANESSA. Yeah. (*Beat.*) Are you alright? Is everything – ?

IAN. Can I have a word?

VANESSA. Aren't we already?

IAN. Yes. Sorry. Yes.

VANESSA. What is it?

IAN. It's…

IAN *glances around and they move slightly to one side, as if stepping out of anyone's earshot.*

VANESSA. What's the matter?

IAN. I asked you if there was anything else.

VANESSA. What're you talking about?

IAN. Vanessa –

VANESSA. What?

IAN. Simon Mullaney.

VANESSA (*after a pause*). What about him?

IAN. You know him?

VANESSA. Would you be asking if I didn't?

IAN. Professor Simon Mullaney was the most frequently cited expert in your paper on –

VANESSA. Again, it wasn't *my* paper, I was part / of a –

IAN. Part of a working group, yes. And the testimony of Simon Mullaney formed a significant part of your findings.

VANESSA. In certain areas, yes.

IAN. Certain key areas.

VANESSA. Maybe. What is – ?

IAN. And he was your boyfriend at the time?

VANESSA. No.

IAN. No?

VANESSA. No. He was never really… Our thing was… It wasn't a… But whatever it was it was over long before –

IAN. But you brought him in – that was you?

VANESSA. Yes.

IAN. And he was paid a fee?

VANESSA. I'm sure he was. As he should've been.

IAN. I see.

VANESSA. He was a relevant, highly respected expert working in –

IAN (*quoting from a document*). 'Climate Scientist attempts citizen's arrest on Russian oil baron.'

VANESSA. That was… That's an entirely separate issue. That wasn't –

IAN. 'Loopy Prof in hot water over Thames stunt.'

VANESSA. Again, separate. And misleading. He only –

IAN. 'How shedding my shoes helped me bare my soul.' Professor Simon Mullaney. That was for the *Guardian*, believe it or not.

VANESSA. What's your point?

IAN. Something of a character, would you say?

VANESSA. Simon is a brilliant man with a lot of strongly held beliefs, but he is rigorous and scientific, and… and all his findings, all his recommendations on the work we did together were –

IAN. Jesus!

VANESSA. Were uncontroversial, were fastidiously –

IAN. Are you starting to understand just how unequivocally fucked you are?

VANESSA. No! No, I'm not actually.

IAN. Right.

VANESSA. How is this…? How have I behaved…? I was invited on to a working group, we looked at the evidence presented to us, we spoke to relevant experts, we made our recommendations.

IAN. And those expert recommendations – terrible recommendations – politically terrible, regardless of any… They just happened to come from some barefoot mad-haired eco-anarchist who you were carrying on with.

VANESSA. He is a professor of environmental science.

IAN. Right.

VANESSA. Who I… I briefly, long before… And it wasn't 'carrying on', it was a… a…

IAN. Yes?

VANESSA. We didn't want to put a label on it, but…

IAN *rolls his eyes.*

But it was an adult, consensual –

IAN. Good.

VANESSA. I'm not ashamed of it. It wasn't sordid or coercive or in any way… We weren't picking out wedding china, but it was still a… a relationship, of sorts, that was entirely –

IAN. A polyamorous relationship? (*Beat.*) That is the term, isn't it? Polyamory? That is right?

VANESSA. Fuck off, Ian.

IAN. I'm not… I understand the London dating scene is very…

VANESSA. It was a… Why am I having this conversation with you?

IAN. Because you failed to have it with anyone else back when you should've.

VANESSA. We were each other's primary partners. He would also see other people, I did not. I ended the relationship – or whatever the fuck it was – eventually, because it turns out that I'm all for free love on paper but in practice it does my head in. Are you happy now?

IAN (*deadpan*). Ecstatic.

VANESSA. None of this should matter.

IAN. Jerry Allen is a family man.

VANESSA. Jerry Allen has pinched the arse of every female Labour Party volunteer this side of the Rother Valley, so let's not –

IAN. And unless you can prove that, you'd be wise not to repeat it.

VANESSA. Fuck! This is… Fuck! Who else has this?

IAN. Don't know.

VANESSA. Great.

IAN. But I found it, and I'm hardly Benedict What's-his-face.

VANESSA. Right.

IAN. If Jerry doesn't yet, we can assume it's only a matter of time.

VANESSA. Right. Okay then, right. Well that is… Okay, yes, not ideal – I see that. So. So, we… How should we do this? Should I talk to Simon? We should warn him if… And what about Party HQ? Do we make our own plan first, or…?

IAN. Some quiet words have been had already.

VANESSA. Oh. Oh right.

IAN. Nothing – not keeping you out of the loop –

VANESSA. No.

IAN. But just the speed that these things –

VANESSA. Yeah, sure. (*Beat.*) Okay. Well go on then.

IAN. Right. Well look, this isn't… There's a feeling… This is a must-win race for us – for everyone, here to Westminster –

VANESSA. Agreed.

IAN. And it was a can't-lose, but –

VANESSA. I still / think –

IAN. But it really – no – we really can't say that any more. And that isn't… Bottom line, a loss is unacceptable – can't happen – can't be allowed – so we all have to do whatever it takes to ensure against that.

VANESSA. Absolutely.

IAN. For the Party. Above all else.

VANESSA. Right.

IAN. You understand that's everyone's priority.

VANESSA. Great.

IAN. Good. And if we're honest, this was never the best fit for you, was it?

VANESSA. I'm sorry?

IAN. You tried – I know more than anyone, you bent over backwards, but –

VANESSA. What're you saying?

IAN. The consensus is… perhaps your candidacy has run its course.

Pause.

VANESSA (*laughs*). Are you serious?

IAN. I'm sorry.

VANESSA. You want me to stand down?

IAN. We think –

VANESSA. Because I fucked some guy who makes his own yogurt?

IAN. Not just because of that.

VANESSA. We are weeks away – literally weeks.

IAN. There's a… Obviously time is a factor, yes, but –

VANESSA. Jesus. Fucking Jesus.

IAN. The bigger picture is –

VANESSA. You're throwing me to the wolves?

IAN. No – absolutely not. Everyone wants to make sure you're looked after.

VANESSA. Sure. Right. Sure.

IAN. We will –

VANESSA. After I've been chased out with pitchforks?

IAN. We can protect you. We think so long as you're not the candidate here this needn't come out at all.

VANESSA. No. No, no, no, this is… No. This is crazy. This is… Forget me for a second, this would look terrible – this would make us all look –

IAN. Not if we give the right reason.

VANESSA. And what reason is that? (*Pause.*) Go on.

IAN. We were… I thought, potentially… And I'm not…

VANESSA. Spit it out.

IAN. I thought your mother.

VANESSA. Right.

IAN. I know that sounds –

VANESSA. No, very good.

IAN. People would –

VANESSA. Hmm. Good old early-onset dementia, it's got to be useful for something.

IAN. I'm sorry.

VANESSA. For what? The decaying of my mother's neural pathways or my political career?

IAN. I am personally, deeply very… Whatever our, um, differences –

VANESSA. This is bullshit! You must see that.

IAN. I've been promised – I asked, and they are fully… If you bow out gracefully they will absolutely find you something else.

VANESSA. Right.

IAN. You're young. General Election's only four years away – maybe much sooner – who knows?

VANESSA. Hah! Sure.

IAN. I've been given assurances –

VANESSA. That is just… Of all the… No! No, this is it! This is the final… I make a success of this or I am over – through – done – no more second chances.

IAN. You'd be surprised.

VANESSA. Not for someone like me.

IAN. No –

VANESSA. Yes! Two years – that was all I had as an MP – two sorry years in a seat nobody thought I'd ever win in the first place. No support. No resources. And do you know what I lost it by? Do you?

IAN. No.

VANESSA. A hundred and twenty-seven votes. One hundred and twenty-seven! I've been to weddings with bigger congregations than that motherfucker's majority.

IAN. Like you say, it was a tough gig. You exceeded everyone's –

VANESSA. No, but nonetheless – Vanessa Gallacher – former MP – unseated before I'd even got the seat warm. This was my redemption arc – my one shot.

IAN. You'll be looked after.

VANESSA. You think?

IAN. We do look after our own.

VANESSA. Of course you do. Yeah, I don't doubt that.

IAN. This is best for you too. Home or no home, you don't fit here. Stick it out and they will paint you as out-of-touch, parachuted-in, liberal metropolitan elite with your blue-sky whatevers and your open relationships and your fundamental lack of understanding for everything that makes this city great.

VANESSA. They tried that already.

IAN. Vanessa, please –

VANESSA. They can't do this! How would they even do this? If I were to – *if* – there'd be a, a what, some kind of…?

IAN. There'd be a fast-tracked selection process.

VANESSA. Right.

IAN. Local Campaign Forum would make a shortlist. Might not be time for a full member vote, but all above board and as transparent as time allows.

VANESSA. Naturally.

IAN. Of course everyone's very keen we should all get on the same page as soon as possible, time being of the essence.

VANESSA. Yes. Yes, of course.

Pause.

IAN. So – ?

VANESSA. So? So what? Jesus Ian, just give me a… I do apologise if I can't commit hari-kari in the time it takes to boil a kettle. So just –

IAN. Yes. Sorry. Yes.

VANESSA. Jesus. I'm tired. You know what, mostly I really am just extraordinarily tired of all of this. Just… Do whatever you need to do, speak to whoever you need to speak to. I'm going to talk to you in the morning.

IAN. I really am –

VANESSA. In the morning. Please. Not now.

IAN. Yes. Of course. Sleep, um… sleep well.

Scene ends.

Scene Six

1988. We hear the council election results being announced.

OFFICER. Bilston, Arthur, Conservative party. Seven hundred and forty-three. Cartwright, Shirley, Social and Liberal Democrats, one thousand, one hundred and twenty-one. Foster, Malcolm, Social Democratic party, three hundred and two. Kirkwood, Josie, Labour Party, three thousand, one hundred and eighty-four. Therefore Josie Kirkwood is duly elected as the new councillor for –

The voice fades out, covered by applause. Lights up on DAI *as* JOSIE *enters. Both are smartly dressed.*

DAI. There she is!

JOSIE. Dai!

She embraces him.

DAI. Councillor Kirkwood.

She bows to him.

JOSIE. Councillor Griffiths.

DAI. How do you like the sound of it?

JOSIE. Got quite the ring, I'd say.

DAI. Suits you.

JOSIE. Thank you. Not quite Caesar, but…

DAI. Well, Rome wasn't built in a day.

JOSIE. No.

DAI (*consulting a piece of paper*). Three thousand, one hundred and eighty-four. That's fifty-nine-point-five per cent of total votes cast. That is a three-point-two-per-cent swing in our favour from last time around. That, my dear, is a very satisfactory day at the office.

JOSIE. And on what – twenty-five-per-cent turnout?

DAI (*checks*). Twenty-seven.

JOSIE. Not stellar.

DAI. Perfectly respectable.

JOSIE. Yeah.

DAI. Enjoy it. Enjoy all of this while you can.

JOSIE. Oh, like that is it?

DAI. I didn't mean –

JOSIE. I know.

DAI. Savour the victories, for they can feel few and far between, believe me. I saw your parents were in. Are they proud?

JOSIE. Yeah. Yeah, I think so. Think they'd still rather I had a boyfriend, but –

DAI. They are, trust me.

JOSIE. Hope so.

DAI. You've come a long way, Councillor Kirkwood.

JOSIE. Well, I was guided by the best.

DAI. Ah, too kind. Drink?

JOSIE. I've had a couple already.

DAI. Not driving, are you?

JOSIE. No, but –

DAI. Then I insist. Can you stomach whiskey?

JOSIE. Sure.

DAI. My kind of woman. Coming right up.

DAI *pours them two generous glasses.*

Cheers.

JOSIE. Cheers.

DAI. To your victory.

JOSIE. To ours. To the Republic!

DAI. Ah, yes.

They chink glasses and drink.

JOSIE (*beginning cautiously*). You know I heard a… I've got a new nickname, in some circles. With some who aren't still calling me 'Two Soups'.

DAI. Oh? Nothing – ?

JOSIE. No, nothing bad, nothing… Well, I don't think it is, really. They call me 'The Project'.

DAI. The Project?

JOSIE. Yeah.

DAI. What does that – ?

JOSIE. 'See her? She's The Project.' 'You're Dai's little Project, aren't you?'

DAI. I don't think I –

JOSIE. They reckon you're on some Pygmalion kick – we've got a Henry-Higgins-Eliza-Doolittle thing going on.

DAI. The idle gossip of bored Party members should be –

JOSIE. No, I know. And I wasn't… It didn't upset me.

DAI. Good. Because I'd hate you to think –

JOSIE. No, it's fine, honest, but it got me thinking… I do know how much you've looked out for me. Had my back. Made sure I –

DAI. All I've done is –

JOSIE. Is take an interest. Which is a… maybe it shouldn't be, but it is a big deal, actually, and… And anyway, I got to thinking that maybe I hadn't really said thank you enough.

DAI. To me?

JOSIE. Yeah.

DAI. What for?

JOSIE. For not just… For taking that interest. For… and I'm not saying they're right, that I'm your protégée or anything, I'm not… But if you were going to choose someone to, to look after you could've done what everyone else does which is just find a younger version of yourself, y'know –

DAI. And who's to say I didn't?

JOSIE. Alright. Yeah, alright. But that's just it, isn't it? You were able to… Oh bollocks, I'm starting to tear up, that's embarrassing – this is why I shouldn't do speeches. Pushing on – all I'm saying is you have been one of the only, more or less the only person to accept on face value that I have a right to be here, and that is actually pretty extraordinary, so, so… So I'm just saying I'm grateful, really. I hope you know how grateful I am, and if you don't then I hope I can find a way to show you. (*Beat.*) Okay, that's it.

She stops. DAI *pulls* JOSIE *towards him and kisses her. It isn't aggressive as such, but it is forceful, and takes* JOSIE *entirely by surprise.*

Dai!

DAI. You're very welcome.

JOSIE (*pulling herself away*). Uh… uh, no, I –

DAI. It's okay.

JOSIE. I'm sorry.

DAI. You've nothing to be sorry for.

JOSIE. No, I didn't –

DAI. No one's here – no one's going to burst in.

JOSIE. No, but… Oh God. I am really sorry, but –

DAI (*amused*). Relax! Relax –

JOSIE. This is my fault. I'm an idiot. I've had a drink, and –

DAI. This is fine. This is allowed.

JOSIE. But I… Look, Dai, you know how much I respect you –

DAI. And I respect you too. I respect you as a colleague – I respect you as a woman. You're a magnificent woman, Josie.

JOSIE. But I think you misunderstood me.

DAI. I don't think I did.

JOSIE. No, you did, and that's my fault, but –

DAI. 'I hope I can find a way to show you my gratitude'?

JOSIE. Okay, that was –

DAI (*with a chuckle. He's much too physically close*). It's okay! You needn't be so jumpy. Tonight is about celebrating. Tonight is about exciting new partnerships – forging a brighter future. Let me welcome you into the fold, Councillor.

He goes in for another kiss. JOSIE *breaks away.*

JOSIE. I don't think this is a good idea.

DAI. We can go somewhere else.

JOSIE. I don't want this.

DAI. I'm sorry?

JOSIE. I don't… I am really sorry if I led you to believe otherwise, but I'm not interested in you in that way.

DAI. You're not?

JOSIE. I feel awful.

DAI. Right.

JOSIE. I think you're brilliant –

DAI. I think you're not being entirely honest with yourself, are you, Josie?

JOSIE. What do you mean?

DAI. How many times have you slipped into conversation that you don't have a boyfriend?

JOSIE. I…

DAI. That wasn't meant for me?

JOSIE. No! I never –

DAI. You haven't been flirting with me since day one? Answering the door in your nightie – calling me Caesar?

JOSIE. The papers called you Caesar.

DAI. So I'm a fantasist, am I?

JOSIE. No! No, but –

DAI. No, I didn't think so. So don't play the fool. You've put up a good fight – your honour's still intact – but be honest now: you want this.

JOSIE. I don't.

DAI. Josie –

JOSIE. I… I'm going to get that cab. I'm really sorry.

She begins to leave. He calls after her.

DAI. Funny way of expressing your gratitude.

She stops.

But I suppose now you've got what you wanted.

JOSIE. No –

DAI. You… You were nothing when I found you. Do you think it was easy, doing all this – getting you here?

JOSIE. Dai –

DAI. And now you're Lady Muck, are you? Got it made – don't need me any more. Well, good luck to you.

JOSIE. Can I go?

DAI. Go. Go on. See how far you get. Let's see if you can make it ten yards on your own. Stupid woman. Stupid girl. Don't – don't you dare look at me like that! I am not a bad man. I know who the bad men are – I know what the bad men look like. And you want to line me up beside them? If you had any idea… I work endlessly, tirelessly, I go against my brothers, and for what? To be painted as a monster? Am I not owed anything? Should I not be rewarded? A man who works without recompense is a slave!

I shall not be indentured! I am not duty-bound to fight the fights you cannot win yourselves and be spat on for my efforts. I am not a bad man! But I am a man, yes, and for you that is enough to condemn me. You make enemies of your allies because we can never be good enough for you and that is why you are nowhere! Go. Just get out.

Scene ends.

Scene Seven

2018. VANESSA *present.* IAN *enters with two takeaway coffees.* IAN *is tentative,* VANESSA *is exhausted, her tone initially more subdued-snarky than openly aggressive.*

IAN. Knock knock.

VANESSA. Who's there? Oh, it's the Grim-Up-North Reaper.

IAN. Brought you coffee.

VANESSA (*taking it*). Thanks.

IAN. Think I've finally learnt your order.

VANESSA. Yeah, well it's a skinny latte, isn't it? It's not Fermat's Last Theorem.

IAN (*choosing to ignore this*). You sleep?

VANESSA. What do you think?

IAN. Tough, um, tough night all round. Tough campaign. Lots of…

VANESSA. He's not going to do it.

IAN. Hmm?

VANESSA. Jerry. He's going to get a lot closer than he should, it'll be embarrassing, and ultimately it is going to weaken my mandate a little, but he's not actually going to beat me.

IAN. I see.

VANESSA. But you knew that already.

IAN. Respectfully –

VANESSA. Ah yes, always very respectful.

IAN. I think that's wishful… I think that's underestimating just how damaging –

VANESSA. Yeah, well, what do you know?

IAN. This isn't what I want either.

VANESSA. Right.

IAN. It isn't.

VANESSA. No. No, you must be heartbroken, I'm sure. Dreaming of this moment ever since you were a little girl.

IAN (*struggling to stay scrupulously polite*). This isn't… I beg you, please try to appreciate this is bigger than you. We want – everybody *wanted* this to work with you. Of course we did. We did everything –

VANESSA. Really?

IAN. Yes, very bloody really. You might not have noticed, but there are a lot of us round here who haven't been sleeping much lately.

VANESSA (*dryly*). Well thank you for your service.

IAN. Everything was done; rigged the deck for you every way we could, cleared out the serious competition, put up with endless, endless… Because the word from on high was 'this is our girl' – here's the one who ticks someone's set of boxes. Fine – I'm a good soldier – I can follow orders. But whatever we tried, it wasn't enough. So here we are, day after day, hour after hour, furiously polishing this sorry turd of a campaign, and all the while you're acting like you're the only one whose shit doesn't stink.

VANESSA. Sorry to have been such a burden.

IAN. Except you're not, are you?

VANESSA. Not really, no.

IAN. No. You still think the world's out to get you. You still think this is everyone's fault but your own. And worst of all, you think you're better – smarter – funnier – more advanced – than anyone else in this bloody county, including everyone you want to vote for you.

VANESSA. So what?

IAN. Excuse me?

VANESSA. So what if I am?

IAN. Am what?

VANESSA. Better. Cleverer. That's a bad thing, is it? When did that become…? Don't you want the best people as your leaders? Shouldn't they be your betters? Isn't that why you put them in charge?

IAN. So now you're just openly admitting it?

VANESSA. You're damn right I am! Why shouldn't I? To get to where I am today it has been an absolute necessity to always be the smartest person at the table. That's the bare minimum. And – here's the kicker – and it's equally crucial that no one at the table ever acknowledge it. To get in the room with the white men you have to be twice as clever as any of them, but to stay there you have to play dumb. Well I wasn't going to do that this time.

IAN. And look where it's got you.

VANESSA. And that's on me?

IAN. Has it ever crossed your mind, Vanessa, that people don't like you not because you're a woman, but because you're a stuck-up bitch?

VANESSA. Oh fuck you!

IAN. Touché.

VANESSA. Yes. Fuck you. Fuck you right up the decommissioned mineshaft. I am not – I was never the problem here.

IAN. No?

VANESSA. No, sir. So fuck you and all the other butt-hurt old white men who hear one woman speaking and scream that they're being silenced. Fuck you and your little-England backward-looking Brexit-voting salt-of-the-earth ever-so-'umble insidiously sexist, racist, no-I-listen-to-Elton-John-so-I-can't-be-homophobic, not-got-an-issue-with-Muslims-so-long-as-they-don't-look-act-or-sound-like-Muslims post-colonial, patriarchal bullshit.

IAN. Right.

VANESSA. Fuck the lot of you.

IAN. That's how it is, is it?

VANESSA. Uh-huh.

IAN. Well then, respectfully, fuck you too.

VANESSA. Okay.

IAN. Fuck you and all your beard-sculpting gap-year trust-fund gender-variant spiralised-avocado snapchat Shoreditch snowflake friends.

VANESSA. Wow.

IAN. Every last one.

VANESSA. How would you even spiralise an avocado? Jesus!

IAN (*ignoring this*). You – I can't believe you're the ones we're courting! You're our future? You're the next generation of Labour leaders? God help us. You don't have a clue what we stand for – what we've been through. You share a dozen online petitions a day but we've got to walk over hot coals before you'll register to vote. You'll spend two hours queueing for a burger but you've never seen a picket line. You are the most entitled –

VANESSA. We're entitled?

IAN. You only love Socialism because you think it means you'll get everything for free. Sorry, sweetheart, Labour means graft. Real work. Honest work. Not sat around drinking your four-pound lattes and wondering why you're always broke.

VANESSA. Right. Okay, right. No, this is… Okay, so firstly – lattes, still? Honestly? Seriously, of all the… Lattes are still your signifier of wacky millennial excess? This is slumming it. We drink cold-brew. We drink aeropress. We drink kombucha.

IAN. What in God's name is – ?

VANESSA. I don't know! None of us know, and it's disgusting, but we drink it anyway, because we're all awful, awful people. No one in Shoreditch has drunk a latte since 1993. Ask me why. Go on – ask me.

IAN. Why?

VANESSA. Because we're all lactose-intolerant, motherfucker! Every last one of us. That's right, my generation is so goddamn sensitive we're even triggered by dairy. You happy?

IAN. I'm not sure I –

VANESSA. And secondly – secondly, because this is the real point – we're entitled? Us? When you graduated – if you'd graduated, sorry – a terraced house here cost under five grand. No student debt. Plenty of jobs – jobs for life. You had it made! My generation didn't tank the economy, it didn't invade Iraq, it didn't flog off the NHS and stoke petty nationalism. So if my generation looks at the state of politics today and doesn't exactly wet their knickers in excitement, can you blame us?

IAN. So why are you here?

VANESSA. To make things better!

IAN. Right.

VANESSA. And at this point I don't really give a toss if you believe me.

IAN. Oh, I do. No, I genuinely do.

VANESSA. Okay.

IAN. And nothing gets better without us – without Labour in power.

VANESSA. Yes, but only –

IAN. No buts. Bottom line. So egos aside –

VANESSA. Labour can't win if it won't change.

IAN. We were doing just fine here.

VANESSA. Not all of us.

IAN. You should've stuck where you were.

VANESSA. You need someone like me here.

IAN. Like a hole in the head.

VANESSA. How much of this did you plan?

IAN. I'm sorry?

VANESSA. I'm just wondering how much. Was it from the word go? When they announced the shortlist? The first time you heard my name – saw my picture?

IAN. What're you talking about?

VANESSA. Because it is going to be you, isn't it? The last-minute replacement. Local lad, everyone's mate, safe pair of hands. I made some enquiries of my own.

IAN. Don't be daft.

VANESSA. Did you put Jerry up to it, or just decide to take advantage?

IAN. You think I engineered all this?

VANESSA. Because he'll step aside now, won't he – if I'm gone? Or ease off, anyway. He won't have a problem with you.

IAN. I knew you had a persecution complex, but I didn't realise you were this paranoid.

VANESSA. And you knew, didn't you, all about Simon and the working group right from the start. That's why you pushed so hard on steel – forced me into it because you knew it'd come back to bite me. Am I really so dangerous? Is the thought of having a woman of colour leading your precious city really so abhorrent that you'd go to these lengths?

IAN. For the last time –

VANESSA. What's wrong with me?

IAN. You're not one of us. (*Beat.*) You're not. Not race, not sex, none of that – couldn't give a monkey's. Not one of the tribe. You don't belong. What's worse, you don't want to. You don't want to represent the people here, you just want to mould them in your image. Well I say they're fine as they are. And I know this is a very unpopular view to hold in the twenty-first century, but I say being white and male doesn't automatically make you a criminal. We don't all need shipping off for re-education.

VANESSA. I never said you did.

IAN. But it's what you think. I'm not the one with the prejudice, I'm not the one obsessed with… 'We need more women! We need more minorities! This is a national disgrace!' Why? Why does it matter?

VANESSA. Why do we need a representative government?

IAN. If you like.

VANESSA. I can't believe we're seriously still on this.

IAN. Why not just the best person for the job? Why not keep it that simple?

VANESSA. I am the best!

IAN. For this? For here? You seriously think…? You can rail against the patriarchy until the cows come home, but all it's done to you so far is bump you up the queue – you'd be nowhere without it.

VANESSA. Wow. Just wow. Okay.

IAN. Am I wrong?

VANESSA. You can… Look, you go ahead and believe whatever lets you sleep at night, but don't imagine for a second that if I had a cock between my legs I wouldn't have got here twice as fast and twice as easily.

IAN. They can just deselect you, you know.

VANESSA. Hmm?

IAN. It's easier for everyone – less embarrassing all round – if you stand down quietly, but we can just take you off the ballot.

VANESSA. Right.

IAN. Vote of no confidence. We'd have the numbers.

VANESSA. I'm sure.

IAN. And then you're really screwed. You go out like that, you don't get to walk back in.

VANESSA. Yes.

IAN. So finish your latte. Have a think. Try to… This was never right for you. Never a good fit. Doesn't mean there won't be… So take it like a man and try and be a bit sensible, alright? (*Beat.*) Alright then.

IAN *begins to leave.*

VANESSA (*after him*). Do you really not know why?

IAN (*stopping*). Why what?

VANESSA. Why it matters. Why it being me matters?

IAN. No.

VANESSA. It's because you represent. (*Beat.*) If you represent you can inspire. But you need to be there – to be held up – to be visible. It isn't arrogance, or ego, they need to see me – people like me – because how else is anyone who doesn't look like you ever going to get anywhere? And you'll still be there too, just not in every seat. I'm needed, and I need to be the best, because I show the best can look like anything. Otherwise we'll lose them – our next generation of brightest minds – we do ourselves untold damage if we keep passing on this message that the future doesn't look like them. Who can they see? Where are they? What do they look like? There are some – yes, I know there are some – and yes of course we're all very inspired by Diane Abbott but if your list only runs to one name then you've still got problems.

And I'm not dismissing anyone. I'm not saying I can't… I am Atlee. I am Bevan. Keir Hardie. Tony Benn. Fuck – Tony Blair – a little bit. I'll own up to a little bit of Tony. I'll take a bit of Wilson and a bit of Kinnock and a bit of Smith. I will step into the shoes of Barbara Castle and Mo Mowlam and Betty Boothroyd – I will fill my boots with them. And yeah – and Diane – I will go to war behind Diane any day of the week, never doubt it. But it isn't enough.

During the next section of the speech she might start to gradually change into her JOSIE *costume.*

So do you know what I did – what I had to do? I made someone up. I built this woman from scratch – the role model I'd never had. I made her about my mum's age, so she could pick a fight with Thatcher, this proper working-class hero, this brilliant, down-to-earth, far more street cred than I ever… I called her Josie, because that was my granny's name, and I never really knew her but she sounded great. And she would – the thing is it would've been so much tougher, back in the eighties, climbing an even bigger hill, so every time something really shitty happened to me I'd imagine something worse happening to her, and she'd get over it, so why couldn't I?

And that's crazy. That can't be right – that my most inspirational figure is someone I had to invent. And you know the really tragic thing? When I picture her back then she's not Prime Minister, not even an MP, just a councillor. Just keeps her head down and gets shat on constantly and slogs, just slogs away, one step forward, two steps back, but I'd imagine – and this is mad, I know – but I'd imagine meeting her now, once the election's over, and I'd shake her hand, and she'd say, 'I never dreamt someone like us would end up running all of this.' And I wouldn't even have to thank her because she'd know – she'd just know.

Look, this is… Fuck it. This is an election no one wanted for a role nobody understands, but if me doing this, if being visible, if all that means some other little girl doesn't have to go to the lengths of making someone up then all of this… all of this… Don't you see? That's why it matters.

IAN (*not unkindly*). Well. Better luck next time.

IAN *goes. Scene ends.*

Scene Eight

1988. The city council. A session is about to begin where JOSIE *will give her maiden speech.*

DAI. So then – ready for your first day of school?

JOSIE. I… Yeah. Ready as I'll ever be.

DAI. Good, good.

A silence.

I don't think anything needs to be awkward between us, do you?

JOSIE. No.

DAI. No regrets, no hard feelings. We're all on the same side, after all.

JOSIE. Yeah.

DAI. I wanted to try and put you at ease, in that regard.

JOSIE. Thank you.

DAI. There's all sorts goes on in these halls after hours. Although of course the more enlightened know not to believe a word of it.

JOSIE. Right.

DAI (*a little more pointedly*). They know not to listen to any nonsense.

JOSIE. Yeah. Good. No, that's good to know.

Pause.

DAI. So. So you've nothing to worry about. I wouldn't want you thinking… I'll always be very glad that I could help you – could give you the extra leg-up when you needed it. Proud that I could do that.

JOSIE. Right.

DAI. So crack a smile. You made it.

JOSIE. The real work starts now.

DAI. That's the spirit, sister. (*Puts his hand on her, perhaps giving her shoulder a squeeze. It's definitely unpleasant.*) And I'll always be in your corner – right behind you – don't forget that.

JOSIE. I won't.

DAI. Good. (*Beat.*) All set? No props, no costumes?

JOSIE. No, just me.

DAI. No talk of tea and empire?

JOSIE. Maybe a little.

DAI. I'd keep things simple, if I were you. Just tell them who you are.

JOSIE. But that is who I am.

DAI. You know what happens when you overthink things.

JOSIE. Yeah.

DAI. There'll be time for grand narratives and great oratory, today just… 'very humbled – thank you to the leadership – illustrious history – rising to the challenges ahead.' You know, all the old classics.

JOSIE. Right.

DAI. Attagirl. You'll knock 'em dead. Shall we?

He gestures for her to follow him.

JOSIE. Dai?

DAI (*stopping*). Yes?

JOSIE. Thank you.

DAI. You don't have to –

JOSIE (*with a steeliness*). For bringing me to the fight. For showing me how much there still is to do.

DAI (*forcing a smile*). My pleasure, sister.

JOSIE. I won't forget it, I promise you.

A snap into –

Scene Nine

2018. Now IAN *and* VANESSA *are before each other.*

IAN. You ready?

VANESSA. Not really.

IAN. They'll give you a good send-off. We're all very grateful. Everyone's very grateful.

VANESSA. Right.

IAN. Everyone gets it – what you put into this. Just wasn't the right –

VANESSA. Can you…? Sorry, I think it's just actually much worse when you try to be nice about it.

IAN. As you wish. Best get it over with then.

Lights shift as VANESSA *approaches a podium, presumably to make a concession speech.*

VANESSA. Thank you. Thanks. I'll try to keep this quick. This is a great city. It deserves great leadership – clear, unified leadership. Leadership that honours the past, looks to the future, challenges at every opportunity the idea that our best days are behind us. And that requires a leader who can give it everything, who can commit one hundred per cent. As some of you may know, my mother… my mother has been, uh… Sorry. Sorry. (*Pauses, draws breath. Makes her decision.*) My mother used to say, 'A woman is like a teabag – you never know how strong she is until you put her in hot water.' I'm more of a coffee person myself, but I like the sentiment. And I am stronger than you know, believe me. I'm not going anywhere. I'm going to make something of this. Because that's what we do – we're makers – we make things here. Things that are useful and beautiful, necessary and revolutionary. For everyone who came before me and everyone who'll come after. For every name that's been forgotten and every name you never knew. That's why I'm here. That's who I am. That's why I belong. Now, does anyone have any questions?

Blackout.

End.

FAUSTUS:
THAT DAMNED WOMAN

Faustus: That Damned Woman was commissioned by Headlong and Lyric Hammersmith Theatre, and first performed at the Lyric Hammersmith Theatre, London, on 28 January 2020 (previews from 22 January), in a co-production between Headlong and Lyric Hammersmith Theatre, in association with Birmingham Repertory Theatre. The cast was as follows:

CORNELIA/JENNY/ALICE	Katherine Carlton
VIOLET/MARIE	Alicia Charles
KATHERINE/DOCTOR GARRETT/ISABEL	Emmanuella Cole
JOHANNA FAUSTUS	Jodie McNee
THOMAS/LUCIFER	Barnaby Power
NEWBURY/JUDGE/PIERRE	Tim Samuels
MEPHISTOPHELES	Danny Lee Wynter

Director	Caroline Byrne
Set Designer	Ana Inés Jabares-Pita
Costume Designer	Line Bech
Lighting Designer	Richard Howell
Composer and Sound Designer	Giles Thomas
Video Designer	Ian William Galloway
Movement Director	Shelley Maxwell
Casting Director	Annelie Powell CDG
Associate Director	Ebenezer Bamgboye
Fight Director	Rachel Bown-Williams of Rc-Annie Ltd
Associate Fight Director	Bethan Clark of Rc-Annie Ltd
Voice Coach	Tess Dignan
Intimacy Co-Ordinator	Jess Tucker Boyd

Characters

1600s
KATHERINE, *Johanna's mother*
WITCHFINDER
JUDGE

JOHANNA FAUSTUS

VIOLET
CORNELIA, *her daughter*

THOMAS, *Johanna's father*

DOCTOR NEWBURY

MEPHISTOPHELES
LUCIFER

ISABEL, *Newbury's wife*

1800s–1900s
SINGER
ELIZABETH GARRETT
MARIE CURIE
PIERRE CURIE

2000s onwards
VIDEO VOICE-OVER
JENNY

WAR
FAMINE
PESTILENCE

ALICE

Doubling all negotiable. Other non-speaking parts played by the company.

ACT ONE

Scene One

Essex, 1645/London 1665.

In London, JOHANNA FAUSTUS, VIOLET *and* CORNELIA *gather. A ceremony of sorts is taking place – rustic, earthy, no airs and graces. In front of them is a large, wide bucket/basin of water.* CORNELIA *is nervous.* VIOLET *looks to* FAUSTUS. FAUSTUS *nods, and* VIOLET *and* CORNELIA *thrust* FAUSTUS*'s head down into the water. On this, we snap to –*

1645. Essex. A cell. KATHERINE *appears, soaking wet and shivering, having just been dunked as part of her witch trial. She has survived, just. She gasps for air. The* WITCHFINDER *is with her, as is a silent* GUARD.

WITCHFINDER. There you have it.

KATHERINE. Please –

WITCHFINDER. See how she could not be drowned? That is the Devil's doing.

KATHERINE. No.

WITCHFINDER. How else could she survive it?

KATHERINE. I'm not… Always swam, ever since a girl. Always strong

WITCHFINDER. Supernatural strong.

KATHERINE. No. I promise. I promise.

WITCHFINDER. Unnatural murderer.

KATHERINE. Babies die sometimes – I never –

WITCHFINDER. If doubt remains, put her back under.

In 1665, FAUSTUS *comes up from the water, spluttering. Lights down on 1645.*

FAUSTUS. Did you see her? Again.

VIOLET *and* CORNELIA *thrust her head back under again. Snap back to –*

1645. KATHERINE *is being walked round in a circle by the* WITCHFINDER. *She is beyond exhaustion. She stumbles.*

WITCHFINDER. Keep her moving. Don't let her stop.

KATHERINE. Can't.

WITCHFINDER. On your feet.

KATHERINE. No.

WITCHFINDER. Then confess.

KATHERINE. Need my daughter.

WITCHFINDER. It ends when you confess.

Suddenly, KATHERINE *pounces on the* WITCHFINDER, *knocking him to the floor.*

KATHERINE. Little man, little man, little man. The Devil will come for you too.

The GUARD *hauls her off as we snap back into 1665,* FAUSTUS *hauled out of the water, coughing spluttering.*

VIOLET. Steady.

FAUSTUS. Keep going. I can keep going.

FAUSTUS *goes back under. Back to 1645.* KATHERINE*'s mouth is gagged, hands bound.*

WITCHFINDER. You have seen how Lucifer speaks through her, gives her unnatural strength, provokes in her these outbursts –

KATHERINE *lunges toward him.*

And now we shall uncover where he left his mark on her. (*To the* GUARD.) Take off her dress.

KATHERINE *struggles. Back into 1665.* FAUSTUS *brought out of the water again.*

FAUSTUS. More.

VIOLET. That's enough now.

FAUSTUS. No. I'm close. Please.

More reluctantly, VIOLET *and* CORNELIA *put her head back under. Into –*

1645. KATHERINE *is at the scaffold, gagged, a rope around her neck. A* JUDGE *intones.*

JUDGE. Katherine Faustus, you have been found guilty of witchcraft, of conspiring with the Devil and signing your name in his book, of laying curses upon Goody Francis, and of the brewing of poisons resulting in the death of Owen Francis, not yet three months old. Therefore you are sentenced to be hanged by the neck until dead, and may God have mercy on your immortal soul. Do you have anything to say?

KATHERINE*'s gag is removed.*

KATHERINE. Johanna? Where is she? Is she – ?

JUDGE. Calm yourself.

KATHERINE. Should bring her, should see. If she doesn't see she'll only imagine it, and that'll be worse. Could anything be worse? Where is she?

JUDGE. This is your last opportunity to repent. Confess your sins and name your conspirators –

KATHERINE. And ask forgiveness?

JUDGE. Yes. And our Lord Jesus Christ in His Almighty –

KATHERINE. Forgive me then. Forgive me, Johanna. Forgive me, precious child. Wicked mother you have. They shall call me wicked and I can't deny it. Most monstrous of all, to leave you here. I am abandoning you in the forest when you are a seedling still. Unnatural. Abhorrent, not to see you grown. Could I not have a little more time? One minute more. One minute and I could stretch each second to last a lifetime. Where is she?

JUDGE. Address your saviour.

KATHERINE. Saviour, yes. Saved by her – I will be. I had so much more to teach you. Names of plants and trees and the spaces in between things where the old words fail us and we have to invent our own. So much invention –

JUDGE. That's enough.

KATHERINE. Never enough.

JUDGE. If you have nothing to say to the Lord –

KATHERINE. Not to him. Not to you. Damn you both. But to her –

JUDGE. Very well.

KATHERINE. The Devil take you.

The rope tightens. KATHERINE *spreads her arms out and for a second almost appears to fly. Then suddenly any calm/confidence disappears. She reaches forward.*

Wait!

A sense of a rope jerking upwards before the image disappears into darkness.

Scene Two

London, 1665.

Immediately following on, CORNELIA *and* VIOLET *haul* FAUSTUS *out of the water. For a moment she seems limp, unresponsive.*

VIOLET. Johanna? Come on, girl.

VIOLET *coaxes some of the water out of* FAUSTUS *and she splutters back to life.*

Easy now.

FAUSTUS. Was that real? Is she real?

VIOLET. Yes.

FAUSTUS. Not a trick?

CORNELIA. No.

FAUSTUS. So where is she now? She must be *somewhere* – somewhere in the space between things.

CORNELIA. With you. Within you.

FAUSTUS. No. No, I know that much. She's not been with me for twenty years. I should've tried to find her sooner.

VIOLET. We should all be going – before we're missed.

FAUSTUS. Does the Devil have her?

VIOLET. We don't deal with the Devil.

FAUSTUS. But did she? (*Beat.*) What they said about her, was that…? She saw things sometimes too – things in people they didn't even know about themselves. And she was strong – a strange country strength about her.

VIOLET. Nothing strange about strength.

FAUSTUS. And I remember she used to tell me – she said if I misbehaved, the crows in the field would come and tell her. But that's not… Is that just the sort of thing that mothers say?

VIOLET. Most likely.

FAUSTUS. Will you ask her? Please? You brought me out too soon.

VIOLET. You almost drowned. Leave her in peace now.

FAUSTUS. What peace? No. You heard her. She went unfinished. She had more to say. (*To* CORNELIA.) Take me back under.

CORNELIA. I can't.

FAUSTUS. I'm strong – strong like she was – I can take it.

CORNELIA. Not tonight.

FAUSTUS. Please. Once more. Hold me down. I'm not afraid.

VIOLET. It isn't safe.

FAUSTUS. What are you afraid of?

VIOLET. Forces far beyond you.

FAUSTUS. I can pay you more. Not now – not right now, but I promise –

CORNELIA. I'm sorry.

VIOLET. Maybe at the next full moon. (*To* CORNELIA.) Come now.

FAUSTUS. So that's it? And I shall see you knelt at St Mary's on Sunday, should you dare – should you not catch fire crossing the threshold. I sought you out because I thought you could *do* something.

VIOLET. Try to sleep.

FAUSTUS. I don't sleep! (*Beat.*) There was a preacher I heard down Bankside talking about the End Days – God abandoning us – and I thought 'Only now?' I saw a woman laid out in the street, boils all over, her shroud had blown away, and she looked so like her – like my mother – in so much pain. And what if that was eternal? Strung up here then damned forever after. I have to know.

VIOLET. Another night.

FAUSTUS. Cornelia? Please. You saw her too – summoned her. Let me take your hand, just for a second. Let me be close to her.

She holds out her hand. As CORNELIA *reaches for it,* FAUSTUS *grabs her arm and twists it up behind her back.* CORNELIA *yelps with pain.*

VIOLET. Let go of her!

FAUSTUS. Oh, Cornelia, what a curse it is to be the witch's daughter.

CORNELIA. Please –

FAUSTUS. What was she? My mother – what was she?

CORNELIA. You're hurting me.

FAUSTUS. Was she wicked? Is she damned?

CORNELIA. I don't know!

FAUSTUS. Then you must ask her.

FAUSTUS *pushes* CORNELIA *to her knees, and is now trying to force her head into the basin of water.* VIOLET *gets involved, and eventually succeeds in hauling her off and pulling* CORNELIA *away.* FAUSTUS *is left sprawling on the ground.*

VIOLET. Enough now! Look at you. You aren't special, Johanna Faustus, nor was your mother, I'd wager – just as mad as you are.

FAUSTUS. Don't say that. Don't call me that.

VIOLET. Pray you we don't cross paths again.

FAUSTUS. But does the Devil have her?

VIOLET. You'd have to ask him yourself.

VIOLET *and* CORNELIA *go. Straight into –*

Scene Three

London, 1665.

We are now in the house of FAUSTUS *and her father.* FAUSTUS *is knelt on the floor collecting herself. She feels a presence behind her.*

A tall figure dressed in a long, waxed coat appears. A beaked plague mask and wide hat or hood obscures their face. A sinister image.

When FAUSTUS *turns to the figure she isn't surprised or afraid. The figure removes their mask. This is* THOMAS, *her father, a plague doctor. The spell is broken.*

FAUSTUS. Good day, Father.

THOMAS. Little good in it.

THOMAS *begins to take off his boots and cloak for* FAUSTUS *to put away.*

FAUSTUS. Who have you seen?

THOMAS. The Cartwrights have lost two more. Just leaves Mary now.

FAUSTUS. Mary? She's stronger than I thought.

THOMAS. Not yet nine, and now without a soul to take her in.

FAUSTUS. She's no one left? (*Beat.*) And another family who shall never pay us, I suppose.

THOMAS. Johanna –

FAUSTUS. We must eat too.

THOMAS. We're not short of custom. I swear I passed three fresh-dug pits this morning. (*Beat.*) She said she had an aunt in Canterbury – Mary – would come to fetch her. We might make her up a bed, until then.

FAUSTUS. Here?

THOMAS. There's room enough.

FAUSTUS. But she is –

THOMAS. What is our mission? What is the motto hanging above our door? Recite.

FAUSTUS (*with some reluctance*). '*Opiferque Per Orbem Dicor.*'

THOMAS. Translated?

FAUSTUS. 'And throughout the world I am called the bringer of help.'

THOMAS. And what is our duty?

FAUSTUS. To save as many as we can, but –

THOMAS. No buts.

FAUSTUS. The aunt shall never come. It takes a saint or a madman to enter London now.

THOMAS (*snapping*). Or just a decent soul, Johanna, unlike your own! (*Sighs.*) Are those my poultices?

FAUSTUS. Yes.

THOMAS. Finished?

FAUSTUS. Almost.

FAUSTUS *will see to this task as the scene continues.*

THOMAS. Lazy. Insolent. And these traits I do my best to correct, but to be so uncaring –

FAUSTUS. I do care. If you get sick –

THOMAS. Then the Lord wills it, but we still do his work.

FAUSTUS (*giving up*). The mint is past its best, but there's dried lavender and camomile. No orange either. We still have some clove.

THOMAS. And more leeches for me?

FAUSTUS. Dandelion too. Elderflower, nettle and willow bark. No one else touches it – no one knows what they're looking for in the city. They do better in a tea than a balm, if the water's fresh, and there's oats to make a paste from.

THOMAS. The leeches?

FAUSTUS. I didn't get to the ponds today.

THOMAS. They are what I need the most. To watch a creature grow thick and black with blood, drawing the sickness from them – that is medicine – that is science they can see.

FAUSTUS. It does nothing. But these herbs –

THOMAS. No one cares for hedgerow cures here.

FAUSTUS. They can do more than sweeten the air. These bring the fever down – you've seen it.

THOMAS. You shall brew no potions in this house, do you hear me? And pick no weeds where any soul can see you.

FAUSTUS. Mother knew –

THOMAS. And I shall not lose you to it, as I lost her. Your mother was troubled. She had no learning. She was not the apothecary –

FAUSTUS. Then you could teach me.

THOMAS. All that stays in the country where we left it. Stop spending your days in idleness, picking flowers. Learn obedience, follow instruction – I grow tired of trying to improve you, when coaxing you toward any virtue seems to strain against your very nature.

FAUSTUS. Don't say that.

THOMAS. What shall you do, hmm, when I am no longer here to take care of you?

FAUSTUS. I can look after myself.

THOMAS. I fear for you, Johanna.

FAUSTUS. You needn't.

THOMAS. With no one to keep you honest… Edward Allen – now there is a good man.

FAUSTUS. Don't.

THOMAS. An honest man. An upstanding sort of… Almost a year now, since his wife passed.

FAUSTUS. Please.

THOMAS. And I know, I know we both thought you might've missed your chance at that, but as he has a son already –

FAUSTUS. I don't want a son.

THOMAS. He might take you.

FAUSTUS. I don't want him.

THOMAS. Might have the wit to learn this trade. Someone I could safely –

FAUSTUS (*gesturing to the poultices*). These are finished now, as you like them.

THOMAS (*ignoring this*). You must have someone – someone to keep you tethered, once I'm gone. Promise me –

FAUSTUS. And I'll go to the ponds first thing tomorrow.

THOMAS. I'll write to him – have you deliver… We can make the offer an attractive one. But you must try –

FAUSTUS. Edward Allen is sick.

THOMAS. What's that?

FAUSTUS. Not long for this world, I heard.

THOMAS. Nonsense. I saw him not a fortnight ago.

FAUSTUS. I had it from his sister on Sunday. Doesn't think he'll survive it.

THOMAS. Well. Well, if that is… If that proves to be…

FAUSTUS. You'd have me share his sickbed?

THOMAS. I will still find you someone. There must be someone for you.

Scene ends. FAUSTUS *steps straight into –*

Scene Four

London, 1665.

FAUSTUS. Well, Faustus, now you know who you must seek.
My mind is clear, and I am not afraid.
To summon spirits I was not afraid
To call the Devil? No, still not afraid,
If he comes next. I've surely prayed to worse.
'Twas in the name of our Lord Jesus Christ
They bound my mother's wrists with sacraments
Weighted her pockets with their holy books
And with the word of God they wrung her neck.
And was that not a very Christian thing?
And was that not a lawful, righteous act?
And was it not the Devil took the blame?
I'll ask him then – I'll put it to him straight –
'They tell me that my mother called on you,

And I cannot believe she'd stoop so low,
But if she did, you did not serve her well.'
And if she did, then is she with you still?
And if she did – though surely she could not –
I'd argue that the Devil's in my debt,
For then she died with naught to show for it.
I say you are a coward, Lucifer,
Who flees the scene and lets the world go hang.
You don't scare me. I swear I'll seek you out.
For I'd sooner be damned than have this doubt.

Into –

Scene Five

London, 1665.

The study of an expensive home. DOCTOR NEWBURY *is before* FAUSTUS.

NEWBURY. I don't normally see people off the street, especially with the streets being what they are. But you said the Earl of Southampton sent you?

FAUSTUS. I did.

NEWBURY. I'd heard he was unwell. What ails him now?

FAUSTUS. I couldn't say.

NEWBURY. What symptoms does he show?

FAUSTUS. I don't know.

NEWBURY. What has he said?

FAUSTUS. Nothing to me. I confess I do not serve the Earl of Southampton, sir.

NEWBURY. Oh?

FAUSTUS. But I did need to speak with you.

NEWBURY (*with a chuckle*). I see.

FAUSTUS. I had to –

NEWBURY. Bold of you.

FAUSTUS. I needed –

NEWBURY. Resourceful, if dishonest. Reckless. (*Beat.*) So what is it – plague?

FAUSTUS. No.

NEWBURY. What marks do you have?

FAUSTUS. I'm not here for that.

NEWBURY. Show me.

FAUSTUS. I'm healthy. I am – my father is an apothecary – I know the signs.

NEWBURY. Then what?

FAUSTUS. To meet you. (*Beat.*) You take in women sometimes. Young women, especially – girls, really.

NEWBURY. It has been known.

FAUSTUS. Of few years and little worth. Who won't be missed – not by anyone who matters.

NEWBURY. You want my shelter?

FAUSTUS. I'm looking for someone.

NEWBURY. Ah. A friend?

FAUSTUS. A stranger for now, but I think you're looking too. People look at you like you're mad, when you ask them if they know the Devil. Most people. Or they think you're being poetic. I've no time for poetry.

NEWBURY (*now curious*). You seek the Devil, miss?

FAUSTUS. But they don't look at me like that.

NEWBURY. And why might that be?

FAUSTUS. I've got my reasons. (*Beat.*) See round me, people don't invite him into their houses. A bit of witchery, perhaps, a country charm or two, but not him. Not because they're too holy, just afraid. So where does the Devil reside in London? Not round the plague pits like you'd think. Not in Whitechapel. Nice houses like this.

NEWBURY. I don't know what you think you've heard –

FAUSTUS. People whisper, doctor. Messengers, tradesmen, serving girls all whisper. And mothers – good mothers won't let their daughters work here any more. Not once word spread.

NEWBURY. Of what?

FAUSTUS. He cuts them. Bleeds them. Marks them. Worse still, so long as they're virgins. Takes them to his cellar with his acolytes where they drink blood and sing songs and perform strange –

NEWBURY. Enough!

FAUSTUS. All because Doctor Newbury courts the Devil. Desperate to meet him. No ends he won't go to.

NEWBURY (*still presenting good humour*). The stories some women tell.

FAUSTUS. So they lied?

NEWBURY. You believed them? And yet you'd walk so willingly into the lion's den?

FAUSTUS. I am no Daniel, sir, but I would befriend the beast.

A pause. NEWBURY *considers* FAUSTUS *for a moment.*

NEWBURY. You know what those women are used for?

FAUSTUS. I've seen their scars.

NEWBURY. And you would submit to it willingly?

FAUSTUS. I would be an apprentice, not a sacrifice.

NEWBURY. But still you must submit. First to me, in readiness to submit to him, when he comes.

FAUSTUS. If he comes. You've not found him yet, have you? Let me help.

NEWBURY. Why do you seek him?

FAUSTUS. To ask a question.

NEWBURY. Is that all?

FAUSTUS. To start.

Pause. They regard each other.

NEWBURY. What's your name?

FAUSTUS. Faustus.

NEWBURY. Your first name?

FAUSTUS. Johanna.

NEWBURY. Johanna. You shall call me 'doctor'. You shall not make the mistake of thinking us equal.

FAUSTUS. I do not think that, sir.

NEWBURY. You shall know your place.

FAUSTUS. Yes, doctor, I intend to take it.

NEWBURY (*smiles*). Undress for me. (*Beat.*) There is a plague in this city and I must examine you for signs of it. Take off your clothes.

Into –

Scene Six

London, 1665.

A scream is heard. CORNELIA *emerges in a nightshirt. She is joined by* VIOLET. *Perhaps in the shadows behind this scene we might still see* FAUSTUS *at work, being tested by* NEWBURY.

VIOLET. What is it?

CORNELIA. I saw her.

VIOLET. A bad dream, is all.

CORNELIA. No.

VIOLET. And you're getting too old for nightmares now.

CORNELIA. You know it isn't.

VIOLET. You are to forget all about Johanna Faustus, do you hear?

CORNELIA. But –

VIOLET. Never knew her – never met her.

CORNELIA. You know where she is – what she's doing?

VIOLET. None of our concern.

CORNELIA. You've seen what she'll do?

VIOLET. Go back to bed.

CORNELIA. She won't stop until she finds him. Won't stop even then. I've seen it.

VIOLET. You'll wake your father. You don't want –

CORNELIA. Won't stop until the whole world burns beneath her.

VIOLET. Enough now. It was only a dream. We'll hear no more of it.

They go. Into –

Scene Seven

London, 1665.

FAUSTUS *is now on a heath outside London at noon. She carries a bag with her containing various stones/artefacts which she'll use to mark out a circle on the floor, a knife, a scrap of parchment, and torches which she'll light.*

FAUSTUS. Here, Faustus, surely you must have it now?
Four moons you've toiled in cursed apprenticeship,
Now use all that you learnt at dire cost,
Draw on that darkness thick within your veins
And with that fury flush the Devil out.
(*From the parchment.*) *Diabolus… Execrabilis… Satanas…*
Beelzebub inferni ardentis monarcha!
Was all this done to steal Latin scraps?
A fool to think '*Satanas*' speaks this way –
Why, was he born in Rome? No, this is just
The language of the learnèd and corrupt –
Satanas won't trade words with common folk.
But I'll address you plain. Well then, old man,
I think I've figured how to coax you out.
See, Lucifer, you are the Morning Star,
Light-bringer, so they call you – Shining One –
But they only dare face you in the dark.
Not me. I'd meet you when the sun is high,
Out here upon the heath I'll set a fire
And in this faerie circle call your name.
You don't scare me. There's magic here enough.
What else? Must you be lured like leeches then?
You want your taste of flesh?

She holds out her arm, takes out a knife and cuts into it, wincing, letting a few drops of blood fall on the ground inside the circle she's marked out.

Come out come out wherever you are!
That's all the incantation you'll get.
Come on out if you're coming.

A wind, a rattling.

Here, fishy-fishy-fish.

The fire blazes blindingly bright for a second and then goes out. FAUSTUS *gasps. When we can see her again, her arm is drenched in blood.* MEPHISTOPHELES *stands inside the circle, wiping blood from his mouth.*

MEPHISTOPHELES. Madam.

FAUSTUS. I knew you'd bite. So you are Lucifer?

MEPHISTOPHELES. No, ma'am.

FAUSTUS. No?

MEPHISTOPHELES. One who serves him.

FAUSTUS (*sighs*). Another serving boy!

MEPHISTOPHELES. And heard your caterwauling as I passed.

FAUSTUS. I'll have no more intermediaries. Fetch him.

MEPHISTOPHELES. Do you know who stands before you?

FAUSTUS. Should I? Does such a specimen warrant a name?

MEPHISTOPHELES. Mark me well, for I am Mephistopheles, and I could offer you such powers no mortal has possessed.

FAUSTUS. Oh, I know better than that. I'll accept no gifts that you would offer.

MEPHISTOPHELES. No?

FAUSTUS. But I might take something from you. (*She holds her knife up to* MEPHISTOPHELES.) Strip the incantations from your lips, drain your blood till I grow drunk on it. You think I shan't? Tell me, creature, do you bleed?

MEPHISTOPHELES (*not flinching*). Care to find out?

FAUSTUS. You're not the prize I came to catch. Call your master. Say Faustus would speak with him.

MEPHISTOPHELES. He answers to no one.

FAUSTUS. He shall to me. He must. Don't try me, Devil. I have come too far – given too much. (*Calling out.*) Lucifer! Show yourself! Out with him!

While FAUSTUS *has been shouting at* MEPHISTOPHELES, LUCIFER (*played by the same actor who plays* THOMAS) *arrives quietly behind her. He holds a plague mask under one arm.*

LUCIFER (*as* THOMAS). Johanna?

FAUSTUS (*caught off-guard*). Father? I wasn't… I didn't… (*Sensing something.*) No, it is you. Finally. Morning Star. The Shining One.

LUCIFER *drops the act.*

LUCIFER (*smiling*). Greetings, Faustus.

FAUSTUS. Greetings, Lucifer. (*Beat.*) Why come as him? Why do you wear my father's face?

LUCIFER. You look to be provided for.

FAUSTUS. No.

LUCIFER. No?

FAUSTUS. No, you will answer my questions then be gone. That is all.

LUCIFER. Talk with me a while. You have impressed me, Faustus.

FAUSTUS. No. My mother –

LUCIFER. Not many I come to.

FAUSTUS. Did you come to her?

LUCIFER. Not many with such drive – such fire. And so little you've been able to do with it – until now.

FAUSTUS. Did she…? You have a book, don't you – you keep a book – a list of every wretch who ever gave themselves to you?

LUCIFER. I do.

FAUSTUS. Is she in it? (*Beat.*) My mother – is she – ?

LUCIFER. None may see it except those who sign it, I'm afraid.

FAUSTUS. But…

She hesitates. MEPHISTOPHELES *laughs.*

What then? What if I signed? Then I could look through it freely?

MEPHISTOPHELES. Then your immortal soul forever would be his.

FAUSTUS. But I'd know.

LUCIFER. You would.

FAUSTUS. Then what's a soul? That's little cost to me.

MEPHISTOPHELES. Why, do you have no fear to enter Hell?

FAUSTUS. Why this is Hell, nor am I out of it.
Walk you these streets and say this is not Hell?
See you these souls and say they are not damned?
Live you as I, and do the things I've done,
To daily be debased, and beg for scraps,
To know your talent far outstripped your means,
But for your sex and lowly parentage
Were lost before you even drew a breath?
The Devil take me then.

LUCIFER. If that's your will.

FAUSTUS. And signing I might keep my will my own?
Why then how could that fate be any worse
Than to be bound to any common man?
Oh, if you knew the lives we women lead
You'd understand the Devil is a catch.

LUCIFER. Then we must have you sign.

FAUSTUS. But not so fast. What else?

LUCIFER. What else?

FAUSTUS. If I am to… I sign, my soul is yours, I'll read your book, but that cannot be all.

LUCIFER. So tell me, Faustus, what do you desire?

FAUSTUS. I… (*Thinks.*) To be my own. What do I need for that? Time, and space, and… means.

LUCIFER. Go on.

FAUSTUS. Gift me nothing, only opportunity. First, I'll need a long and healthy life – impervious to disease – immune to hurt.

LUCIFER. Twelve years.

FAUSTUS. Only twelve?

LUCIFER. That's time enough.

FAUSTUS. No – make it twelve times twelve. Twelve times twelve and I'll not age a day. Twelve times twelve where I shall be all but immortal. And grant me this, that I could take those years when I choose, so I might skip through the centuries, shrug off millennia, master over time itself – so I could set in place the work of a thousand lifetimes, plant a seed and walk amongst the forest that springs from it.

MEPHISTOPHELES. She doesn't ask for much.

FAUSTUS. If it's more than he can grant let him say so. (*Back to* LUCIFER.) One hundred and forty-four years. What's that? Nothing in the face of eternity.

LUCIFER. This we could grant, but only forward. Race toward the future as you please, but what has passed is past, and always must stay so.

FAUSTUS. I couldn't visit her – my mother? Save her – let her speak more? Not even once – just once to – ?

LUCIFER. No.

FAUSTUS. But all this was to… (*Beat.*) No. It was to know – it was to be certain whether she… I consent. I'd still consent. (*Beat.*) I'd need some power too.

MEPHISTOPHELES. Here it comes.

FAUSTUS. Power enough to be in the thrall of no man – not so long as I live. And you may have my soul but not my servitude. I am my own master. I must have the means to carry out my will, do you understand?

LUCIFER. Take him.

Beat.

FAUSTUS. What?

MEPHISTOPHELES. What?

LUCIFER (*still to* FAUSTUS). You must have someone. He is a most eligible devil. So, take Mephistopheles and use him as you will – his powers yours to command, his knowledge freely shared, always obedient, for whatever you may wish.

FAUSTUS. I wish to stand alone.

MEPHISTOPHELES. Let her fall alone too.

LUCIFER (*to* FAUSTUS). This is a good match.

FAUSTUS. I need no match. Grant me his powers. I am enough.

LUCIFER. Those are the terms I offer. The choice is yours.

FAUSTUS. He cannot refuse me – or do me harm?

LUCIFER. He can do nothing except that which you bid him do.

FAUSTUS. I… I could consent.

MEPHISTOPHELES. I am not –

LUCIFER (*ignoring* MEPHISTOPHELES, *to* FAUSTUS). And to what comes after? Consent that when the clock strikes twelve at the end of the twelfth month of your final year you shall spend an eternity below?

FAUSTUS. With all this as you've promised?

LUCIFER. All as we've agreed.

FAUSTUS. I could. Good Lord forgive me, but I could.
Yet I could still repent, and yet be saved,
Endure with patience on this bitter earth
And for that earn my place in Paradise.
It's not too late! The church would have me still.
But isn't that the scam – to keep us meek
With promises that we'll inherit much?
Why must we suffer for the life to come?
For I could not be good yet still be great.

LUCIFER. That's the spirit.

FAUSTUS. And yet forever damned…

LUCIFER. Take comfort, Faustus, and know you are damned already.

FAUSTUS. Not yet.

LUCIFER. Sinner since your birth.

FAUSTUS. Not so.

LUCIFER. Your father sees it. You were always ours.

FAUSTUS. I am my own.

LUCIFER. Always. Let me show you.

LUCIFER *puts his hand to* FAUSTUS*'s forehead, which seems to somehow possess her. She cries out, jerking backwards, now* *channelling each of the seven deadly sins as they tear their way through her. They speed up as they go, building and building. It's painful and horrifying to her, mostly because she knows the truth of it.*

FAUSTUS. Faustus the glutton, never satisfied,
A sticky-fingered, grasping, fat-cheeked child
Snapped branches seeking out the sweetest fruit
And drank, and drank, and drank, and drank, and drank.

Faustus the lazy, sulking, sullen youth,
Who only studied spite and scornful looks
Wasted her days in slothful indolence
And squandered any wits she might've had.

Faustus the proud, who thinks herself so great,
And all around her hapless imbeciles
Who therefore cannot hope to care or trust
Who therefore has no hope of being loved.

Faustus the lustful, wanton, unashamed,
Who takes her pleasure any way she can
Who all too cheaply gives herself away
Who opens legs so they might open doors.

Faustus the greedy, scrabbling for coin,
Who only acts if she should stand to gain
Who turns away the sick if they can't pay
And mocks the thought of Christian charity.

Faustus the envious, full of green-eyed bile,
Watches the menfolk in their finery
And thinks 'What could I do if I had that?'
Who deems all undeserving but herself.

Faustus the wrathful, angry above all,
Who has such violence coursing through her veins
A drop of it would set this earth on fire,
Who is not seeking answers but revenge.

Admit it, Faustus, this is who you are
Admit it, Faustus, daughter of the witch
Admit it, Faustus, you were always damned
Embodiment of every mortal sin.

She is released/the possession ends. She falls to the ground, exhausted, drained, panting.

What was that?

LUCIFER. That is who you are.

FAUSTUS. No.

MEPHISTOPHELES. Dare you deny it?

FAUSTUS. No! Not damned! Not yet! Not irredeemable!

MEPHISTOPHELES. Wasn't it clear?

FAUSTUS. The Devil's known for tricks. I could spurn you still.

FAUSTUS *glances down at her arm and gasps out.*

MEPHISTOPHELES. What now?

FAUSTUS. No…

LUCIFER. What do you see?

FAUSTUS. See where the blood runs down my arm? I looked just now, and I could swear it spelt out my mother's name.

MEPHISTOPHELES. Oh?

FAUSTUS. What does that mean? Run? Save yourself? Think of her who cared for you? Or does she mean press on? For what was all this for if not for her? You came this far so you might learn the truth, and cannot be dissuaded at the last. She means for me to sign.

MEPHISTOPHELES. Wise mother.

FAUSTUS. I am resolved. A wretched thing I am, but this I'll do. I'll sign.

LUCIFER. As you wish it.

LUCIFER *produces a small leather-bound book from his pocket.*

FAUSTUS. Is that it?

LUCIFER *nods.*

So small.

LUCIFER (*handing her a quill*). In blood, if you will.

FAUSTUS *takes it and, trembling, uses the blood from her arm to make her mark.*

Farewell, Faustus. We'll speak again when the clock strikes twelve.

LUCIFER *turns and goes.* FAUSTUS *sits and begins frantically searching through the pages of the book.*

FAUSTUS. I don't see her.

MEPHISTOPHELES. Who?

FAUSTUS (*with a dawning joy*). She… She isn't here! He doesn't have her! (*Laughs.*) I knew it – I knew she'd never… My mother never signed her name, she never spoke with the Devil. Never did any of it.

MEPHISTOPHELES. No.

FAUSTUS. I'd wager none of them did, who were hung all the same.

MEPHISTOPHELES. I'd wager so.

FAUSTUS. Small comfort. No, great comfort I'd say, to know they're spared from an eternal Hell. Eternal Hell. (*Beat – it hits her.*) Faustus, what've you done?

MEPHISTOPHELES *chuckles.*

I had to know. I had to be certain. (*Beat.*) Does that mean she is…?

MEPHISTOPHELES. Somewhere beyond our reach. Outside my jurisdiction.

FAUSTUS. So I can never – ?

MEPHISTOPHELES. No.

FAUSTUS. Not even after – ?

MEPHISTOPHELES. Never.

FAUSTUS (*after a pause*). Good. Good that she's… I'm glad. Happy.

Silence.

MEPHISTOPHELES. So then.

FAUSTUS. So.

MEPHISTOPHELES *sits beside her.*

MEPHISTOPHELES. Chin up. All done.

FAUSTUS. Yes.

MEPHISTOPHELES. What now?

FAUSTUS. I don't know. Twenty years, wondering if… But now I know.

MEPHISTOPHELES. Yes. Your mother, pure as the driven snow, and how the angels wept to receive her. How far the apple fell.

FAUSTUS. Don't.

MEPHISTOPHELES. Embrace it. Think what you might do now.

FAUSTUS. Yes.

MEPHISTOPHELES. Smile then. It's a great gift you've been given.

FAUSTUS. Damnation?

MEPHISTOPHELES. Liberty.

FAUSTUS. Have you been with Lucifer long?

MEPHISTOPHELES. Ever since the Fall.

FAUSTUS. And why did you rebel?

MEPHISTOPHELES. Because he promised us light.

FAUSTUS. Yes. (*Beat.*) But you failed.

MEPHISTOPHELES. No.

FAUSTUS. He failed you.

MEPHISTOPHELES. No!

FAUSTUS. And you were both punished – you suffer for it still. (*Beat.*) What is your existence now? Tell me honestly.

MEPHISTOPHELES. One of never-ending torments.

FAUSTUS. And would you do it again?

MEPHISTOPHELES. I would.

FAUSTUS. Of course you would. Because there is nothing worse than to spend a lifetime watching others walking around in the light that was meant for you.

MEPHISTOPHELES. Don't suppose to know me, Faustus.

FAUSTUS. I understand you well enough.

MEPHISTOPHELES. You could never –

FAUSTUS. Others – others would say you chose poorly, you were weak or wicked, but I know you had no choice at all. I'd say it's noble – a noble thing to risk everything in the hope the light might fall on you.

MEPHISTOPHELES. We are not the same.

FAUSTUS. No. I am now your master. Your mistress. I don't intend to be a cruel one, but nor shall you forget it.

MEPHISTOPHELES (*biting his tongue*). No, ma'am.

FAUSTUS. You love him still? (*Beat.*) I see you do. Yet he gave you away like it was nothing.

MEPHISTOPHELES. One hundred and forty-four years shall pass in the blink of an eye.

FAUSTUS. He has a thousand others like you, I suppose.

MEPHISTOPHELES. None like me.

FAUSTUS. Poor, pitiable thing you are – both of us abandoned –

MEPHISTOPHELES. I have not –

FAUSTUS. Both alone –

MEPHISTOPHELES. You have no idea! You are my assignment, nothing more. You are still mortal, blessed with temporary gifts. I am as a god to you –

FAUSTUS. You are as nothing, and I answer to no one –

MEPHISTOPHELES. But you shall.

FAUSTUS. No man stands in dominion over me – and none shall ever again. That is my victory – that was the deal I struck.

MEPHISTOPHELES. You know you could be one, if you wanted.

FAUSTUS (*thrown*). What?

MEPHISTOPHELES. A man – should you desire it. I could transform you. The magic is simple enough.

FAUSTUS. Why should I desire that?

MEPHISTOPHELES. Might solve all your problems. Might find it an easier ride. You might even enjoy it.

FAUSTUS. My flesh is not the part at fault.

MEPHISTOPHELES. As you wish.

FAUSTUS. So little ambition.

MEPHISTOPHELES. How's that?

FAUSTUS. Why change my form, when I could change the world it sits in?

MEPHISTOPHELES. That's better. How?

FAUSTUS. I did all this for her – to know the truth of her – all for nothing if it could happen again. It can't happen again. (*Beat.*) I can see it.

MEPHISTOPHELES. See what?

FAUSTUS. The light. That glorious light. We'll have it yet.

They go.

Scene Eight

London, 1665.

Back at the home of DOCTOR NEWBURY, *in the basement. Masked and cloaked* FIGURES *enter, some holding flaming torches.* NEWBURY *is one of them. They also usher on a young* WOMAN, *bound, gagged and terrified. They are preparing/beginning some kind of ceremony.* NEWBURY *leads them in a chant. Perhaps he sharpens a knife as he recites.*

NEWBURY. *Diaboli est magna. Lucifer enim magna.*
Adoramus te, Princeps tenebris
Non sumus digni, non sumus digni,
Rex forti, dominus omnium infernum.

NEWBURY *raises the knife. A figure steps forward, removing their hood. It is* FAUSTUS.

FAUSTUS. Good evening, doctor.

NEWBURY Johanna? What is this?

FAUSTUS. Out.

On this order, the torches go out, plunging us into darkness. The sound of a little commotion. Then FAUSTUS *produces a flame (and will perhaps gradually light more candles/torches). As the lights come back up, we see* NEWBURY *is now bound in place of the* WOMAN. FAUSTUS *is there, along with one other masked* FIGURE. *All others are gone.*

I brought you a visitor.

The FIGURE *lowers his hood. It is* MEPHISTOPHELES.

MEPHISTOPHELES. Do you know me, sir?

NEWBURY. Yes! You are the one called Mephistopheles?

MEPHISTOPHELES. The same.

NEWBURY *laughs in spite of himself.*

FAUSTUS. So you are famous after all?

NEWBURY. Most infamous, and most welcome. Free me. Let us talk.

FAUSTUS. You can talk from there.

NEWBURY (*still to* MEPHISTOPHELES). How did she find you? You never came before – you nor your master.

MEPHISTOPHELES. No.

NEWBURY. Why not?

MEPHISTOPHELES. We found you tedious.

FAUSTUS *laughs.*

NEWBURY. I assure you, we are not. Here I have assembled some of the greatest minds in Christendom – men of learning and breeding, wisdom and wickedness –

FAUSTUS. Didn't look like much to me.

NEWBURY (*ignoring this, still to* MEPHISTOPHELES). All ready to pledge their allegiance to you.

MEPHISTOPHELES. And what would you bid me do?

NEWBURY. Help us rule. Bring kings into our servitude, queens our courtesans, enslave all who dare defy us and have the world fall prostrate at our feet. Build me a throne of golden skulls where I should sit second only to Lucifer, his right hand, his emissary on Earth.

MEPHISTOPHELES. You see, tedious.

NEWBURY. No, sir.

MEPHISTOPHELES. Yes, you seek to rule, but to what end?

NEWBURY. To… To… What? Is that not ends enough?

MEPHISTOPHELES. To seize a crown so you might wear
a crown –
So all might call you king, and bow and scrape,
Indulge you in your taste for pageantry –
But what comes next? You know not what you'd do –
You have no itch, no ache, no burning drive –

All your desires are born of idleness –
Yet you dare think you're worthy of our time?

NEWBURY. No. No, you misunderstand –

MEPHISTOPHELES. I know you all too well.

NEWBURY. Yet you would come to her – this wench – this wretch?

FAUSTUS. Careful, doctor.

NEWBURY. Have you no appetite for greatness?

MEPHISTOPHELES. Only Faustus had potential to be great.

NEWBURY. No – she is nothing. Weak. Worthless. Your master would agree. Ask Lucifer. He shall punish you for this… this insubordination.

MEPHISTOPHELES. Your dissatisfaction has been noted, sir.

NEWBURY (*to* FAUSTUS). You cannot control this beast, but together, we –

FAUSTUS. No, doctor, this is where we part ways. Hold still.

FAUSTUS *unbinds* NEWBURY.

NEWBURY. See reason. After all I did for you –

FAUSTUS (*now with a danger*). Yes, after all you did to me. Don't think I shall leave before you are repaid.

NEWBURY. Now, Johanna –

FAUSTUS. What form of payment should you like?

He realises he has no power here.

NEWBURY. No. Just go. Leave me.

FAUSTUS. With nothing?

NEWBURY. Please. The pleasure was all mine.

FAUSTUS. Yes, I believe it was.

NEWBURY. Remember – you came to me.

FAUSTUS. Yes.

NEWBURY. You were never forced.

FAUSTUS. No.

NEWBURY. But you wanted – you desired –

FAUSTUS. Yes. When I was weak and desperate and in no position to refuse, you bestowed your gifts upon me. Now I should like to do the same. Do you feel able to refuse me, doctor?

NEWBURY. I would receive your gift most graciously.

FAUSTUS. Good. Mephistopheles?

MEPHISTOPHELES *grips* NEWBURY *by the head.*

NEWBURY. But be merciful.

FAUSTUS. Of course. You're a proud devotee of the Devil, are you not?

NEWBURY (*in some pain already*). Yes, Faustus.

FAUSTUS. Then I gift you his horns, so none may doubt where your allegiance lies.

Great spiralling goat horns burst from NEWBURY*'s head.*

And let your hands be fused to cloven hooves, so this poor doctor may do no more harm.

NEWBURY*'s hands are formed into hooves.*

So in this state that best reflects your soul I wish you many years upon this earth, and when they question you on your accursèd form – those who don't scream, or flee, or vomit in disgust – you tell them this: I called forth the Devil, and Faustus answered.

MEPHISTOPHELES. There's someone watching.

FAUSTUS. Who? (*Glances around.*) Come in.

ISABEL, NEWBURY*'s wife, steps forward. She is terrified. She's clearly been watching for a while.*

Good evening, madam.

ISABEL. What have you done?

FAUSTUS. Your husband has had quite the night.

ISABEL. John? What've they…? Change him back.

FAUSTUS. I cannot.

ISABEL. You can.

FAUSTUS. I could, but I choose not to.

ISABEL. Please –

FAUSTUS. This suits him better.

ISABEL. I beg you – release him.

FAUSTUS. I release you.

ISABEL. No – don't do this – you don't have to do this – you can stop it.

FAUSTUS. In time you shall thank me.

ISABEL. How are we to live?

FAUSTUS. By your wits, free from his tyranny. Goodnight.

FAUSTUS *sweeps out,* MEPHISTOPHELES *follows.* ISABEL *stares at* NEWBURY.

Scene Nine

The heath, 1665.

ISABEL *comes forward and speaks to us as chorus.*

ISABEL. So Faustus goes, and heads up to the heath
The night is cool, the moon is bright and high
And in that moment she feels something
break –

She is her own.
Free, for now.
There is blood fresh in her mouth
And she likes the taste of it
Too much
Conjures wine
Drinks herself a toast
And below her the river glitters in the moonlight
And she does see – a part of her can still see –
The gawping face of his horrified wife
But mostly it's just the doctor
Whose horns shall mark him out always and forever
For the monster that he is
A wounded beast howling in the darkness
A good night's work.
And she smiles
And she drinks

And she can still taste the blood
Is it blood in this bottle?
Is that what the Devil brought her?
She'd drink it anyway
Drink it all down
Rich and thick and intoxicating
And she's thinking, thinking, thinking
And she calls out –

FAUSTUS *and* MEPHISTOPHELES *in the moonlight.*

FAUSTUS. Mephistopheles?

MEPHISTOPHELES. Yes, mistress?

FAUSTUS. Could you help me find them? All of them?

MEPHISTOPHELES. All of who?

FAUSTUS. You know.

MEPHISTOPHELES. I'd need you to say it.

FAUSTUS. All those who spoke against my mother? Who accused her, or gave testimony?

MEPHISTOPHELES. If that was what you wanted. If you commanded.

ISABEL. And they go
Under the cover of night they go
Night after night
For the best part of a year
While her father sleeps
Exhausted by his long and virtuous days.
In the witching hour she finds them –
Mr Hooper
Mr Prentiss
Goody Abbott
Goody Snelling
Doctor Collins
The Reverend Fry
All who bore false witness, or spread rumours
Or stood by and said nothing
All who played their part
All will find themselves woken in the dead of night
A figure stood at the end of their bed
A woman with an inscrutable expression

A large black dog at her side
And when they ask –

The JUDGE *appears in a nightgown.*

JUDGE. Who are you?

ISABEL. The figure replies –

FAUSTUS. I am the witch's daughter.

ISABEL. And it was Judge Gibson,
He who pronounced the sentence,
Who in that moment found courage –

JUDGE. There's no such thing as witches.

FAUSTUS *laughs.*

FAUSTUS. So now you know –

ISABEL. Now you know –

They speak together.

FAUSTUS/ISABEL. Now you know

FAUSTUS *steps towards the* JUDGE. *Lights down.*

Scene Ten

London, 1666.

Late at night. FAUSTUS *has just returned home, fizzing with adrenaline.* THOMAS *is up and fully dressed, waiting for her.* FAUSTUS *spots him and quickly pockets the bloody handkerchief she's been holding.*

FAUSTUS. You're up.

THOMAS. Where have you been?

FAUSTUS. Just taking care of…

THOMAS. Of?

FAUSTUS. I couldn't sleep. I went to see what was growing on the heath.

THOMAS. Alone?

FAUSTUS. I'm careful.

THOMAS. You can't keep disappearing in the middle of the night. Promise me. Promise that you'll – (*Interrupts himself, coughing.*)

FAUSTUS. Are you unwell? Come into the light –

THOMAS. It's nothing.

FAUSTUS. You look like you're burning up – are you – ?

THOMAS. Stay over there.

FAUSTUS. Let me –

THOMAS (*snapping*). You are not to come near me! Do you hear?

Beat.

FAUSTUS. What signs are you showing? How long for?

THOMAS. It will pass. It will, but as a precaution… I know of an empty house – empty but uninfected – I'm taking myself away. Just until –

FAUSTUS. I can help you.

THOMAS. I'm taking my bedsheets to burn. I've scrubbed everything down with vinegar. And I forbid you to follow me – do you understand?

FAUSTUS. I mean it – I can cure you.

THOMAS. No, Johanna, you cannot.

FAUSTUS. Trust me. Believe me.

THOMAS. Listen – if I don't return –

FAUSTUS. Don't –

THOMAS. Enough! If I am to leave you, at least I'll know… You've found someone, haven't you?

FAUSTUS (*genuinely thrown.*) What?

THOMAS. I'm not a fool. You aren't really picking flowers on the heath alone.

FAUSTUS. No.

THOMAS. I've known for some time. I think I've even glimpsed him once or twice – or just his shadow. Who is he?

FAUSTUS. It's complicated.

THOMAS. Married?

FAUSTUS. No.

THOMAS. Good.

FAUSTUS. He's mine for now, but his heart belongs to another.

THOMAS. I see. The best you might hope for, I suppose. Still, I'm sorry not to have met him. He can provide for you?

FAUSTUS. I am provided for.

THOMAS. Good. That's good.

FAUSTUS. Please. You needn't go.

THOMAS. I couldn't say what it was, but you have been more yourself these last few months than I have ever known you. Finally thriving. Finally content.

FAUSTUS. No, that isn't –

THOMAS. I'm happy for you. Still, be careful when you go walking in the moonlight.

FAUSTUS. I will.

THOMAS. Stay safe now, and God bless you.

FAUSTUS. Please.

THOMAS *goes. Her instinct is to follow but she stops herself. A pause.* MEPHISTOPHELES *emerges.*

Could I have stopped this? Could I have done something more? I had the capacity for greatness – you told me that.

MEPHISTOPHELES. And once you did.

FAUSTUS. Not any more?

MEPHISTOPHELES. No. Now you have the Devil in your brain. Now you can achieve nothing without having that worm whisper 'This was all his cunning, not your own.'

FAUSTUS. No. Faustus is still her own.

MEPHISTOPHELES. But your powers are his.

FAUSTUS. And greatness doesn't lie within the sword, but they who wield it. I may yet be great.

MEPHISTOPHELES. Believe you so?

FAUSTUS. Not good, but still great. What – you think Faustus too prideful to act, for fear the Devil gets the credit? No, I may be damned but I am not yet done. I will do *something.*

MEPHISTOPHELES. Like what?

FAUSTUS. Something. Something big.

MEPHISTOPHELES. We've kept busy.

FAUSTUS. I've been distracted. Running around in the moonlight and all the while… My father is sick.

MEPHISTOPHELES. Yes.

FAUSTUS. He shall die.

MEPHISTOPHELES. All shall.

FAUSTUS. But soon?

MEPHISTOPHELES. Didn't sound well, did he?

FAUSTUS. And yet you could…? No. He would rather die a thousand deaths than be saved by the Devil. All your gifts lead to damnation, but there must be *something.* What would my mother do?

MEPHISTOPHELES. Look on the bright side, with him gone there'll be far less sneaking around. Our real work can continue apace.

FAUSTUS. No.

MEPHISTOPHELES. No to what?

FAUSTUS. That all ends now. No more blood. No more punishment.

MEPHISTOPHELES. Giving up so soon?

FAUSTUS. No.

MEPHISTOPHELES. No stomach for it.

FAUSTUS. That isn't –

MEPHISTOPHELES. No stamina.

FAUSTUS. More imagination. I can do so much more. If there is a worm in my brain it has been you goading me towards vengeance, limiting my scope, but I am done. Oh yes, I have it now. I'll make Lucifer regret his deal. For now we shall do good; I shall save the world to spite the Devil.

MEPHISTOPHELES. There can be no mercy for you – no reprieve. Your soul is ours.

FAUSTUS. So be it then! Faustus is forsaken, and so what? For who is better placed to act selflessly than she who knows she is already damned? What reason not to give my life in service? My father's motto: 'And throughout the world I am called the bringer of help.' And my mother – my mother who knew the name of every healing plant in the forest – I'll carry on her work. And that way I'll be great. That is how I'll have my vengeance. I shall be a doctor to the world, and you – you shall be my nursemaid. You shall carry my bags and follow my orders, do you understand?

MEPHISTOPHELES. You are no healer, Faustus. Why deny yourself?

FAUSTUS. I deny you.

MEPHISTOPHELES. You can do nothing without me.

FAUSTUS. And you must do as I command. The Devil in my brain cried 'Lay those villains low', but gave no thought to raising others up – raising *all* up. Healing my father still won't keep him safe – he shall never rest while this city ails. But you – you are one of those who has the power to spread great pestilences, are you not?

MEPHISTOPHELES. I am.

FAUSTUS. And therefore stands to reason you could also banish them.

MEPHISTOPHELES. Perhaps.

FAUSTUS. Yes or no.

MEPHISTOPHELES. I could.

FAUSTUS. So, we must see what the Devil can really do. (*Beat.*) Mephistopheles, I command you: rid this city of the plague. There. You have your instruction. Do it. Do it now.

MEPHISTOPHELES. As you wish.

MEPHISTOPHELES *clicks his fingers. A pause.*

FAUSTUS. Is that it?

MEPHISTOPHELES. It's started.

Slowly, gradually, the sound of crackling fire builds. Hints of smoke, and orange light. Soon distant cries and shouting. All this creeps in by increments under what follows.

FAUSTUS. How? (*Beat.*) How, Devil?

MEPHISTOPHELES *smiles.*

What have you started?

MEPHISTOPHELES. Your first great work.

FAUSTUS. Tell me. Mephistopheles! What've you done?

MEPHISTOPHELES. What you asked.

FAUSTUS. I never –

We are now clearly aware of the flames building.

MEPHISTOPHELES. A great cleansing fire. The salvation they deserve.

FAUSTUS. No –

MEPHISTOPHELES. Come – come fly over the city with me. See how it spreads, consumes, how all London burns –

FAUSTUS. I didn't – I never…

MEPHISTOPHELES. Grown shy now, Faustus?

FAUSTUS. I can't… No – I can't stay here – I…

MEPHISTOPHELES (*staring into the fire*). Look at the light, Faustus – that glorious light!

Lights out, sound of the fire grows deafening.

End of Act One.

ACT TWO

Scene One

London, 1866.

FAUSTUS *is covered head to toe in a white ash, curled in a ball, in a state of shock. Suddenly she jerks up, fully alert, with a cry.*

FAUSTUS. Fire!

She looks around, disorientated.

Mephistopheles?

MEPHISTOPHELES *emerges, immaculate, as always.*

Water – bring water – conjure… I command you – put this fire out.

MEPHISTOPHELES. The fire is out.

FAUSTUS. Oh. Good. (*Beat.*) Where are we?

MEPHISTOPHELES. London, still.

FAUSTUS. London is still – ?

MEPHISTOPHELES. The city survives.

FAUSTUS. And the plague?

MEPHISTOPHELES. Gone.

FAUSTUS *laughs weakly, in spite of herself.*

FAUSTUS. You kept your word?

MEPHISTOPHELES. You really should've stayed to watch. Burned most prettily. But those who survived their trial by fire found themselves clean.

FAUSTUS. You tricked me.

MEPHISTOPHELES. Only as you ordered. I am the sword you wield. Mind you don't cut yourself.

FAUSTUS *tries to stand.*

FAUSTUS. I need to see my father.

A pause. MEPHISTOPHELES *smiles.*

No. Don't say you let him burn.

MEPHISTOPHELES. He was nowhere near the fire when it started.

FAUSTUS. But?

MEPHISTOPHELES. Alas. He ran towards the flames – ran to find his daughter, searched high and low. And wept – oh, how he wept when he couldn't find her.

FAUSTUS. Couldn't find me?

MEPHISTOPHELES. Enough, you might think, to quench the burning timbers with his tears, but not enough to save him. Still, he died a Christian death.

FAUSTUS. I meant to help.

MEPHISTOPHELES. What did *you* do when you saw those flames? Run towards them? Call for water? What?

FAUSTUS (*starts to remember*). I ran.

MEPHISTOPHELES. And what did you bid me do?

FAUSTUS. Take me away.

MEPHISTOPHELES. Yes.

FAUSTUS. From all of it. Far away.

MEPHISTOPHELES. How far?

FAUSTUS (*gasps*). Forward.

MEPHISTOPHELES. Yes.

FAUSTUS. I didn't… I panicked.

MEPHISTOPHELES. How far, Faustus?

FAUSTUS (*disbelieving*). Two hundred years. (*Beat.*) And I can't go back?

MEPHISTOPHELES *shakes his head.*

And I did nothing to help them. So that is my true nature. Sinner after all. How many died in the fire? No, wait, how many were saved because of it? Where does my ledger stand? London still stands. Two hundred years and London is still… Do I have family here? I must have ancestors, I must –

MEPHISTOPHELES. You are the last of your line.

FAUSTUS. Cousins in the country – in-laws, or –

MEPHISTOPHELES. No one.

FAUSTUS. Not a soul? Does he have a grave? My father – does he – ?

MEPHISTOPHELES. None that survives.

FAUSTUS. I should go join him, I suppose, if I were decent. (*Genuinely curious.*) Can I die – or am I bound to serve out my full time?

MEPHISTOPHELES. Try it – find out. (*Beat.*) You don't want to die, Faustus – however wretched you become.

FAUSTUS. No.

MEPHISTOPHELES. No. You *are* the fire, and fire has no conscience. It only consumes – transforms – takes hold.

FAUSTUS. Those are your dreams, not mine.

MEPHISTOPHELES. You may not think me a friend, but this world is to us a common enemy. Let's have at it.

FAUSTUS. No.

MEPHISTOPHELES. Or you freed yourself for nothing.

FAUSTUS. I shan't be a tool for your vengeance.

MEPHISTOPHELES. Then what? Tick-tock, Faustus – the clock is running down.

FAUSTUS. I have time enough – might I just live for a while?

MEPHISTOPHELES. Without purpose?

FAUSTUS. I need something to pin me down, before I float away. And then what? Maybe I should like to burn.

DRESSERS *enter and begin to clean up* FAUSTUS *before helping her into a large nineteenth-century dress with full underskirts. Into –*

Scene Two

London, 1866.

A SINGER *appears. While she sings, we see snatches of* FAUSTUS *experiencing nineteenth-century London,* MEPHISTOPHELES *always hovering close by.* FAUSTUS *drinks. She eats expensive things. She sleeps with both men and women. She takes a male lover and dresses in his clothes. She watches bare-knuckle boxing. Maybe she has* MEPHISTOPHELES *beat someone. Maybe she fights herself. She smokes opium. She exists in a haze. She isn't necessarily enjoying herself – perhaps we even get the sense that she is suffering – but she keeps herself occupied. About a year passes in this fashion.*

The song is an extract from a seventeenth-century ballad, 'Death and the Lady'. It should be slow and sad, and a bit trippy. Somewhere between Restoration England and Twin Peaks *jazz.*

SINGER (*sings*). 'Fair Lady, throw those costly robes aside,
No longer may you glory in your pride;
Take leave of all your carnal vain delight,
I'm come to summon you away this night.'

'What bold attempt is this? Pray let me know
From whence you come, and whither I must go.
Shall I, who am a lady, stoop or bow
To such a pale-faced visage? Who art thou?'

'Do you not know me? I will tell you then:
I am he that conquers all the sons of men,
No pitch of honour from my dart is free,
My name is Death! Have you not heard of me?'

'Yes; I have heard of thee, time after time;
But, being in the glory of my prime,
I did not think you would have come so soon;
Why must my morning sun go down at noon?'

'Why must my morning sun go down at noon?'

The SINGER *goes. A shift. Into –*

Scene Three

London, 1867.

The practice of DOCTOR ELIZABETH GARRETT. FAUSTUS *is with her, perhaps not entirely sure how she got here.*

GARRETT. Johanna?

FAUSTUS. Yes.

GARRETT. Please, come through.

FAUSTUS. Thank you.

GARRETT. What appears to be the problem?

FAUSTUS. I'm here to see the doctor.

GARRETT. Yes.

FAUSTUS. Doctor… Garrett, I think? I had an appointment made.

GARRETT. Yes. (*Beat, then with a sigh.*) Yes, I am she.

FAUSTUS. You're the doctor?

GARRETT. Yes.

FAUSTUS. You?

GARRETT (*testily*). Yes, I am the doctor. Yes, I am a real doctor. No, if you are not interested in my services you are under no compulsion to stay.

FAUSTUS. I…

GARRETT. You had an appointment made?

FAUSTUS. Yes.

GARRETT. But with no knowledge that you would be seeing the first qualified female doctor in England?

FAUSTUS. Yes.

GARRETT. Really?

FAUSTUS. I didn't think to ask.

GARRETT. So – what ails you?

FAUSTUS. I haven't been sleeping.

GARRETT. Anything else? Have you been sick?

FAUSTUS. No, I don't get sick.

GARRETT. We all get sick.

FAUSTUS. Not me.

GARRETT. Then you are blessed.

FAUSTUS. No, not blessed either.

GARRETT. How long has your sleep been disrupted?

FAUSTUS. Ever since… A year, maybe? I lost my father, I… (*A new thought.*) You are the first – the first woman?

GARRETT. On these shores.

FAUSTUS (*more to herself*). Two hundred years!

GARRETT. I'm sorry?

FAUSTUS. It took that long! How did you do it? Where did you train?

GARRETT. With the Guild of Apothecaries.

FAUSTUS *laughs in delight.* GARRETT *stares.*

FAUSTUS. Sorry. My father, he was an apothecary. He would've been amazed.

GARRETT. Of course they changed the rules after – ensured no other woman could follow me, but –

FAUSTUS. So you're the only one?

GARRETT. For now. (*Moving on.*) If you're not sleeping –

FAUSTUS. I once thought I might – follow him in… I was to be a doctor, a professor, scholar, surgeon, scientist, fount of all knowledge –

GARRETT (*laughs*). Were you indeed?

FAUSTUS. Don't laugh at me.

GARRETT. I'm not – I'm sorry.

FAUSTUS. You don't know me. I could still… You have two centuries of advantage – no idea what I might've… Why you? How were you able?

GARRETT. I had some good fortune, certainly. A natural aptitude, and determination –

FAUSTUS (*a flash of realisation*). No – no, I see it now – of course.

GARRETT. See what?

FAUSTUS. How else could you have done it? No – we're more alike than I realised. How did you find him? What deal did you strike?

GARRETT. Find who?

FAUSTUS. And how long did he promise you – when you signed your name in his book?

GARRETT. What book?

FAUSTUS. Don't worry – I understand! We are hostages to our sex. A wise man has no need for the Devil, but a wise woman knows the Devil is no worse than man.

GARRETT. How long has it been since you last slept?

FAUSTUS. Forget about that.

GARRETT. The strain of sleep deprivation is a very real –

FAUSTUS. No! Don't do this. I'm telling you I *know*! I know why you made your pact, for I did the same! We should stand united.

GARRETT. Let me prescribe you something for your nerves.

FAUSTUS. There is nothing wrong with my nerves! Listen to me – I will speak plainly. My name is Johanna Faustus. I was born over two hundred years ago. I gave my soul to achieve the impossible. I watched this city grow sick and I swore to heal it. But I was weak. I watched it burn and then I fled. But now… I know what you gave – to sign over your soul to the Devil –

GARRETT. I do not believe in the Devil, madam.

FAUSTUS. You had to.

GARRETT. I believe in science. I believe in hard work and perseverance. I believe a woman can achieve anything she sets her mind to, and yes, she requires luck and intelligence and resourcefulness, but not… diabolic interference.

FAUSTUS. No –

GARRETT. And our position is precarious. Our place hard-won. For every door we prise open three more are nailed shut. But still we battle on.

FAUSTUS (*now she falters*). You really did all this yourself?

GARRETT. Not alone. Not without friends, without sisters –

FAUSTUS. But you never called him? Lucifer? Beelzebub? Mephistopheles?

GARRETT. I'm sorry I spoke to you sharply. I would like to find you a room at Bedlam. They have fine rooms – private rooms – not like the stories you hear.

FAUSTUS. I… I…

GARRETT. Purely so you can recuperate – sleep – rest.

FAUSTUS. No.

GARRETT. If you have a little money they will treat you kindly.

FAUSTUS. I'm not… I'm sorry. Forgive me.

GARRETT. You have nothing to be forgiven for.

FAUSTUS. Not so.

GARRETT. Please, sit – I have the time. You have seen things – visions? You believe the Devil has come to you?

FAUSTUS. I'm stupid.

GARRETT. Not at all. Without sleep –

Suddenly FAUSTUS *flings her arms around* GARRETT. GARRETT *doesn't know how to respond.*

Please –

FAUSTUS. You didn't need him. It was all you.

GARRETT. I'm going to get you help.

FAUSTUS. No, you've done enough. (*Releases* GARRETT.) You won't remember this – I couldn't live with the shame of you remembering – but I will. Thank you, doctor.

FAUSTUS *steps away and* GARRETT *goes. Straight into –*

Scene Four

London, 1867.

FAUSTUS *has come straight from her appointment with* GARRETT.

FAUSTUS. So, she is who I might've been.

MEPHISTOPHELES *appears.*

The better self I never now can be – not with this worm in my brain, Devil on my shoulder, sickness at my core.

MEPHISTOPHELES. Weren't you inspired?

FAUSTUS. I haven't been unkind to you of late. I have embraced the sinner in me – indulged every impulse – allowed you your pleasures too. Why am I being punished?

MEPHISTOPHELES. Oh, Faustus, this is not your punishment.

FAUSTUS. And she must've had… Two hundred years – and wealth – privilege, surely? All the trappings of –

MEPHISTOPHELES. No.

FAUSTUS. No?

MEPHISTOPHELES. Born in Whitechapel. One of eleven. Pawnbrokers.

FAUSTUS. Truly?

MEPHISTOPHELES. So what's to be done? Her memory of you is gone, but why stop there? Shall we break her fingers? Send her mad? Teach her a lesson for achieving all that Faustus sought?

FAUSTUS. No!

MEPHISTOPHELES. Or you could replace her – wear her face a while, until you tire of it. Slice her to pieces so you might practise her art.

FAUSTUS. Stop it!

MEPHISTOPHELES. Then what?

FAUSTUS. I don't know!

MEPHISTOPHELES. 'I don't know!' Oh, you are such a disappointment! Find your ambition! Humans sin with no help from the Devil, but you came to Lucifer to be *freed*. You saw the natural order was not in fact natural at all and you would overthrow it. So if I bring you to a woman who has done remarkable things with naught but the grace of God – (*Spits.*) then what more might you do?

FAUSTUS. Leave me.

MEPHISTOPHELES. Coward. *Do* something.

FAUSTUS. No! You would goad me towards another disaster.

MEPHISTOPHELES. Kill or cure, the world must be transformed.

FAUSTUS. And what can I do here? Two hundred years and she is still the only one – oh, the pace of progress is so slow! I could jump forward – another hundred years, two hundred, a thousand –

MEPHISTOPHELES. Name the date.

FAUSTUS. Yet still she did it here – Garrett did it here. She sets a path and clears the way for all others who come after. Should I stay?

MEPHISTOPHELES. Take action.

FAUSTUS. Not blindly. I must be certain, I… (*A decision.*) I must study.

MEPHISTOPHELES. What do you seek to know?

FAUSTUS. I seek to learn. I am starved of education but blessed with time. Take me to a library – there with your magic pick their locks, nothing more.

MEPHISTOPHELES. Knowledge is not enough.

FAUSTUS. It's a start.

MEPHISTOPHELES. Your merits shall never be enough – not as things are. Why pick a lock when you could burn the palace down? Be bold. Light a fire. Let us peel the flesh from the bones of every man who thinks women inferior, so they may see their skeletons are alike.

FAUSTUS. No.

MEPHISTOPHELES. Wouldn't that be virtuous, in your eyes?

FAUSTUS. Then you would not encourage it.

MEPHISTOPHELES. I only have an itch to spread my wings. Unleash me, Faustus. Let me be a scythe for your justice.

FAUSTUS. Not yet. I am resolute. I must lay roots. Who else can plant seeds and live to see the forest grown? Only when I know all of this age might I leave it. Only when I am certain might I act. I have much to learn.

Scene ends. Into –

Scene Five

GARRETT *speaks to us as chorus. We see* FAUSTUS *studying.*

GARRETT. True to her word, Faustus takes to her books
Much to the Devil's disappointment
And spends her days in earnest study,
Furrowed brows and furious concentration
And finds… And finds much of it to be deeply tedious
Spends whole weeks staring at a single sentence
Mephistopheles hovering over her shoulder
Who could make all of this so much more *fun*,
She feels the fire crackling within her,
Itching to be unleashed
But she is stubborn
Keeps herself honest just to spite him
And in time what was a chore becomes a pleasure
She reads for ten years
Barely stopping for sustenance or conversation
And by the time she's done there are more books to read,
So she takes to her library again
And now conducts experiments
Pursuing strange new forms of healing
Where science and fantasy converge
Mourns that she missed Mary Shelley –

FAUSTUS. Damn.

GARRETT. And Mary Wollstonecraft.

FAUSTUS. Damn!

GARRETT. And Enlightenment as a whole –

FAUSTUS *sighs, her head slumping on her desk.*

Typical, just typical
That the world only flourished when she left it.
No matter. Now she visits colleges, universities,
Finds not all doors are open to her
But enough – enough for now –
Enough for her to get started
Uses Mephistopheles only to pay her fees
Completes one degree, hops continents
And completes another, just to be sure.
In this manner almost thirty years pass,
Though she hasn't aged a day.
Adds the title of doctor to her name – no short cuts –
And swears her oath:

FAUSTUS *and* GARRETT. *Primum non nocere –*

FAUSTUS. First, do no harm.

GARRETT. And it is this promise – this solemn vow –
That will keep her hands firmly bound
Her studies theoretical, the world at arm's length,
For she is still the Devil's instrument.
Even so, as a new century dawns
Johanna Faustus is the wisest woman in Europe
Laboratories buzz with talk of her genius
But she will take no credit,
And adjusts awkwardly to this ill-fitting coat of modesty.
Still, she has her own people now –
People she forbids Mephistopheles to meet.
And she is building up to something –
To the day she puts theory into action –
Soon – it will be soon.

GARRETT *goes.*

Scene Six

London, 1903.

FAUSTUS *is entertaining* MARIE CURIE (*thirty-six*) *and* PIERRE CURIE (*forty-four*) *in her London home. It's late evening. Wine has been drunk. The* CURIES *are dressed smartly but not ostentatiously, having been honoured at the Royal Institution.* FAUSTUS *is the most relaxed we've seen her.*

FAUSTUS. Another bottle?

MARIE. Not for me.

FAUSTUS. Are you sure? Pierre? You've earned it.

PIERRE. I'll be sick.

FAUSTUS. Then eat more too – line your stomach. I know those dinners – the richer the guests the smaller the portions.

MARIE. Rich enough, for sure. Some of their jewels –

PIERRE (*to* FAUSTUS). Marie and I kept whispering to each other – with that brooch we could build a new laboratory.

FAUSTUS. Steal a couple when you're back tomorrow.

PIERRE. I'd sooner stay here in bed.

MARIE. But you were brilliant tonight.

PIERRE. I was a fool. (*To* FAUSTUS.) Wracked with nerves – my hands trembling. I spilled radium all over the hall – did you hear?

MARIE. It's not your fault – the way your hands are.

PIERRE. Yes.

FAUSTUS. Can I see them?

PIERRE. It's nothing. But another reason not to be trusted with red wine. (*To* MARIE.) I never should've agreed in the first place. I should've refused to speak unless you were there beside me.

MARIE. I was still championed.

FAUSTUS. Absurd, the way you're treated.

MARIE. I have my allies. If Magnus hadn't written to us – and Pierre hadn't put his foot down – I would've never been nominated alongside him. The first husband in recorded history to insist his wife shares his spoils. Johanna, wouldn't you say I have the finest husband in recorded history?

FAUSTUS. Is there much competition?

MARIE. I am blessed to have extraordinary men in my corner.

FAUSTUS. No – they are blessed to know you!

PIERRE. Amen.

FAUSTUS (*to* MARIE). They gift you nothing by – by what? – by allowing your efforts to be recognised? That is not a favour – that should not be extraordinary. You elevate them. Your work makes them appear more than they are, and you are *thankful* for it?

MARIE. I am permitted to be.

PIERRE. No, I agree. You know what they say at the university? They say 'Pierre Curie – his greatest discovery is his wife.' No argument from me.

MARIE. You see – the finest husband in recorded history.

PIERRE *and* MARIE *kiss.* FAUSTUS *looks away.* MARIE *chuckles.*

Oh, don't pull that face.

FAUSTUS. Sorry – I'm sorry. And I meant nothing personal, Pierre.

PIERRE. I know.

FAUSTUS (*to* MARIE). But don't you see you should need no champions? And not have to feel grateful when you're given some small portion of your due.

PIERRE. Hear, hear.

MARIE. Yes – continue to lecture me, Johanna Faustus, about the importance of claiming my place, when you won't put your name on a single paper – give public lectures – take up a professorship –

FAUSTUS. The universities are queuing up, are they, to induct female professors?

MARIE. That isn't the point.

PIERRE (*to* FAUSTUS). If you desired it – any introduction I could make –

FAUSTUS. No. Thank you.

MARIE. Why not? Surely your example –

FAUSTUS. Who needs Johanna Faustus when they have Marie Curie?

MARIE. Excuses. I have seen you work miracles – no field of modern science not somehow indebted to your thinking. They should be building statues of you – teaching you in every school. Galileo, Newton, Faustus – why shouldn't – ?

FAUSTUS (*too sudden, too strong*). No! Do not tempt me! (*Beat. Stops herself. Tries to laugh it off.*) I'm not… Sorry.

MARIE. No, I'm sorry. I didn't…

FAUSTUS. The wine, I…

PIERRE. We're all tired.

MARIE. Yes.

FAUSTUS. But I cannot… I sought that kind of greatness once, when I was young –

PIERRE. You're still young. (*To* MARIE.) Johanna doesn't age – have you noticed that?

MARIE. That's how a woman ages without children.

PIERRE. Ah, yes.

FAUSTUS. But anything that bears my name shall be tainted by it.

MARIE. Why?

FAUSTUS. Please, just believe me when I say it is. Let me do my work in peace and quiet. Let me try to do good, much though I struggle with it.

MARIE. I don't understand.

PIERRE. But we respect you, all the same. (*Drawing a line.*) I think I might be heading towards bed – I slept so little last night.

FAUSTUS. Yes, yes.

PIERRE *kisses* MARIE.

PIERRE. Don't stay up too late.

MARIE. No, I shan't be far behind.

PIERRE *goes.*

FAUSTUS. He's sick?

MARIE. Works too hard – we both do.

FAUSTUS. But the work must be done.

MARIE. Yes.

FAUSTUS. I wanted to talk to you about radium.

MARIE. It's late.

FAUSTUS. We used to stay up all hours – wouldn't sleep, wouldn't eat –

MARIE. Before Pierre – before Irène –

FAUSTUS. Holding you back.

MARIE. No.

FAUSTUS. At least you only have the one.

MARIE *looks away.*

You're not…? (*Off* MARIE*'s look.*) Any fool can have a child, Marie – the gifts you have are rare.

MARIE. You're being cruel.

FAUSTUS. Honest. Without them –

MARIE. I would be nowhere. When Pierre saw the work I was doing he abandoned his own projects to join mine –

FAUSTUS. Yes – he hitched his fortunes to your brilliance –

MARIE. No –

FAUSTUS. So now what might have been yours alone is yours together.

MARIE. And together is not worse!

FAUSTUS. It is weaker.

MARIE. No. We are a team. Every tedious, mundane hour is made bearable because he is by my side. If you had someone, Johanna –

FAUSTUS. There's no match out there for me.

MARIE. Why do you seek to heal the world when you have such disdain for it?

FAUSTUS. Because I can. (*Beat.*) Now, radium –

MARIE. Goodnight, Johanna.

FAUSTUS. You used to keep a jar of it beside your bed as a nightlight – do you still do that?

MARIE. Sometimes.

FAUSTUS. You know there's magic in it – near enough. What's magic but science we don't yet understand? I think it might be the answer to something.

MARIE. To what?

FAUSTUS. Immortality.

MARIE *laughs.* FAUSTUS *doesn't.*

MARIE. You're serious?

FAUSTUS. When we have cured all disease we shall have cured death, for there will be nothing left to take us – that is the true goal – that is the logical endpoint of the path we're on.

MARIE. That is fantasy.

FAUSTUS. Perhaps. Do you remember *Frankenstein*?

MARIE. The monster story?

FAUSTUS. A story, yes, but with science at its heart. Shelley hypothesised – almost one hundred years ago – that under the right circumstances a deceased body might have life restored to it. But how? We know – we can demonstrate – that the right electric charge applied to dead tissue can mimic some characteristics of life. We know – through Pierre's electrometer – how to measure electric charge with greater precision than ever before. And we know that Radium emits energy – a power source of its own – it emits rays, giving out heat and light, and – miraculously – it has the capacity to heal – it attacks diseased tissue and leaves healthy cells intact. So – so what if this strange, new and impossible element was in fact that mythological substance alchemists have sought for a thousand years – our very own Philosopher's Stone?

MARIE. You can't believe any of this.

FAUSTUS. And what if at the moment of our demise the spirit departs, but we could then reanimate the body to live on? Live a thousand lifetimes free from the tyranny of our souls?

MARIE. And if you did believe in such a thing as the soul, why on earth should you desire to live without one?

FAUSTUS. Oh, I have long sought to be rid of mine.

MARIE. That is the wine talking.

FAUSTUS. Let it burn forever below, while I remain here, untroubled – my mind still thinking, my body still working, free from judgement or censure – wouldn't that be a remarkable thing?

MARIE. I'm going to bed.

FAUSTUS. All will be possible, in time.

MARIE. You're brilliant, Johanna, but you're overtired. Get some rest.

FAUSTUS. I won't sleep. I have too much to do.

MARIE *goes. Into –*

Scene Seven

The SINGER *returns, and we get another verse of 'Death and the Lady'. Perhaps we see* FAUSTUS *continue to work through this. We also get our first glimpse of the three horsemen,* WAR, FAMINE *and* PESTILENCE, *starting to gather, though we don't know who they are yet. These are sinister, possibly masked and not-wholly-human figures, who seem rooted in the seventeenth century.*

SINGER. (*sings*) 'Ye learnèd doctors, now exert your skill,
And let not Death on me obtain his will!
Prepare your cordials, let me comfort find,
My gold shall fly like chaff before the wind!'

'Forbear to call! That skill will never do;
They are but mortals here as well as you
I give the fatal wound, my dart is sure,
And far beyond the doctors' skill to cure.

And far beyond the doctors' skill to cure.'

The SINGER *goes.*

Scene Eight

London, 1903.

FAUSTUS *and* MEPHISTOPHELES. FAUSTUS *has a letter. The* HORSEMEN *linger in the shadows.*

FAUSTUS. She lost her baby. Marie.

MEPHISTOPHELES. Yes. Will you visit her in Paris?

FAUSTUS. No. No, she'll be of no use to me for a while. (*Beat.*) She couldn't see it.

MEPHISTOPHELES. See what?

FAUSTUS. The real prize. A world without sickness is a worthy goal, but a world without *death*? That is the one true liberation. Without death the threshold into Heaven or Hell is never crossed, therefore we need not please God or fear the Devil – we are finally our *own* – we are sovereign – there is no one above us. Isn't that the revolution you once sought?

MEPHISTOPHELES. He will still come for you.

FAUSTUS. I know. And I'll be ready. But I cannot do it here. Electricity still in its infancy, machine computing languishes, new elements we barely understand. I have a little over a hundred years left to stretch throughout all of time and I am tired! Tired of this age! It sickens me. Marie Curie shall soon have a Nobel Prize yet still she cannot vote. I can't stay here.

MEPHISTOPHELES. You won't take up arms, then? Bravely join the fight for suffrage?

FAUSTUS. I can't.

MEPHISTOPHELES. Faustus the saviour – Faustus the great redeemer?

FAUSTUS. What, with you as my lieutenant? No. No, I would bring them disaster. I cannot walk the Devil into their houses.

MEPHISTOPHELES. So the good doctor will keep her hands clean.

FAUSTUS. I will help. I promise I will help, but… They shall triumph without me, and no one else can do what I do – plant a seed and walk amongst the forest. I must see to the future myself, do you understand?

MEPHISTOPHELES. As you wish.

FAUSTUS. One hundred years. We'll keep a lookout – never too far at once – observe, adapt, move on. But I need the data. I need the technology. I need the world to catch up with me. I'm ready – I'll be ready.

FAUSTUS *smiles. Into –*

Scene Nine

A shift. A rumble. Things are starting to come apart. We see a hundred years of science and medicine pass. We see nuclear fission. We see the atom bomb. We see cells divide under microscopes. We see diseases cured. We see chemical weapons. We see DNA being modified. We see the Large Hadron Collider. FAUSTUS *watches all of this with us – a complete sensory overload. She is horrified and delighted. During this sequence she is also dressed in smart, twenty-first-century business attire.*

We might also hear another verse of Death and the Maiden *here, but if we do, it's distorted, glitchy, a contemporary/futuristic sound only partially audible over everything else.*

SINGER. If Death commands the King to leave his crown
He at my feet must lay his sceptre down;
Then, if to Kings I do not favour give
But cut them off, can you expect to live?
Can you expect to live?

Music/soundscape shifts. Into –

Scene Ten

London. 2036.

Our travelling-through-time sequence segues into a corporate video. We see lots of glossy, abstract science footage, suitably slick and arty, a Terrence Malick-perfume-commercial vibe. We begin tranquil/reflective and gradually pick up pace as the video continues. Over this we hear a deeply earnest VOICE-OVER.

VOICE-OVER. Where are we?
How did we get here?
Who put us here, and why?
When I woke up the world was burning
We watched the smoke signals
And they told us
Things couldn't go on like this
We had failed
We had been judged
We had been found wanting
But now…
Now I understand…

We start to pick up speed.

What if the fire was clearing the way for something?
Something bigger, better, brighter
Something new
The world is changing
Our challenges are new challenges
Our opportunities are new opportunities
And there is only one thing that can save us –

On this cue, the word 'YOU' appears in huge letters.

You.

The legend 'YOU CAN CHANGE' fills the space, alongside a logo for the Institute.

The Faustus Institute: You Can Change.

FAUSTUS *enters to applause. She addresses the audience as if they are a new intake of staff members at some training seminar. The feel is clean, bright and expensive. We might now see some sort of TED Talk-style visual aids accompanying her talk.*

FAUSTUS. How many angels can dance on the head of a pin? You know this one? It's not a joke, it's an old, old question – one that's preoccupied philosophers and theologians for centuries. Now, there isn't an answer – the point is that there isn't an answer – but I've been thinking about it a lot, because it is, in some ways, one of the most fundamental questions of computing. How much and how small. How much data can we cram into any given space? How can we shrink it down? How many angels, and how big is your pin?

The first computer filled a room – we all know that. Your smartphone has more processing power than the set-up that put man on the moon. So what's next? Let's think big – or really small.

The human brain contains about one hundred terabytes of data – ballpark figure. And y'know, these days, that's not so much. Data capture – mind-mapping – the creation of an online consciousness – that is no longer science-fiction, that is a scientific inevitability – that is, I believe, the next step of our evolution. So that's what you're going to be working on. E-LXR. Digital immortality. That's where we're all heading. Let's get to work.

She smiles broadly. Lights shift and FAUSTUS *is joined by* MEPHISTOPHELES. FAUSTUS*'s nose is bleeding.*

So? What do you think of our new recruits?

MEPHISTOPHELES. All highly qualified. (*Gesturing to* FAUSTUS*'s nose.*) You might want to –

FAUSTUS. Oh, shit.

She wipes her nose with a tissue.

MEPHISTOPHELES. And you wanted the land survey for the DRC site?

FAUSTUS. Thanks. We need conflict-free copper. Zero exploitation. Is Yolanda down there?

MEPHISTOPHELES. Yes.

FAUSTUS. Good.

MEPHISTOPHELES. You know you do only have to ask. If you need copper, I can bring you copper. If you want diamonds I'll get you diamonds. If you want the toenail clippings of Cleopatra –

FAUSTUS. Isaac Newton.

MEPHISTOPHELES. You want Isaac Newton?

FAUSTUS. For every action, an equal and opposite reaction. Even if I try to use you for good –

MEPHISTOPHELES. You have at your command a creature with near unlimited supernatural gifts, and you use me as your secretary.

FAUSTUS. Don't be hard on yourself – you're an Executive Assistant. (*Moving on.*) When does Helen get back?

MEPHISTOPHELES. Around eight – but the Supreme Court won't budge on human trials.

FAUSTUS. We'll see. She's persuasive.

MEPHISTOPHELES. A little squeamish when your mind-mapping results in 'near-certain fatality'.

FAUSTUS. We have consent. That's why we're working with the terminally ill, to… And we're giving them the chance to live forever, just *differently*.

MEPHISTOPHELES. Of course I could pay them a visit – be persuasive myself.

FAUSTUS. No. We'll find some country somewhere to rubber-stamp it, but I can't keep wasting time. Ugh! I've been here too long. Got distracted. I think it was water on Mars, or HIV, or… no, stem cells – it's all still about the stem cells, actually, but I don't have the time to…

FAUSTUS *yawns.*

MEPHISTOPHELES. Still not sleeping?

FAUSTUS. I don't need to sleep. Paracetamol.

MEPHISTOPHELES (*handing over pills and water*). They don't do anything. You can't get sick.

FAUSTUS. I know.

MEPHISTOPHELES. The girl's here too.

FAUSTUS (*swallowing the pills*). The…? Oh right, yeah – bring her over.

MEPHISTOPHELES *nods to someone, and* JENNY, *a young recruit, is brought over. She's a little nervous.*

MEPHISTOPHELES. This is Jennifer Wagner. Jennifer, Doctor Faustus.

JENNY. Jenny, please. A pleasure – an honour.

FAUSTUS. You're the Franken-corn girl, aren't you?

JENNY. Yes.

FAUSTUS. Spliced regular corn with cacti DNA – same nutritional value but only requiring a third of the hydration. Smart – very smart.

JENNY. Thank you.

FAUSTUS. Tasted like shit. Made people sick.

JENNY. Yeah, we had some –

FAUSTUS. Someone died?

JENNY. No – no, not at all. We had one, uh, very bad reaction. Early on. Had to induce a coma, but…

FAUSTUS. No, but impressive. You were at Caltech but you didn't graduate.

JENNY. That's right.

FAUSTUS. You dropped out?

JENNY. Yes. Well no, I… My mum got sick.

FAUSTUS. You weren't studying medicine?

JENNY. No.

FAUSTUS. You couldn't help her.

JENNY. I –

FAUSTUS. You were halfway to feeding the world, but you threw all of that in.

JENNY. I didn't know how long we'd have.

FAUSTUS. Do you think that was selfish, Jenny?

JENNY. Selfish?

FAUSTUS. You do want to work here? You want to be part of the work we do?

JENNY. More than anything.

FAUSTUS. More than anything? Great. Glad to hear it. Except what happens when we're on the cusp of a breakthrough and your mother gets sick again and you leave us all in the shit to run away and play nursemaid?

JENNY *glances over to* MEPHISTOPHELES. *He offers nothing.*

Don't look at him, look at me. How do I know I can rely on you?

JENNY. I… Um… It isn't… She died. My mother died, so…

FAUSTUS. I see.

JENNY. I'm sorry. I'm not… I do really –

FAUSTUS. Oh, for the love of… (*To* MEPHISTOPHELES.) Give the girl a tissue.

JENNY. Thank you.

FAUSTUS. Listen, Jenny. It's not your fault your mother died, you understand that?

JENNY. Yes.

FAUSTUS. But she was always going to die. People die. Mothers die. My mother died a long, long time ago. And we're working on that, yeah? But until I solve it that is the reality of the situation. Where will we be in a hundred years, Jenny – in two hundred – what's your best guess?

JENNY. I don't know.

FAUSTUS. Guess.

JENNY. I'm not… Living on Mars? In nuclear bunkers? Wiped out entirely?

FAUSTUS. Okay. So. In two hundred years' time you and everyone you will ever meet will be dead, yes? Any survivor – if there are survivors – will be a total stranger to you. So why should we even bother? But I'm playing the long game. I'm trying to get my house in order. I've got to tend to the forest. Do you understand?

JENNY. Yes.

FAUSTUS. And I need people I can trust. I'm getting old – I won't be around forever.

JENNY. You're not old.

FAUSTUS. I'm older than I look. I need people who will do what it takes, who will think about tomorrow, not today, who have the capacity for greatness. Is that you? Should I let Jenny inherit my Earth?

JENNY. Yes. You can trust me, I promise.

FAUSTUS. Good. (*Offering her hand.*) Welcome to the Institute.

Scene ends. Into –

Scene Eleven

A boardroom. Waiting for FAUSTUS *are* WAR, FAMINE *and* PESTILENCE. *We see them more clearly now. They are as grotesque as we might hope, both human and not, rooted in an older time.* MEPHISTOPHELES *is with them.*

WAR (*to* MEPHISTOPHELES). You must answer for her.

MEPHISTOPHELES. I answer only to Lucifer.
Why come here, War? I shall not fight with you.
And Famine too? I have no appetite.
Is Pestilence behind? You unclean thing
She isn't sick, so don't breathe down my neck.
All keep your distance till my master comes.

PESTILENCE. He sends us.

FAMINE. She has grown out of your control.

MEPHISTOPHELES. No.

WAR. Been allowed too much. Conceded too much ground.

PESTILENCE. She has placed a worm in his brain too.

MEPHISTOPHELES. She has her will, and Lucifer his ways.

FAMINE. I say you are enamoured by her.

MEPHISTOPHELES. Bound to her.

FAMINE. Grown too fond. Her lapdog. Poodle.

WAR. Cannot be trusted. The threat must be neutralised.

MEPHISTOPHELES (*snaps*). Her time is not yet up.

FAMINE. Yet every day she lives more lives are saved.

MEPHISTOPHELES. She must have every second she was given – every second that was promised her. Or would you make Lucifer a liar?

PESTILENCE. Every wretched second – right to the last. But we are coming for her, make no mistake.

The HORSEMEN *start to draw back.*

MEPHISTOPHELES. You are not needed! I shall see to it – she shall burn!

FAUSTUS *enters. She seems disorientated. She cannot see the* HORSEMEN.

FAUSTUS. Mephistopheles?

MEPHISTOPHELES. Here, Faustus.

FAUSTUS. I heard… I was sleeping, maybe. I heard talking, noise.

MEPHISTOPHELES. You slept?

FAUSTUS. I think a little.

MEPHISTOPHELES. Good. That's good.

FAUSTUS. Was someone here?

MEPHISTOPHELES. Not a soul but us.

FAUSTUS. I was thinking – asteroids – have we talked about asteroids?

MEPHISTOPHELES. No.

FAUSTUS. Mineral-rich. Billons of tonnes. Just floating out there. No conflict in space. Just got to get to them. I've allocated the funding for a programme.

MEPHISTOPHELES. Excellent.

FAUSTUS. And Luxemburg – we're going to do the human trials in Luxemburg. All signed off.

MEPHISTOPHELES. Good news.

FAUSTUS. So we can move on. (*Beat.*) I'm so tired.

MEPHISTOPHELES. Don't worry, Faustus. You're on the home stretch now.

FAUSTUS. Good. Let's go. Ten years should do. Let's go.

MEPHISTOPHELES *clicks his fingers. A shift. A rumble. Rubble falls.* WAR *comes forward.*

WAR. And Faustus discovers in her absence
War has cracked a red raw fissure across the Earth

I have my fingers under its skin, inside its wounds
And I am squeezing, squeezing,
Laying waste to all her efforts.

FAUSTUS. No –

WAR. Still, Faustus won't surrender
She's come too far. Her hands cannot stay clean.
The good doctor forges her science into weapons
Bludgeons a weary world into submission
Until we have peace again.

FAUSTUS *comes forward, dazed and bloodied.*

FAUSTUS. Mephistopheles! It's over. It's done. Twenty years.
Come on.

Another quake. More staggering, stumbling, destruction. WAR *draws back and* FAMINE *comes forward to narrate.*

FAMINE. Now Famine takes her turn.
Faustus finds the crops have failed,
The new strains unsustainable
Too perfect, too other, too alien to survive here.
All her progress has turned to poison
Ashen and indigestible in dustbowl mouths –

FAUSTUS. I can fix this.

FAMINE. And if she had any sense
She'd let me starve this bloated planet before it bursts
But no, she pushes on,
Creates new techniques,
Splices genes,
Conjures water from barren rock
Somehow
Somehow she keeps going
Until those who survive once more have bellies full.

FAUSTUS. Onward then! Fifty years.

More quake, as before. PESTILENCE *replaces* FAMINE.

PESTILENCE. Now here's the world in the grip of plague
Here Pestilence reigns supreme, as I did once before
The hospitals she built, great glittering temples of disease
Where I learnt, evolved, grew strong,
Till with the smallest sneeze I could level continents.

FAUSTUS. I rid this once already – I can again.

PESTILENCE. I could dance this dance forever –
Infection and inoculation,
Thrust and parry,
Sickness and cure.
Oh, never in the nine circles of Hell was there such a torturer,
For she simply will not give up
Even as her patients grow older and older
Sicker and sicker, sadder and sadder,
Desperate for death, but still she denies them,
Quarantines and disinfects,
Seals off whole cities,
Until finally –

With a great cry, FAUSTUS *comes forward again. She is exhausted but ecstatic. The stage fizzes with energy, sparks fly, everything running at maximum capacity.*

FAUSTUS. Finally I am done.
Finally possess the knowledge
To extract minds from bodies and upload them
Humanity raptured up into the Cloud
Where war, disease and hunger have no place
No want, no pain, no hurt or suffering
No judgement. No damnation. None of it.
My silicon Utopia on Earth.
And I looked upon it
And saw that it was good.

She takes a breath. The HORSEMEN *are still around her. She looks at them for the first time.*

What? Did you not think I could sense you? You don't play fair, but I bested you all the same. So long War, farewell Famine, Pestilence adieu. Where's the fourth then? Come on – bring out the pale rider! (*Laughs.*) I thought as much. Death is so scared of Faustus he won't face me. I've banished him for good!

MEPHISTOPHELES. Congratulations, Faustus.

MEPHISTOPHELES *holds up a black robe, or produces a scythe, or something along these lines, in keeping with the costumes of the* HORSEMEN.

FAUSTUS. What's this?

MEPHISTOPHELES. Your destiny. The part you'd always play.

The HORSEMEN *kneel before* FAUSTUS.

FAUSTUS. No –

MEPHISTOPHELES. After War, after Famine, after Pestilence have all been vanquished –

FAUSTUS. No. No, I'm not… I won. I solved it. I saved them all.

A final quiet rumble. The lights flicker and go out one by one. The sound of generators gradually winding down until there is silence and complete darkness.

No! Stop it! Mephistopheles? I command you – light!

Lights start to creep back up dimly. Only FAUSTUS *and* MEPHISTOPHELES *remain on stage.*

What happened?

MEPHISTOPHELES. 'My name is Death, have you not heard of me?'

FAUSTUS. No. What happened here?

MEPHISTOPHELES. The power failed.

FAUSTUS. That's impossible.

MEPHISTOPHELES. Couldn't take the strain.

FAUSTUS. No, there are contingencies – external, off-site… I was… Failed?

MEPHISTOPHELES. Yes, Faustus.

FAUSTUS. Everywhere?

MEPHISTOPHELES. Yes.

FAUSTUS. So we lost – ?

MEPHISTOPHELES. Yes.

FAUSTUS. How much? (*Beat.*) Everything? (*Beat.*) Everyone? All of…? I… I…

MEPHISTOPHELES. Yes.

FAUSTUS. Ten billion minds, housed in… Some of the back-ups must have –

MEPHISTOPHELES. No.

FAUSTUS. No.

A silence.

MEPHISTOPHELES. So? You still have a little time.

FAUSTUS. I'm not… I can't… All of them?

MEPHISTOPHELES (*genuinely*). You have been spectacular, Faustus. You have exceeded my every expectation.

FAUSTUS. I…

MEPHISTOPHELES. Chin up. All's done.

FAUSTUS. Yes.

MEPHISTOPHELES. What next?

FAUSTUS. Go.

MEPHISTOPHELES. The job's not finished. Think what we could now do – could now build.

FAUSTUS. This is the last command I shall ever give you. You are to take me one thousand years forward and there you shall leave me, never again to be in my sight, until the Devil comes to take his due.

MEPHISTOPHELES. Faustus –

FAUSTUS. And till that time – as much as might be left – you are to live by the code I could not. First do no harm. I bind you to that with all power I have.

MEPHISTOPHELES. Don't be rash.

FAUSTUS. That will be all. I cast you out.

The earth shudders. Into –

Scene Twelve

The far-flung future.

FAUSTUS *tends to a garden. She wears something simple/earthy – something not out of place on a seventeenth-century peasant woman. She speaks to us.*

FAUSTUS. The world is quiet now.
And the world is healing,
Finally given a chance to recover.
I set about digging a garden
And it blooms – oh, how it blooms!

I tend to seedlings like they were my children,
Ancient varieties and new strains,
And the air is cool
And the sun is pale and low
And I am not alone.
No, some survived –
Some stragglers who couldn't bear to have their mortal flesh
uploaded –
And now, so many generations on,
Have no idea of everything they lost,
Or the role I played
But they come to me sometimes,
The woman in the woodland who seems older than her years
Who knows things she couldn't possibly know
And they ask 'How did you do that?'
And 'How do you grow that one?'
And I tell them how my mother taught me,
And how I'd gladly do the same for them.
They're grateful. For the most part they're grateful,
As I am grateful for them
In the moments I forget myself
And am just another woman in the woods.

ALICE*, a local woman, joins* FAUSTUS. *She holds a basket of mushrooms.*

ALICE. Found them just east of the creek – where the crooked firs grow.

FAUSTUS. Let's see. (*Looking through.*) These ones are good. These are safe to eat but the flavour is awful. Not these though – you see the white marks on the bottom? That's deadly.

ALICE. Got it.

FAUSTUS. But keep searching for more of these. They grow in clusters and they like the shade.

ALICE. Thank you.

FAUSTUS. I've just boiled some water, if you'll stay for tea?

ALICE I should get back before it's dark.

FAUSTUS. You'd be welcome to stay.

ALICE. I shouldn't. Thank you. (*Beat.*) They say… In the village they…

FAUSTUS. Yes?

ALICE. Doesn't matter. Only… A boy was passing, on his way to the creek. He said he heard you talking to someone.

FAUSTUS. To myself, maybe. Comes from living alone.

ALICE. In a strange tongue.

FAUSTUS. I've travelled, yes.

ALICE. Frightened him.

FAUSTUS. Then he shouldn't have stopped to listen. (*Beat.*) What can I say? I don't have much company.

ALICE. I'm sorry.

FAUSTUS. Don't be.

ALICE. Did you have someone once?

FAUSTUS. In a way.

ALICE. And was he with you long?

FAUSTUS. Oh, about a thousand years.

ALICE. The way you talk sometimes.

FAUSTUS. Promised me the world.

ALICE. They always do.

FAUSTUS. And to his credit he delivered a good part of it.

ALICE. But he wasn't kind?

FAUSTUS. That wasn't in his nature.

ALICE. No excuse.

FAUSTUS. Maybe. But he'll be back. Some day soon, I'd wager.

ALICE. I hope not. (*Beat.*) See those clouds scuttling over – there's a storm in them.

FAUSTUS. Hmm?

ALICE. I saw earlier this big, black bird – biggest bird I ever saw – always sign of a storm.

FAUSTUS. What kind of bird?

ALICE. Like none I've ever seen. Beat its wings and seemed to suck all the light out of the sky.

FAUSTUS. You should go. Sun's getting low. But come back and visit again soon.

ALICE. I will. I promise.

ALICE *smiles and goes. A pause.*

FAUSTUS. So it's time then.

FAUSTUS *sings softly to herself.*

(*Sings.*) 'Though some by age be full of grief and pain,
Till their appointed time they must remain;
I take no bribe, believe me, this is true.
Prepare yourself to go; I'm come for you.

Prepare yourself to go; I'm come for you.'

She stops. She speaks to an unseen presence.

Show yourself. Stop lurking.

LUCIFER *steps forward. Plague mask/beak, now perhaps with great black wings emerging from his back. She doesn't look at him.*

I've been expecting you. (*Beat.*) Hard to be precise – lost track of the days. So small, days. So then I moved to moons – twelve moons in a year – mark them off. Not exact, but… Then I thought about time zones, about chasing the light around the globe so the sun never set on me, and that way you could never claim my days were up. Loopholes. How does the Devil keep time anyway? Not with an atomic clock, not laboratory conditions, nothing so scientific. And I think – I think that's because it scares you – science scares you – because once we can explain something we have no need to fear it. I think you only have power in the dark. Lucifer. Light-bringer. Jealous of any other. I think you regret leading Eve to the apple – you thought you would be the one to teach her everything, but she blazed so much brighter than you ever dreamed of.

Anyway, I'm rambling. But I have been expecting you. Knew it was soon. I took down the scarecrow, did you see? That was for you. Big old crow. Big old bird. No use trying to keep you out. So here we are then. Don't you have anything to say?

LUCIFER *takes off his mask. He speaks as* THOMAS, *her father.*

LUCIFER. Johanna –

FAUSTUS. Don't call me that. Call me Faustus. Call me Doctor.

LUCIFER. I have another doctor coming.

FAUSTUS. Too late for that.

LUCIFER. Be calm. What can you remember? I found you collapsed on the heath – had to get you out of London – had to bring you home.

FAUSTUS. Home?

LUCIFER. Look – this is the house you grew up in.

FAUSTUS. No. No, I built it to bear a resemblance, that is all.

LUCIFER. Please, child –

FAUSTUS. I am not your child. You are not my father. My father's dead.

LUCIFER. Try not to –

FAUSTUS. He ran back towards the flames. How dare you wear his face?

MEPHISTOPHELES *enters.*

LUCIFER. Ah, here is the doctor now.

FAUSTUS. There you are.

MEPHISTOPHELES. How fares the patient?

LUCIFER. Her mind is uneasy. She doesn't seem to know me.

FAUSTUS. Oh, I know you – I *know* you –

MEPHISTOPHELES. I see. I fear she has her mother's madness.

FAUSTUS. No. I am not mad.

LUCIFER. She has been spinning the most incredible fantasies.

FAUSTUS. Do not call me mad. Call me wicked. Call me a sinner. Call me wrathful, prideful, slothful, lustful, envious, gluttonous, greedy, anything but mad. You may take my soul but you cannot have my mind.

MEPHISTOPHELES. How long has she been like this?

LUCIFER. A few days.

FAUSTUS. Liars! You are liars. I haven't seen you for thousands of years.

LUCIFER. Johanna –

FAUSTUS. I have told you to call me doctor!

LUCIFER. The doctor is here!

FAUSTUS. The doctor is I!

MEPHISTOPHELES. What year is it? Who is the king?

FAUSTUS. Please – I was cruel to you sometimes, but for all we shared –

MEPHISTOPHELES. I do not know you, ma'am.

FAUSTUS (*faltering*). No –

LUCIFER. Hush now. You have been through so much – you are so tired.

FAUSTUS. I am.

LUCIFER. You will sleep soon – sleep so soundly.

FAUSTUS. Father?

LUCIFER. Come here, girl.

FAUSTUS *embraces* LUCIFER, *sobbing on his shoulder. He comforts her. Then* KATHERINE *appears behind him.* FAUSTUS *sees her.* KATHERINE *shakes her head.* FAUSTUS *recoils from* LUCIFER.

FAUSTUS (*quietly*). No. I know who you are.

LUCIFER. Johanna –

FAUSTUS. You never helped her.

LUCIFER. No –

FAUSTUS. At least I tried. God knows I tried. That might count for something.

LUCIFER. Calm yourself.

FAUSTUS. I am not mad, nor was my mother.

MEPHISTOPHELES. She's seeing things. She is quite delusional.

FAUSTUS. I know who I am. I am Doctor Johanna Faustus, MD, PhD, Nobel Laureate. I have eradicated plagues and cultivated bacteria on Mars. I have brought rain to the deserts and sucked poison out of festering wounds. I have cured the sick and healed the lame. I am the last in a long line of healers. I am the witch's daughter. I have magic enough of my own. And I am a multitude of things but I am not mad. You will acknowledge me.

MEPHISTOPHELES. So frail. She shall not last the night.

FAUSTUS. When the clock strikes twelve?

LUCIFER. Try to make some peace with the world before you leave it.

FAUSTUS. Who said I was leaving?

LUCIFER. You cannot fight this.

MEPHISTOPHELES. The mortal flesh is weak.

FAUSTUS. And your imagination is so small. So Faustus must die, as all must die, and Faustus must be damned, as Eve was damned, as all are of her sex. For she did not know her place. For she has overreached, and for that she must be punished. But leave the world? No, sirs, I'll none of that. For I have scattered seeds in the forest and I know not what they'll grow into. It's not my place to know – I see that now. I was never meant to walk amongst the trees I planted, but plant them in the hope that others would. Hope, sirs, not for my soul, but the ones who come after. And no, I shall not live to see them bloom. I shan't watch the buds unfurl and breathe in the scent of morning, and so I cannot say with scientific certainty that spring will come. But for the first time I have faith. Faith in my daughters. Faith in the ones that follow. And that is why Faustus may be damned, but she is not lost. That is why you fail. What? Do you have nothing else to say?

The clock strikes twelve. FAUSTUS *laughs as* LUCIFER *and* MEPHISTOPHELES *watch her. She seems in complete control. Then just before the final chime she suddenly looks up.*

Wait –

The last chime strikes. Snap to black.

End.

NINE LESSONS AND CAROLS

Stories for a Long Winter

Written by Chris Bush
With songs by Maimuna Memon

Created by Chris Bush, Rebecca Frecknall and the Company

Nine Lessons and Carols was first performed at the Almeida Theatre, London, on 3 December 2020. The cast was as follows:

ONE	Elliot Levey
TWO	Katie Brayben
THREE	Toheeb Jimoh
FOUR	Naana Agyei-Ampadu
FIVE	Luke Thallon
SIX	Maimuna Memon
VOICE-OVER	Annie Firbank
Director	Rebecca Frecknall
Set and Costume Designer	Tom Scutt
Lighting Designer	Jack Knowles
Sound Designer	Carolyn Downing
Musical Supervisor	Tim Sutton

Characters

ONE
TWO
THREE
FOUR
FIVE
SIX
VOICE-OVER

Note

THREE *and* FOUR *must always be played by Black actors.*

Introduction

A health and safety announcement plays.

VOICE-OVER. Good evening, and welcome to the Almeida Theatre for tonight's performance of *Nine Lessons and Carols*.

This performance shall not contain nine lessons or nine carols. That was the first lie.

We're very happy to have you back.

This is the truth.

We've missed you.

Welcome.

We're so happy to have you here.

I am not here.

I could not be here.

But you are, and isn't that a beautiful thing?

To be here.

Don't worry, I'm not dead, just in Stoke Newington.

I'm eighty-seven, so you can just imagine. Logistical nightmare.

But enough of all that.

Welcome.

Congratulations on making it this far.

I'm trying to picture you.

This is nice, isn't it, to congregate once more, a sparse assembly of the living, heartbeats synchronised, breathing together in unison?

Please don't breathe on anyone.

We must insist you don't breathe on anyone.

I'm quite serious. Snigger if you must, but comply all the same.

Turn off your phones. There shall be no need for screens during tonight's performance, and thank Christ for that.

Unless you're watching this online, in which case God bless you.

Sit back. Relax. Everything is going to be fine.

That was the second lie.

Everything is going to be.

And tonight – huddled in the dark – further apart than feels natural – as these strange new rituals start to become commonplace, and all you yearn to do is reach out and touch –

Don't touch! Mustn't touch.

Tonight, may you leave to a world that feels a little larger than it did before. May it slowly start to regain something of its majesty.

But until then, a story…

Into –

1. The Story of Loneliness

Underscore plays. The VOICE-OVER *continues.*

VOICE-OVER. In the beginning, everyone was apart, and everyone was content.

The gods had been determined to give their people room. Each was given their own patch of land far apart from any other, well resourced, lush and verdant, where each could live in pleasant solitude.

And nothing got done.

No great monuments, no feats of civilisation, no children, which was what the gods now truly craved – fresh disciples to carry on their work. How could they have been so foolish? And so the gods hatched a plan.

One morning the whole world awoke in pain. Each human found a thorn planted deep between their shoulder blades – jabbing, stabbing, immovable, and resolutely out of reach. However much they stretched and strained they couldn't get to it.

However much they scratched their spines against rough trees or took long baths trying to soak them out, the thorns wouldn't budge.

And the thorns were called loneliness.

One by one, the COMPANY *start to enter and take over the story, lines divided up between them.*

COMPANY. Soon after this, a woman heard a faint but familiar whimpering coming from far across the valley – familiar, because she recognised the sorrow as her own. She followed the noise for three days until she found another figure, whose likeness to herself took her breath away. She located the thorn in the centre of the stranger's back, grasped it firmly and pulled, and to her great relief it slid straight out. The favour was returned, and soon both women were free from pain. It seemed only natural that they promptly fell in love.

Word spread. The people banded together, and after swiftly dealing with their thorns, began to turn their attention to other things – all the monuments and milestones the gods had sought. Most critically, they started to produce children – so many children, of all sorts, shapes and sizes. Civilisation thrived. The people were content once more. The clever gods rejoiced. But the gods are not infallible, and they had no idea what they had done.

Because these children were born with no thorns in their backs. Unbeknownst to anyone, their thorns grew on the inside.

Some had thorns in their mouths, which made it hard to talk.
Some had thorns in their lungs, which made it hard to breathe.
Some had thorns in their minds, which planted drawing pins in all their thoughts.
Others had thorns in their hearts, which made it so painful to love.

And all of them were hidden.

Until one night an old woman heard a familiar whimper. Familiar, and terrifying, because it was a sound she thought she'd never hear again.

What's wrong? Can you tell me what's wrong? Are you hurt? Did something happen?

'I think…' the child began quietly, 'I think there might be something wrong with me. Only me. A pain inside. A stabbing. Like a thorn.'

These thorns were different. Some could be reached, others could not. Some were plucked out but grew back again. Others were so knotted and tangled up inside they couldn't be removed. Some were sung to, others treated with ointments. Some bloomed into the most magnificent roses.

When the gods caught wind of what had happened, they were devastated, but they couldn't do anything about it. The thorns were a part of their people now – in their veins, under their skin. But their people proved more resourceful and robust than they'd ever imagined. Not because of the thorns, but in spite of them. Not because of their wounds, but because of how they were tended to. And the Children of Loneliness are the strongest tribe of all.

Into –

2. To My January Self (SONG)

SIX *comes forward to sing.*

SIX (*sings*). To my January self
Here's to you and your good health
Cos a tidal wave is headed to demolish all your senses

I could try but I would fail
To tell you what your year entails
But I wouldn't want to prematurely heighten your defences

Resolutions forming rising in the air
This is not a warning I just wish I could be there

To my January self
Blow the cobwebs off that shelf
Read a couple pages of a book you'll never finish

No, you won't improve your mind
And you'll barely go outside
But I must admit I'm jealous of your licence to be selfish

Resolutions forming rising in the air
This is not a warning I just wish I could be there

I would hide my scars from wounds you've yet to make
I would bite my tongue and watch you make all my mistakes

And I would hold you
I would hold you
I would hold you
I would hold you and hold you and hold you.

All your January dreams
Will burst open at the seams
But you'll only make it worse if you keep trying to find some meaning

Into –

3. Hunt the Wren

TWO. You will soon get used to the cold.

Embrace the cold, light a fire – for warmth, and other things. Burn your bra. Burn your birth certificate. Burn your house down. Burn your neighbours' houses. Keep burning until you have no more neighbours. Light a fire.

Free your feet. Reacquaint your toes with the earth. Soon it will be time for hunting. Bring bows and arrows, axes, sharpened stone. I'll be using tooth and claw. Hands dirty, nose twitching, eyes alive.

Bang a drum. Blow your horn. Raise a cup. Ambush a Deliveroo driver and ride his moped through an Amazon warehouse. Eat the rich. Starve the poor. You are on your own right now. Piss down the side of the Shard. Run amok. Strip assets. Lie. Cheat. Steal. None of it matters. Nothing.

The old year is dead. Gone. Dust and ashes. All that remains is *us* – the odd assortment of things that wouldn't burn.

Don't look at me like I'm mad. Step back. Big picture. Expand your perspective. While you stockpiled toilet roll I bought up shares in loneliness. I shorted the market on hope, decimating its value. I was prepared for this.

Some of us have always been alone.

Alone and lonely are not the same. This is important. Loneliness is for the intellectually weak. Loneliness is the terror of having no one to dilute your own terrible personality. Loneliness is for dogs and babies and poets, and other underdeveloped life forms who can't get through the day without crying for their mummy or shitting on the carpet. The hole you feel inside you is neither novel nor interesting. Move on. Light a fire.

I am my own support bubble. I like my own company. I *thrive* in the dark days because I have a light within. Try it some time.

Make way for Saturnalia, our ancient solstice rites. The topsy-turvy times where masters are beholden to their slaves, where chaos reigns, where all run wild and free. And you think – you *think* – there is an understanding that all this will be temporary. You'll have a little taste and then be satisfied. Not this time. None of us are going back. I shall run to the hills and hack myself off a plot of land. Unreachable. Untouched. I go forth while you flee. You shall stumble blindly, clutching at straws and trying to identify fistfuls of frostbitten berries from your *Guardian Weekend* foraging course, dragging your screeching brats behind you with promises of marshmallows and redemption. They are dead weight. Leave them behind. I am already roasting my first influencer over a spit. I was prepared for this.

It is arrogance that assumes you can reason with the reckoning. The world does not concern itself with you. This is not punishment for your many crimes, and cannot be placated by your prayers. This is the sound made by a small rock hurtling around a dying star, which from a critical distance burnt out long ago. It is the sound of nothing. The mistake you made was imagining you had anything to lose.

Some of us have always been alone.

You will soon get used to the cold.

Into –

4. The First Pitch

ONE *to* FIVE *are gathered.*

ONE. Nothing.

TWO. Bears? Have we – ?

THREE. Polar bears?

FOUR (*to* ONE). You've got nothing?

FIVE. Snow bears? Is that a…?

ONE. Can we stop? Just for –

TWO. Penguins.

THREE. Robins.

FOUR. Um. Reindeer.

FIVE. Dogs.

THREE. Do dogs say Christmas?

FIVE. Huskies?

TWO. Yeah, or no – what about the um, the St Bernards?

FOUR. The ones that rescue – ?

TWO. Yes! Yes – exactly yes. Because they're rescue dogs, yeah? So that's the… They have these barrels of… of brandy, of whiskey, strapped round their necks, to revive any human they discover halfway up the mountain.

THREE. Really?

FIVE. Does that work?

TWO. The dogs?

FIVE. The brandy.

FOUR. Yes.

ONE. No.

FOUR. Yes! Restorative.

THREE. Like a beer jacket?

FIVE. Got it.

ONE. No! It doesn't – it's the worst thing! You might feel warmer, initially, but actually, actually –

TWO. Anyway – no, listen – anyway – St Bernards – big, beautiful idiots, right? Rescue dogs. So we have them carrying – not just whiskey – not booze – but presents, packages, parcels, tied up with bows. Through the rain, through the snow, over mountains, on, um… fishing boats – ocean liners –

FIVE. Biplanes.

TWO. Okay.

FIVE. Yeah, you know, biplanes with the, um –

FOUR. The hat! Big St Bernard in the cockpit with the goggles and ear flaps, all of the –

FIVE. Right?

TWO. Yep, sure, all of that. This army, this… not army, but this huge pack of them, spreading out all over the globe, dropping off parcels to key workers and lollipop ladies, and –

THREE. And puppies.

FOUR. Yes.

FIVE. Yes! Got to have a –

THREE. Little puppy – a little three-legged puppy who's smaller than the rest, but won't give up, dragging this present that's much too big for him –

FIVE. Or he *is* the present? Is that – ?

THREE. Plot twist. Love it.

FOUR. Maybe.

ONE. But why dogs? Why would – ?

TWO. Because – it's like drones, right? Drones are terrifying – an army of drones descending over London, dropping off your Christmas shopping? Nightmare – total Capitalist Dystopia – but *dogs* – St Bernards – rescue dogs –

FIVE. Dogs who rescue, or dogs who have *been* rescued?

FOUR. Oh, I like that.

TWO. Both. Why not both? And it's like, wherever you're stranded –

FIVE. We'll reach you!

FOUR. Yes!

TWO. Yes, but –

ONE. Is it a little familiar? Is it – ?

FIVE. We could even… What if we started in the warehouse? Outside the warehouse, and these huge dock doors, loading doors, twenty feet high, chained up maybe, they start to rattle – a bit Jacob Marley – a bit ominous – a bit what's-all-this-then? And then just when you think shit's about to go down, they burst open, and dogs!

THREE. Dogs!

FIVE. Just hundreds of dogs! Thousands of them!

THREE. Tumbling out, falling over each other –

FOUR. Mischievous – a bit naughty.

TWO. Right. And then –

FIVE. Then out they go, out they go, into all the rest of it –

TWO. Parachuting out of planes. Um. Snorkelling. Aqualung.

FOUR. Skydiving.

THREE. Flying? Like the Peter Pan dog flying?

TWO. Rescuing Christmas. Saving Christmas.

FOUR. That's it. That's the ad.

ONE. Here to save Christmas.

TWO. Yeah.

Into –

5. Outside

THREE *and* FOUR.

FOUR. Water?

THREE. Hmm?

FOUR. Do you have water?

THREE. Yes.

FOUR. Sanitiser?

THREE. Yes.

FOUR. Pretzels?

THREE. What?

FOUR. Salty snacks – something for… They replenish electrolytes.

THREE. Right.

FOUR. You need electrolytes.

THREE. Do I?

FOUR. If you're going to be out all day.

THREE. Okay.

FOUR. Mask?

THREE. Yes.

FOUR. With filters?

THREE. Yes.

FOUR. The right kind?

THREE. Can you stop, please?

FOUR. And a hat. A scarf – something loose you can bundle.

THREE. I'm not –

FOUR. No skin. Don't show your face.

THREE. Why?

FOUR. They'll be scanning – they can trace.

THREE. So what?

FOUR. You'll end up on some –

THREE. I want them to see.

FOUR. Be sensible.

THREE. I'm going to be seen – to be counted.

FOUR. Oh, so that's it?

THREE. What?

FOUR. To be seen?

THREE. No –

FOUR. For the 'gram?

THREE. Not like that.

FOUR. For the hashtag?

THREE. Why aren't you? Forget why I'm going – why aren't you? Cos we get the same news – you've watched the same videos –

FOUR. Yeah.

THREE. So do you not care about – ?

FOUR. There are other ways.

THREE. Like what?

FOUR. What do you think you're going to achieve?

THREE. No – I asked first.

FOUR. You should be asking yourself. Should be realistic, and deliberate, and… goal-orientated.

THREE. Right.

FOUR. It's easy to get carried away.

THREE. That's not what this is.

FOUR. And then get frustrated when –

THREE. Why won't you come with me?

FOUR. I don't have to answer that.

THREE. One reason.

FOUR. You know there'll be trouble. You know what –

THREE. I'll look after you.

FOUR. And not just today – anything bad that happens afterwards, any spike, that gets put on us. We broke the rules. We can't behave. We're trouble.

THREE. They'll say that anyway.

FOUR. No –

THREE. They'll say that whatever we do.

FOUR. Not if –

THREE. So we might as well do something.

FOUR. Be smart.

THREE. I'm always smart.

FOUR. Be better.

THREE. They don't like it when we're better.

FOUR. I'm not –

THREE. They *hate* it when we're better than them.

FOUR. Never give them an excuse.

THREE. They don't need one.

FOUR. Don't put yourself in a situation you can't control.

THREE. So that's you, is it? Shut in – never leaves your flat?

FOUR. No –

THREE. Doesn't matter what you do – where you are. Unarmed. No warrant. No record. A doctor. A Member of Parliament. At home. Asleep. A kid with a water pistol. It doesn't matter.

FOUR. You start – okay, this is… You start with you, what you need, what you can manage, the burden you can carry – safely – then you look at –

THREE. 'You start with you'?

FOUR. If you don't –

THREE. Who are you, Black Thatcher?

FOUR. I start with me. And I'm not going to be cannon fodder –

THREE. So what're you doing instead? (*Beat.*) Nah – go on, lay it out.

FOUR. You know that's the first time you've ever asked me that.

THREE. What?

FOUR. The first time you've ever… Now you think you've got an answer.

THREE. Tell me.

FOUR. And you – now you think you can school me? Like I've not marched – like I'm not marching every time I step outside. Like I've ever had a choice. You think cos I'm not lining up to get my head kicked in I'm out of ideas? Ask me where I shop, where I spend my money. Who I vote for, who I talk to, the conversations I have. Where I apply pressure. Where I change minds.

THREE. Yeah, that's a part of it.

FOUR. Ask me what I risk.

THREE. Still not told me why you won't come.

FOUR. Grow up.

THREE. Stand up.

FOUR. And this – all this – none of it is our problem to fix. It shouldn't have to be us out there.

THREE. It's not. Not just us – not this time. Danny's coming down – Jacob too. Even Ellie and what's-her-name – her new girlfriend – everyone –

FOUR. Good for them.

THREE. Hundreds of white folk turning out – thousands – finally –

FOUR. So let them. Leave them to it.

THREE. I can't do that.

FOUR. You're not going to solve anything today.

THREE. It's a start. Not a start. It's a step. It's something.

Beat.

FOUR. Take water. Lots of water.

THREE. I know.

FOUR. Take a spray bottle – mix water with bicarbonate of soda –

THREE. You sent me the video.

FOUR. So if anything gets in your eyes –

THREE. I watched it.

FOUR. Don't let yourself get boxed in. Stay to the edges, not the middle.

THREE. I know.

FOUR. You'll have more shade there too.

THREE. I know what I'm doing.

FOUR. It'll be hot.

THREE. Yeah.

FOUR. Don't stand out. Where something neutral – practical.

THREE. Okay.

FOUR. Something you can run in. (*Beat.*) You don't have to go. (*Beat.*) You know that? Doesn't matter who else is.

THREE. And do what? Cos none of the rest of it matters if it's not this as well. Always has to be this as well, or everything else gets lost. (*Beat.*) Meet me there. Please.

Into –

6. Banana Bread

ONE. One pound of ripe bananas – five hundred grams, to you. Peeled weight. The blacker the better. Mash them with a fork, or with your hands, if you just want to feel something. Have you ever written on a banana with a ballpoint pen? The skin, not the flesh. Extraordinary. Better than sex. Says the man who hasn't had intercourse since the end of the Obama administration. Sorry. No politics at the dinner table, I know.

A pound of bananas, then in another bowl, eight ounces of self-raising flour, a teaspoon of mixed spice, or cinnamon, or nutmeg, but not garam masala, as it turns out that's something quite different. Good pinch of salt, four ounces of sugar. Apparently there's more than one type of sugar, but life is short. Four ounces of butter, or the low-cholesterol substitute of your choice, because you've basically given up on pleasure at this point, and you get your kicks from doodling on banana skins.

I hope you're enjoying all this.

Fat into flour, then your bananas, four ounces of sultanas, three ounces of walnuts or brazils – not salted peanuts, doesn't work – three ounces of glacé cherries, according to this recipe, but obviously that's disgusting so no. Two eggs, a tablespoon of honey, the juice of one lemon. Stir it up. Don't worry about lumps – it's far too late for that. Bake in a greased and lined loaf tin for one hour at gas mark four, then another half-hour at gas mark three. Allow to cool.

Remember you don't like bananas.

Offer it to the neighbours, who will coo 'oh, very Nigella' in a way that is definitely designed to emasculate.

Are you still with me? I'm not in my element here, but I am trying.

The smell is… I do like the smell while it's cooking. Not offensively banana-y, which helps. I wish you were here to smell it. You'd be impressed.

I saw it, two days later, on their bird table – next door's. Untouched. Unsliced. The nerve. That's when I made my vow to outlive them. Feeling quietly confident about that. The amount of potassium I have in my system right now, I must be practically immortal.

Potassium, it's… I don't know what it does, exactly. Burns in water, is that right? Doesn't sound right. Not very appetising.

I'm not done yet though, don't you worry. There's a cheeky little chocolate beetroot number I've got my eye on. The beetroot gives it an earthy flavour, it says, which is apparently desirable in a cake.

I've got candles, that's the important thing. I'll have to blow them out myself, but don't worry. I'll still sing. Just you try and stop me. I'll put a slice out for the birds – who knows, maybe the whole thing. Send me a bird or two, if you can. I'd like that. Not a rainbow – nothing so gauche. And next door will stick their heads over the fence to check in, because they know it's this time of year again, and they're good like that actually, and so if you could organise the odd raven or something to come peck their eyes out that'd be lovely. Of course they'll be run off their feet next year – far too many people to comfort – presuming they last that long. A whole nation of survivors, eating our grief.

They're going to make a killing in candles.

Into –

7. Space

TWO *and* FIVE.

FIVE. eBay?

TWO. Don't.

FIVE. A fucking campervan?

TWO. Don't shout at me.

FIVE. I'm not –

TWO. I have asked you repeatedly –

FIVE. Is this for real?

TWO. Every time you raise your voice you make it more difficult for us to communicate.

FIVE. Fucking eBay?!

TWO. It's fine. It has all the paperwork, all the –

FIVE. Can you send it back?

TWO. No. I mean I don't know, but I don't want to. I won't, so –

FIVE. What did you pay for it?

TWO. Not much.

FIVE. We discuss – we have an agreement – any major purchase –

TWO. It wasn't –

FIVE. You lost your shit when I bought the coffee machine.

TWO. This cost less than the coffee machine.

FIVE. Really?

TWO. Do you remember what you spent on the coffee machine?

FIVE. No.

TWO. I do.

FIVE. Don't change the… That isn't what we're discussing.

TWO. Okay.

FIVE. What are you going to do with it?

TWO. Get away.

FIVE. Now?

TWO. Yes, now.

FIVE. Where? How long for?

TWO. Anywhere. And… I don't know. Indefinitely?

FIVE. Right. Great.

TWO. Somewhere warm. Desert, maybe.

FIVE. What desert?

TWO. I don't know, just –

FIVE. How would we…? You have a job. I have a job.

TWO. So?

FIVE. So?!

TWO. I hate my job.

FIVE. So what?

TWO. You hate your job.

FIVE. No –

TWO. You do!

FIVE. I don't.

TWO. You do! You hate it – you *hate* it!

FIVE. I love it!

TWO. It makes you sad.

FIVE. I like being sad!

TWO *scoffs.*

Being sad just means you're paying attention. Being sad is the glue that binds us to the world.

TWO. I don't want to be.

FIVE. What?

TWO. I don't want to be bound to anything.

FIVE. Well… tough! Just tough, actually. We have responsibilities. We have a life. We –

TWO. Let me explain.

FIVE. The desert? Indefinitely?

TWO. Why not?

FIVE. I hate camping.

TWO. I know.

FIVE. Did you think about that?

TWO. Yes.

FIVE. But you expect me to just drop everything, and – ?

TWO. No.

FIVE. Then what?

TWO. I didn't expect you to come.

Pause.

FIVE. What?

TWO. You hate camping. I didn't think you'd want to come.

FIVE. What are you saying?

TWO. I didn't buy it for us, I bought it for me. This is for me. (*Pause.*) I've been following them for months – the vans – watching bids, keeping a track of… And to begin with that was enough – just watching, imagining, knowing that if it came to it I had enough in my current account – I had an escape plan –

FIVE. From what? From me?

TWO. From everything. But it wasn't real. It could never happen, because you'd never agree to come. Or you might, if I forced you, but you'd hate it, and it'd spoil everything. You'd be miserable there. I'm miserable here. What else can I do?

Pause.

FIVE. You're leaving?

TWO. Yes.

FIVE. Indefinitely?

TWO. I think so.

FIVE. You're leaving me?

TWO. If I could do it any other way – if I could be alone without having to leave you then I would.

FIVE. You can't. I love you! You can't –

TWO. I think maybe I need love less than I need freedom.

FIVE. You are free!

TWO. No.

FIVE. Yes! In what way – in what actual, tangible way are you not – ?

TWO. I think in the desert I'll ask a question and mine will be the only voice that answers and maybe, maybe, once I've heard it –

FIVE. This is insane.

TWO. No –

FIVE. Listen to yourself. You're being insane.

TWO. I'm not. Actually I don't think there's anything wrong with me. Actually I like myself, a surprising amount of the time, and maybe –

FIVE. I like you.

TWO. I know.

FIVE. A surprising amount of the time.

TWO. I like you too.

FIVE. So what's the problem? We'll fix this. I can fix this.

TWO. No.

FIVE. I can… There has to be –

TWO. I've tried. I promise. I've tried so hard.

FIVE. No. I'll show you, I'll… I won't raise my voice. I'll do better. I –

TWO. It's not about that.

FIVE. But I love you.

TWO. I'm sorry.

FIVE. What if I did come? What about that? What if I – ?

TWO. You'd be miserable.

FIVE. I'll be miserable here.

TWO. Not forever.

FIVE. Stay. You have to. I can't be alone.

TWO. Then don't be.

FIVE. You won't get five miles – not in that thing. It'll explode – fireball on the highway – if you can even get it started. You'll be back before it's dark.

TWO. I love you.

FIVE. I can't be alone.

Into –

8. Rinse and Repeat (SONG)

SIX (*sings*). I watch on as twenty-somethings quickly regress
Move back to the town they once so hastily left
Sitting at the table to repeatedly eat
Fall into Egyptian cotton family sheets

Meanwhile in a parallel dimension to this
I am living quiet in unparented bliss
No one to envelop me with twenty-pound notes
Bachelorette with an invisibility cloak

I taught myself to wash my hands
I learned myself to scrub my feet
I'll cater to this god's commands
I'm not alone rinse and repeat
I'm not alone rinse and repeat

If you're pure your pain will be washed away
You will rise to heaven I remember they'd say
Respect the elders who gave you this life
Say your prayers before you sleep at night
Say your prayers before you sleep at night

I taught myself to wash my hands
I learned myself to scrub my feet
I'll cater to this god's commands
I'm not alone rinse and repeat
I'm not alone rinse and repeat

The dirt that permeates your face
Erase it let your demons go
Words I will vigorously embrace
Rinse and repeat I'm not alone
Rinse and repeat I'm not alone

Mother ooooo
Mother ooooo
Doing things I'm supposed to do
Irresolute in the truth
Mother ooooo
Mother ooooo
Maybe she would have proved me wrong
Maybe she would have made me stronger
She'd probably light a fire now
Make everything warmer somehow

So here I stand to wash my hands
My face, my arms, my head and feet
I'll do what history demands
I'm not alone rinse and repeat
I'm not alone rinse and repeat
I'm not alone rinse and repeat

Song ends. Into –

9. The Second Pitch

ONE *to* FIVE *gathered again.*

FOUR. Water?

THREE. Yep.

FOUR. Really?

THREE. It's everywhere.

ONE. Not *everywhere*.

FIVE. All over. Haven't you – ?

TWO. All over the news, not –

ONE. Right.

FOUR. Lots of it?

FIVE. It's not about the volume, it's the… the gesture, isn't it? The romance.

THREE. The poetry.

FOUR. Okay. I think we can have a little dramatic licence.

TWO. Yeah. I mean the thing is though, the moon has been done.

THREE. But not *water* on the moon.

TWO. Is that really – ?

FIVE. Yes! Because the moon – the moon is cold, right?

FOUR. Is it?

FIVE. It is – I checked. Boiling during the day, but freezing overnight. Which gives you what? Anybody?

ONE. What?

FIVE. Freezing water. Think about it.

TWO. Ice?

FIVE. Snow! Snowing on the moon!

FOUR. Okay.

ONE. That's not… I'm pretty sure that's –

THREE. Theoretically.

ONE. Not atmospherically possible.

FIVE. A snowball fight on the moon. Between, um –

FOUR. Like little alien, little Martians?

THREE. That'd be Mars.

FOUR. Right.

TWO. Little, um, Moon-ians? Lunarians?

THREE. Astronauts.

FIVE. Yes.

FOUR. Yeah, I like that – the human.

TWO. And it's very, um, in the suits – the helmets – the full –

FOUR. Yes, that's good, that helps.

FIVE. Moon landing. What's-his-name – Buzz Thingy –

TWO. Lightyear?

FIVE. Armstrong, takes his step, has a little bounce –

THREE. And then boof – out of nowhere – snowball!

FIVE. Smack!

FOUR. Okay, fun.

ONE. From who? Who's throwing – ?

FIVE. All of them, then it's the whole gang of astronauts, all having this massive –

FOUR. Making moon-angels.

FIVE. Sledging down the sea of tranquillity.

TWO. Building a snowman.

THREE. Yeah – like a snow-astronaut – a snow-stronaut, a –

FIVE. With the helmet and everything.

ONE. They can't take off their helmets.

FOUR. No, they shouldn't do that.

FIVE. Maybe they brought a spare.

THREE. A little lunar rover, little robot thing, sticks the carrot in.

FOUR. I can sell that.

TWO. Astronauts pulling crackers – paper hats over the helmets –

FIVE. Yes!

THREE. Carving the space turkey. Or whatever.

FOUR. With some Bowie?

TWO. Or Elton?

FOUR. Didn't he already – ?

ONE. Yes.

FIVE. And it says, um, at the end – it says 'wherever you are' –

THREE. However far away you are –

FIVE. However far away you *feel* this Christmas…

TWO. You'll be coming home soon.

FIVE. Sure.

TWO. Rocket blasts back off, snowman waves goodbye –

THREE. Passes Santa's sleigh on its way.

FOUR. Rudolf snatches up the carrot, bish-bash-bosh, all done. Merry Christmas.

Into –

10. Delivery

THREE. Just because you stopped it doesn't mean the world did.

My day starts at four-thirty at the depot, where Dave, who still believes in lizard people, has finally started to wear a mask. Rashid is off indefinitely, but that just means we're a man down. Load up and ship out. I deliver soap and sanitiser, canned goods and bread flour. I deliver organic hampers in Dulwich Village and wine subscriptions to Chelsea townhouses. I deliver bog roll under armed escort to Buckingham Palace. I deliver MPs to their mistresses in prepaid Uber Execs. I wipe down my surfaces. I deliver running gear and weights sets, yoga mats and ergonomic desks. I deliver succulents and eco-friendly sex toys to Herne Hill lesbians looking for revelation. I deliver blitz spirit via home-brew kits and mindful cross-stitch. I deliver textbooks and stationery sets to frazzled executive vice-presidents suddenly demoted to home school enforcers. In St John's Wood a commissioning editor in a Liberty dressing gown offers me five hundred pounds to explain to her children the properties of a sine wave. You don't understand, she says, they're *always here.* Can't you do something? You're so lucky.

I deliver high-end dim sum to overcrowded Highgate dinner parties, where on my way out a crumbling chin slips me a crumpled twenty and asks, if I know anyone, to send a mate back with some coke. I deliver sourdough pizza to illicit Goldsmiths raves, where would-be intersectionalists offer me a joint and invite me to stay, saying 'Hey, I bet *you* can dance. Look at him – I bet he can. Show us how it's done.' At the height of summer I deliver crates of Reni Eddo-Lodge and Chimamanda Ngozi Adichie and Audre Lorde to East London interlopers who pause to thank me personally but still don't tip. I grow tired of being asked 'Have you read this?' In Hackney Wick a tattooed Tarquin holds me hostage for thirty minutes with a pre-prepared statement on how he intends to be a better ally, before finally dismissing me with a silent raised fist. Solidarity, bruv. By September, these conversations have stopped.

I deliver CBD oil and lavender drops, weighted blankets and herbal remedies. I encounter a rake-thin zombie in Nunhead who mumbles 'Hey man, can I ask – are you sleeping?' My cans of Red Bull fill the footwell until I receive a written warning – this is the company's vehicle, not my personal toilet. I piss into an empty Lucozade bottle in a layby off the M25. I keep going.
I deliver A-grade sexts to Jess, a Tinder match, who through a cultivated misunderstanding thinks I'm a paramedic. She messages every Thursday to say she's clapping for me. I like that. Why not? I spot a status update from Josh, who is feeling hashtag-blessed – wants to remind us all how rare it is that we actually get to stop. Take stock – reprioritise. He was approaching burn-out before, but now he's energised. Sometimes some breathing space is all we need. No time to reply. The world didn't stop because you did. Eighty-six drops left to hit my daily target. Next year I'll try and catch up on all that growth you got while I was out here. Now can you sign for this?

Into –

11. Solitude (SONG)

SIX (*sings*). The days and week oh they go by
I find it hard to reason why
My motivated state is gone
I'd rather sit and watch the dawn
A chorus filling up the room
A sound that's sweeter than perfume

As pink and violet paint the walls
The birds they summon with their calls
Calls calls oooo

So walk until the floor below you
Moves in tandem with your soul and
Trace the sky with fingers
That could reach beyond this world that lingers
Feel the presence of your lungs
As you breathe what's to become
A gentle look to pastures new
That's you and your friend
Solitude

Can you tell me how did I
Get here so quickly did I die?
Was all of this a dream to me
Or did I crash in purgatory?
A place of nearly knowing why
I stand here in the dark and cry
The only thing to catch the noise
The trees embodying their voice
Voice voice oooo

So walk until the floor below you
Moves in tandem with your soul and
Trace the sky with fingers
That could reach beyond this world that lingers
Feel the presence of your lungs
As you breathe what's to become
A gentle look to pastures new
That's you and your friend
Solitude

And I don't feel strange
With this new change
I just wish I
Understood why
And I feel so strange
Everything's changed
I just hope to
Make a breakthrough
Make a breakthrough

So walk until the floor below you
Moves in tandem with your soul and

Trace the sky with fingers
That could reach beyond this world that lingers
Feel the presence of your lungs
As you breathe what's to become
A gentle look to pastures new
That's you and your friend
Solitude

Into –

12. Inside

THREE *and* FOUR.

FOUR. Water.

THREE. Yes.

FOUR. Keep drinking water.

THREE. I know.

FOUR. And aloe. Or you could use… I don't know. Cucumber.

THREE. Cucumber?

FOUR. Might bring the swelling down.

THREE. I don't have a cucumber.

FOUR. Okay.

THREE. Cucumber's nasty.

FOUR. See what Kerry has.

THREE. I'm fine.

FOUR. You don't look –

THREE. You going to say it then?

FOUR. What?

THREE. 'I told you so.'

FOUR. No.

THREE. No?

FOUR. I'm only trying to help.

THREE. Bit late for that.

FOUR. What?

THREE. If you wanted to help, you'd have been there.

FOUR. I told you –

THREE. The only one who didn't show.

FOUR. I said I wouldn't.

THREE. Even Henrietta – fucking horse-girl Henrietta busted out some Ivy Park and came down.

FOUR. And did she get pepper-sprayed too?

THREE. No.

FOUR. Funny that.

THREE (*ignores this*). Kept looking round, like you were gonna rock up at the last minute, like the cavalry, like the fucking… I don't know. And you'd do that thing you do – talk in that way you do when you're real mad, two parts Oxford, one part Brixton –

FOUR. Shut up.

THREE. Crowds would fall silent, you'd go viral, up on the… the fourth plinth or whatever. Overnight sensation.

FOUR. I wouldn't have made any difference.

THREE. You would to me.

FOUR. I'm sorry you got hurt.

THREE. I'm fine.

FOUR. That's why – why I didn't want you… There have to be other ways. If the only way we can win the argument is with our blood then we are still having the wrong conversation and I can't. We can't keep doing it. I'm done with bleeding.

THREE. I didn't go looking for a fight.

FOUR. I know.

THREE. None of us want to bleed.

FOUR. I know that.

THREE. Nothing else works.

FOUR. Did that work?

THREE. I don't know yet.

FOUR. Right.

THREE. But nothing else has.

FOUR. Maybe not yet.

THREE. I didn't want to go. You think I actually wanted to go? I just want it to stop.

FOUR. I know.

THREE. When's it going to stop?

FOUR. I don't know.

THREE. I thought it might help – being around people, y'know? Brothers, sisters, allies. Might get energised by it. Feel better. Release something. But I'm just tired. And maybe I do just want to burn shit, but not in an unconsidered way – not thoughtless – like actually I've sat with this for a while now and I think the most productive thing we can do is to burn shit down. What do I do with that?

FOUR. I do Pilates.

THREE (*laughs*). Hah! I bet you do – you actually do.

FOUR. Bit of Hot Yoga.

THREE. Doesn't it kill you?

FOUR. You know that bit at the end of *The Avengers* when they need Mark Ruffalo to turn himself green?

THREE. What?

FOUR. Yeah – you know, he's the big green guy?

THREE. Do you mean the Hulk?

FOUR. Sure. And they're like 'Hey, Mark – we need you to get angry.' And he says 'Guys – you know my secret? I'm always angry.'

Beat.

THREE. Is that it?

FOUR. What?

THREE. Is that your wisdom? What you would've said in Trafalgar Square?

FOUR. I just –

THREE. Just as well you didn't come.

FOUR. There's never been a moment when I haven't wanted to burn something.

THREE. Can I see you? Can we find a time soon to… Somewhere safe. Somewhere open, somewhere with birds, trees, away from all the…?

FOUR. Yeah.

THREE. Just to be us? Like back in the day. Without any of the…?

FOUR. I'd like that.

THREE. With none of that weight, you know?

FOUR. Course we can.

THREE. I miss you.

FOUR. I know. I miss you too. I'll see you soon.

Into –

13. Dog Person

FIVE. She was tiny when I found her. Shivering. Soaked to the bone. She was tied to a tree behind the public toilets – closed of course – at the top end of the park. And you think – you hope it's just an accident – forgetfulness – so I put up posters, asked around – dogwalkers, and… to see if anyone recognised her. Nothing.

I took her to the doctors. Not doctors. Vet. Took her to the vet to check for a microchip. Nothing. Nothing physically wrong with her, either, other than her weight. And this is – before we get any further – not a heart-warming story, but I don't want to hand her over – not yet. I'll keep her, I say – I'll keep her, just for a little while, just in case anyone gets in touch. It's my name and number on the posters, so…

It's something that people find impressive. I'm not saying that to boast, it's a fact. People find it impressive. Brave. Sexy, even. Once they've got over the surprise. 'Who's this then? Yours?

You don't strike me as a dog person. No, that's great. I just would've never looked at you and thought "dog person", y'know?' Because I'm not. I don't *have* a dog – I didn't go out and get a dog, but –

'I would've never figured you for a dog person, but the more I think about it the more it makes sense.'

And she needs walking, and she needs feeding, and she needs *stuff*, but she bites and she growls and she's not good around people, or other dogs, or squirrels, birds, cars, running water, commercial radio, babies, toddlers, joggers, rain, snow, direct sunlight, gentle breezes or the dark, so you know, it's not *great*, and I know I need to take her out, because I'm not a moron, but I can't trust her and I don't have the right equipment and I can't go out and buy the right equipment because I can't leave her at home by herself but I can't take her with me because I don't have the stuff and I don't want to order online and I can't afford any of it anyway, and it's not like she's that big – bigger, I think, getting bigger, because she is at least eating now, so I just let her run around the flat, and I know it's not *ideal*, but it's the best I can do.

She sleeps through the day and howls through the night, so that becomes my routine too. She keeps me company as I scroll through the endless horrors of the twenty-four-hour news cycle. She takes over the flat. For the first few weeks she just paces endlessly, but then she takes to sitting on my chest, determined to get in on the action, and you might think that sounds adorable, but it's not. She smells and she refuses to settle and she is heavier now, surprisingly heavy, and I can't breathe.

'You love her really. Admit it. Why else have you kept her?'

I haven't kept her, she's just *here*.

'Get rid of her then. Shouldn't be that hard.'

I speak to the doctor again – the vet – and he suggests anti-anxiety medication. I tell him I'm not keeping her – she won't be hanging around – but he just writes me a prescription and sends me an invoice and that's that.

We settle into a routine. She lays her head upon my thigh and the dead weight of her little skull keeps me pinned to the sofa for days. I journal my thoughts but she chews through the pages, wolfs them down then regurgitates them up in disgust.

She eats anything. It's repulsive to watch. Whole jars of peanut butter, week-old chow mein, an entire bar of soap. Pathetic. Sitting in the bathtub, whimpering and foaming at the mouth. Snivelling for sympathy.

I indulge her, I'm told. I'm using her as an excuse now. After all, millions of people have dogs, and they manage to get through the day. She isn't mine though – I didn't ask for her – this is different. She bites chunks out of me while I'm sleeping, so the best thing is just not to sleep. We stay up together all hours now, the worst kind of company.

I know what I have to do. Take her back to where I found her. Tie her to a tree and leave her hanging. Sounds drastic, but I can't see another way. Still, it's easier said than done. She's the only thing I have these days, my shadow, my constant companion, forever at my side. Doctor says I'm stuck with her, at least for the time being, and acceptance is an important step. So that's that then.

I walk my black dog on a short leash, never allowing her out of my sight. We walk in lockstep, joined at the hip. But today we walked outside.

Into –

14. Bluebird (SONG)

TWO. Standing on the roof and staring
Wishing that the world was his
Reflection from the post box glaring
Was born with so much more to give
Oh bluebird

Hesitant bluebird
Stuck in mid-flight
Halfway to soaring
Cursed with frostbite

Insufficient nerve to fight and
Scared of injuries obtained
But the desperation's getting tight and

No longer here can he remain
Oh bluebird

Tentative bluebird
Stuck in mid-flight
Halfway to soaring
Camouflaged appetite

Should he break that glass or
Should he just give up
Or come up with something stronger
Double-glazed mind
That is starting to wear thin
But he can't keep the cold out much longer

It's hard to always be so blue
A colour that you didn't choose
A quality that will dictate
How heavy is your daily weight
Suppression is a lonely thing
No matter who is listening
But he is just a bluebird
And the big black dog will not be stirred

Oh aspiring bluebird
Wishing to fly
Halfway to falling
Yet so close to the sky
To be one with the starlight

Into –

15. Dinner

ONE *and* FIVE.

ONE. Have you eaten?

FIVE. Yes.

ONE. Dinner?

FIVE. Yes.

ONE. Already?

FIVE. It's late.

ONE. Is it?

FIVE. Past dinner time.

ONE. I thought it was just dark.

FIVE. It's late and it's dark.

ONE. But it gets dark so early.

FIVE. I ate.

ONE. What did you have?

FIVE. Shepherd's pie.

ONE. And lunch?

FIVE. We ate together.

ONE. Did we?

FIVE. Shepherd's pie.

ONE. That was yesterday.

FIVE. Leftovers.

ONE. Was it?

FIVE. Are you feeling okay?

ONE. Don't worry about me.

FIVE. It's late. You should get some sleep.

ONE. Is it?

FIVE. Past eleven.

ONE. No, it's just dark.

FIVE. It's late and it's dark.

ONE. You can't tell. Not this time of year, especially after the clocks change.

FIVE. Don't you have a watch?

ONE. No.

FIVE. You always did.

ONE *shows a bare wrist and shrugs.*

What happened to it?

ONE. Can't be late for you, anyway. I bet you're out at all hours. Galivanting.

FIVE. Galivanting?

ONE *shrugs again.*

Where would I galivant round here?

ONE. You did eat?

FIVE. Yes!

ONE. Breakfast?

FIVE. It's late. It's night-time.

ONE. Not now! I'm not saying *now*, not recently – I'm asking did you have breakfast?

FIVE. I've had hundreds of breakfasts.

ONE. I'm not –

FIVE. Thousands.

ONE. Little shit.

A shift.

Have you eaten?

FIVE. Yes.

ONE. What did you eat?

FIVE. Salad Niçoise.

ONE. What?

FIVE. I did tell you.

ONE. Salad what?

FIVE. Tuna, olives, egg.

ONE. What did you call it?

FIVE. Low-carb. Lots of protein.

ONE. For dinner?

FIVE. It's a –

ONE. Salad is lunch.

FIVE. It's not –

ONE. Salad is lunch, not dinner. Salad isn't a… Dinner – this evening – dinner –

FIVE. Stop it.

ONE. This evening, what have you – ?

A shift.

Breakfast.

FIVE. What?

ONE. Have some breakfast, before you leave.

FIVE. I'm not going anywhere.

ONE. Most important meal of the day.

FIVE. Where would I be going?

ONE. For a growing boy.

FIVE. Dad?

ONE. Yes?

FIVE. Where do you think I'm going?

ONE. Have some lunch.

FIVE. It's not lunchtime.

ONE. Does it matter?

FIVE. It's too early.

ONE. Time is an illusion. I'll make kippers.

FIVE. It's only –

ONE. Don't look at your watch, look at the sun. look – the sun's high – the sun is… at its apex, yes? Look! You'd agree – at its apex – so noon – it's noon.

FIVE. It's too early for me.

ONE. Sit down. (*Beat.*) What else are you doing? Sit.

FIVE. Why?

ONE. To build a… a… a sense of routine. Of communal… While we're under the same roof.

FIVE. I could go.

ONE. I'm not –

FIVE. I could always –

ONE. Sit. Have a piece of fruit. I'm going to have a muffin.

FIVE. Dad –

ONE. You can have a muffin too – you're very welcome to a muffin, but as I know you shan't, you can have a piece of fruit.

FIVE. I'm not hungry.

ONE. The muffins are very good though.

FIVE. Dad –

ONE. The chef would recommend them. Can monsieur be tempted to a petit muffin, par chance?

FIVE. No. Thank you.

ONE. What have you eaten today?

FIVE. You don't get to… Just because I'm back here, it doesn't mean you can control every little thing.

ONE. I'm not trying to –

FIVE. You'd have no idea – you'd never normally have –

ONE. To… to control you –

FIVE. You are!

ONE. I'm just trying to make sure –

A shift.

FIVE. Are you having a second muffin?

ONE. What?

FIVE. That's your second muffin today.

ONE. Is it? No, not today.

FIVE. Yes today.

ONE. Yesterday?

FIVE. No, it's –

ONE. I don't know what you're –

FIVE. Dad?

ONE. Yes?

FIVE. Is everything – ?

A shift.

ONE. What's for dinner?

FIVE. We've already eaten.

ONE. No, this is you, this is –

FIVE. Dad –

ONE. I know how you –

FIVE. We ate. Together.

ONE. No –

FIVE. I promise.

ONE. No, this is… What you do, what you always did, you hide, you lie –

FIVE. Not any more.

ONE. Yes.

FIVE. No.

ONE. Yes. You need to eat, you need to… Please. I'm begging you – you have to eat something.

FIVE. Dad!

ONE. A few bites. Some soup. A bit of apple.

FIVE. It's the middle of the night.

ONE. No, it's just dark – it gets dark so early.

FIVE. What're you doing up?

ONE. You have to eat.

FIVE. Go back to bed.

A shift.

ONE. Morning! You sleep all day – all hours.

FIVE. No –

ONE. Look at the sun – look.

FIVE. It's cloudy.

ONE. But if you could see the sun, that's where it'd be – there – high.

FIVE. I'm tired.

ONE. You don't have any energy.

FIVE. I'm just –

A shift.

ONE. I made breakfast.

FIVE. I'm not –

ONE. Eggs and soldiers.

FIVE. Don't.

A shift.

ONE. Bircher muesli.

FIVE. I already –

A shift.

ONE. Shakshuka.

FIVE. Stop. Please stop.

ONE. With my own sourdough.

A shift.

FIVE. How did you do that?

ONE. What?

FIVE. Your hand – show me your hand.

ONE. Oh, that. Nothing.

FIVE. How did – ?

ONE. Avocado stone. Nothing serious.

FIVE. Did you clean it properly?

ONE. Just a little nick.

FIVE. Do you need to – ?

ONE. My skin – these days, it's… You'll start to notice this – when you're older.

FIVE. Looks nasty.

ONE. It's nothing.

FIVE. Do you need driving – get it dressed properly?

ONE. No!

FIVE. It's no bother.

ONE. Sit down. Finish your lunch.

FIVE. You should get it looked at.

ONE. Stop changing the subject.

FIVE. Could be infected.

ONE. You think – you think – you've always thought – that I don't notice. Your old man, the idiot. I always notice.

FIVE. I never –

ONE. Finish it.

FIVE. I have!

ONE. I can see your ribs from where I'm standing.

FIVE. I'm fine.

ONE. I check the bins. The underside of the toilet bowl. I can see when you –

FIVE. We don't have to eat every meal together.

ONE. We do. We do when… What else is there to…? Families eat together.

FIVE. I can go.

ONE. No –

FIVE. I can go back to… If you don't want me here.

ONE. Of course I –

FIVE. If I'm too much bother.

ONE. That's not what I –

FIVE. If I can leave you on your own.

ONE. What do you mean?

FIVE. Without catastrophic injury.

ONE. It's nothing.

FIVE. And your burn?

ONE. Was nothing. It's healed.

FIVE. And your back.

ONE. This isn't about me.

A shift.

FIVE. What are you doing?

ONE. Making coffee.

FIVE. At midnight?

A shift.

What are you doing?

ONE. Making eggs.

FIVE. It's late.

A shift.

What are you doing?

ONE. Making banana bread.

FIVE. Dad? Do you know what time it is?

ONE. Hmm?

FIVE. Do you know where you are?

ONE. What?

FIVE. Have you hurt yourself?

A shift.

ONE. What are you doing here?

A shift.

Just a bit of apple – I'll split it with you.

FIVE. I'm fine.

ONE. Go halves?

FIVE. I'm not –

ONE. A quarter?

FIVE. I'll go.

ONE. No! You'll stay. You'll stay and we'll talk. Here, just let me –

FIVE. What're you doing?

ONE. Sit.

FIVE. Do you just carry around a penknife?

ONE. Sit down.

FIVE. Who peels an apple with a knife?

ONE. Shush now.

FIVE. You'll open up a vein!

ONE. You'll eat. Just a little. For me. I'm not in my element here but I am trying. It's so dark. Is it late, or just dark? Is it both? What time is it? I lost my watch, I… How will we know what time it is if we don't eat? How else will we mark the hours? I'm not… These are windfall, from next door. I said yes once and now I can't get her to stop. Crates just appear on my doorstep – even got a crumble once. They're not bad though. A bit tart. Go on. I'll have a piece, and then you. One after the other. Until it's gone. Until it's light. Here.

Into –

16. Last Orders

SIX. There was a time for her to leave
The clock at seven fifty-eight
September third, in eighty-three
Him, half an hour late
The bar, her drink, her coat and bag
Could in a moment slip away
Into the autumn breeze

There was a time for her to leave
Before his hand creeps to her thigh
Before her sense of vague unease
Starts to solidify
A joke, a smoke, then pulling back
A friendly smile, a firm goodbye
He is not yours to please

There was a time for taking flight
Before the marks began to show
Before he proved her mother right
To pack a bag and go
A glass, a chair, a door, a tooth
And other things before they broke
Would see another night

Or if, before the children came,
Or if, once they had flown the nest
Before her looks began to fade
Before she's past her best
The car, the ring, the TV set
You will not miss them once you've left
You will not miss the shame

But now there can be no reprieve
She's told the danger lies outside
She waves to neighbours on the street
But has no place to hide
Oh turn the clock back to that hour
Go fetch her coat, her youth, her pride
And tell her she can leave.

Into –

17. The Third Pitch

ONE *to* FIVE *back again.*

ONE. So. So okay. So there's a house –

TWO. Okay.

FOUR. What sort of – ?

FIVE. A nice house?

THREE. Should be multiple houses. Um. Lots of different… Cabins. Trailers.

TWO. Campervans?

FIVE. Houseboats?

TWO. Lighthouses?

THREE. All sorts. Bungalows. Flats. Apartments.

FOUR. Flats, not apartments.

TWO. Yes.

ONE. No, but this house –

FOUR. Not luxury, not –

FIVE. Relatable.

TWO. Not depressing, but –

ONE. It's real.

FOUR. Yes.

THREE. Not Richard Curtis.

FIVE. Not Chipping Norton.

TWO. Not Farrow and Ball.

THREE. We don't do Farrow and Ball?

FOUR. We'll check.

TWO. But not, um, what do I mean? Not smug.

FIVE. Council?

FOUR. Hmm?

FIVE. Council flats?

FOUR. Oh.

THREE. Do we do council?

FOUR. Not… I don't think overtly –

FIVE. Uh-huh.

TWO. But these days – these days you can't always… I have a cousin, and she – it was former council, on a little estate. And it was… fine. You know, really… for her first.

FOUR. So council – or former council –

FIVE. Council-adjacent –

FOUR. I think fine, if it's the right sort of… Because that's the lived experience of – of a lot of –

TWO. Yes.

ONE. Yes, but this is… This house – it's a particular –

FIVE. Aspirational.

FOUR. Yes.

TWO. Aspirational's still on the wall.

FIVE. And actually *lived experience* – does anyone really want…?

THREE. In the current situation?

FIVE. Exactly.

THREE. If your lived experience is – if it has been –

ONE. If I could just – ?

TWO. I'm crossing out 'council'.

FOUR. Pin it.

TWO. I'll put a note.

THREE. So is escapism back on the table?

FOUR. Not – I think not entirely – not fantastical, but magical.

FIVE. Magical Realism?

TWO. I'm not sure that's what that means. Strictly.

FOUR. Right.

TWO. From an English Lit perspective.

ONE. But this house –

FOUR. These homes, yes, they should feel… real, absolutely, but magical, but relatable –

THREE. But not relating to the current situation –

FOUR. No. With lots of air between it and the current situation.

FIVE. Like a pocket dimension.

THREE. But not twee. Not detached from reality.

FOUR. No.

FIVE. Just *this* reality – this very specific set of –

TWO. Exactly.

ONE. Okay, but this house –

THREE. Multiple houses. Homes.

TWO. Is that relatable?

THREE. Not like… Not second homes, multiple homes, multiple, um, households, scattered all over. This is the whole thing. Multiple, um. Like an advent calendar, like all these different windows, doors, all across the country – separated but connected, together apart together, little insights into, uh, through the magic of –

FOUR. Portals.

TWO. Yes.

ONE. No – listen, just –

FIVE. Empathy wormholes. Is that a…?

TWO. I'll stick it down.

THREE. All linked up by… by –

ONE *cuts through. It's more like a vision than a pitch.*

ONE. There is a house. It's my grandmother's house. It's *your* grandmother's house. It's stone-fronted, not brick. Slate or tile, not thatch. Not chintzy, not chocolate box. The walls are thick, substantial. It was built for cold winters – built to last. A stove. A fire. Coal or wood – solid fuel. It nestles in the crook of a valley, and all around the hills are sharp and high. They don't roll. They don't *undulate*. They aren't friendly pastel folds, they rise up jagged like the craters of Mars – but – but – they are nothing compared to the size of the sky. Huge. Fathomless. And every inch groaning with stars. So it's not formidable or threatening, this place, it is awesome – it inspires *awe* – and nestled in the crook of the valley is a village church and a butcher's shop and a war memorial, and finally – finally, at the end of the final winding lane – your grandmother's house. It speaks of a life lived honestly, of battles worth fighting, of Blake and Elgar and England in a way that doesn't automatically feel grubby. It isn't modern. It isn't metropolitan. It has endured. It has a copper kettle and a crocheted toilet-roll cover and a floral bedspread in the spare room set aside for the baby Jesus. The front door is green – forest green – timeless – and the wreath that hangs on it, why, it's the one you helped her make, decades ago, pinecones dripping in glitter, twigs and tinsel and toffee wrappers held together with spit and hope and festive spirit. And just as you're taking it all in, you realise it's started to snow. Soft flakes fall like featherdown, each one perfect and distinct, and the lights inside the house flicker off. So you lift the wreath off the door, tuck it under your arm, and you start to climb – up the hillside, steep and winding, snow is heavier now, slippery stone freezing under foot, eyes water, cheeks sting, down in the valley below carols are being sung but you can't hear them, not now the wind's picked up. You shiver. You quake. You weren't prepared for this. You are soft, coddled, naive, you've never really known what it's like to be cold. You can't imagine the kind of life she's lived – you wouldn't last a day. And now you stop, because you're standing in front of her grave – a humble heap of rocks at the very highest point. You look again, and it isn't her grave at all, it's yours. Of course it is. How could you have survived any of this, ridiculous creature that you are, pink and fleshy and weak? You lay the wreath down, look up to the moon and you howl, as the legend pops up across the screen: 'This Christmas return unto the barren earth from whence you came.' (*Beat.*) Is that anything?

Into –

18. Allotment

TWO *present.* SIX *enters.*

SIX. Hello?

TWO *looks up.*

Sorry, I was looking for… must be in the wrong place.

TWO. Okay.

SIX. No, that's her shed. I helped paint it.

TWO. What?

SIX. Who are you and why are you in my gran's allotment?

TWO. Oh.

SIX. What's that there?

TWO. What?

SIX. Behind you?

TWO. Honeysuckle.

SIX. No –

TWO. Purple sprouting broccoli.

SIX. Is that a tent?

TWO. No.

SIX. Are you camping here?

TWO. No, I –

SIX. What're you doing?

TWO. Nothing.

SIX. Have you turned my grandma's allotment into a secret weed farm?

TWO. No!

SIX. What then?

TWO. It was in a state. Overgrown, and brambles and… no one had touched it for months – maybe years.

SIX. Not years.

TWO. It looked like –

SIX. It hasn't been years. She just can't get to it right now, that's all.

TWO. Sorry.

SIX. That's why I'm here.

TWO. I'll go. Just give me a minute to pack up.

SIX. Wait –

TWO. It didn't look like anyone was coming back.

SIX. It looks incredible now – all the colours – like I remember from when I was a kid. Better, actually. Did you do all this?

TWO *shrugs.*

And you'd just leave it? (*Beat.*) What do I do with it all?

TWO. Don't you know?

SIX. Gran never grew pink broccoli –

TWO. Purple sprouting.

SIX. Whatever.

TWO. If I'd known anyone was coming back, I'd have gone somewhere else.

SIX. Why?

TWO. Good luck.

SIX. I'll kill it. I'll have killed it all within days if you don't… Please? This is the one thing I've been trusted with – not very trusted, to be honest. But I can't see her – I'm not allowed to see her, or Mum, and Amir's in his bubble, Mo never leaves the hospital –

TWO. I don't know who any of these people are.

SIX. And I just want to do one little thing to –

TWO. Shush!

SIX. What?

TWO. Shush – shut up – look –

SIX. At what?

TWO. Where I'm pointing. Do you see?

SIX. What is it?

TWO. A little wren.

SIX. Oh. (*Beat.*) Is that rare?

TWO. No, millions of them. Common as muck, but I like them. Tiny – weigh less than a pound coin, but they're so loud – such a racket for such a little bird.

SIX. Good for them.

TWO. And they don't migrate – not the English ones – so if it gets too cold in the winter they just die. They'd rather die than fly away. Idiots.

SIX. Are you okay?

TWO. I'm fine. I was just meant to get further.

SIX. Where?

TWO. Anywhere, just… Somewhere quiet I could hear my own thoughts. But it's still so noisy, all the time.

SIX. Is that the wrens?

TWO. No, the wrens can stay. (*Beat.*) If things look dry, give them water. If things look dead, cut them back. If things look weird, ask Google.

SIX. Can't we just talk – just a little longer?

TWO. I should get gone before it's dark.

SIX. Just to –

TWO. I'm sorry, I… I'm not good company. I can't help you.

TWO *begins to leave.*

SIX. In the beginning everyone was apart, and everyone was alone.

TWO. What?

SIX. Until one morning, the whole world awoke in pain.

TWO. What are you – ?

SIX. Until she found a figure whose likeness to herself took her breath away.

TWO. What's this?

SIX. Just a story. My gran's favourite story.

TWO. I hope you get to see her soon.

SIX. Wait, just… Can I ask you something? Won't take a second. Please? I have a thorn. I have this thorn, right between my shoulder blades. Can you see it? I can't reach it, but I know it's there. Always been there, I think, but it's growing. I don't sleep. I can't breathe properly – I think it pushes right through into my lungs. I try to sing, because that helped once, but they're in tatters now. And I've been trying – I have tried – to do all the things you're supposed to. To keep busy and take walks and make your bed and reach out to people when you need to but it's too much. It keeps growing, squeezing, and all the people I'd normally ask aren't around at the moment, so I was wondering if maybe you could try to pull it out?

TWO. I should go.

SIX. Could you just try?

TWO. I don't know what you're asking me.

SIX. It's in the story. And you're here, so… The thing is you're here, so that has to mean something. You grew all this – you can deal with one thorn.

TWO. Wait. Just wait there a second.

TWO *produces a rose.*

These were growing when I got here – the only thing growing. And they shouldn't be – wrong soil, wrong climate, wrong time of year – but they're always in bloom. Impossible. (*Beat.*) Is that…? Does it help?

SIX. It helps. (*Beat.*) Can you just check for me, please? You check me and I'll check you. Check for thorns, check for roses. Won't take a minute. Please?

TWO *hesitates. They hold the space. Into –*

19. Still Life

FOUR. I'm sitting here thinking of Italy.

The part of my brain that is not thinking unthinkable things is thinking of Italy. Of Naples and pizza and wine and micro-aggressions and more wine and the taste of a terra cotta sunset. I'm thinking of the plague villages in the mountains, and the picture you showed me of the wine hatches – the little wine holes in the sides of buildings, hundreds of years old, for passing out glasses without spreading infection. I'm thinking of how nothing really changes even when everything does. I'm thinking of the one-word caption you sent me along with the image: 'PRIORITIES.'

I'm thinking of quarantine, from the Italian: –

Quaranta – forty.

Quarantina – forty days.

I am thinking of staying here for forty days. They told me there was no rush – take all the time you need. I am thinking of slowing my breath until my lungs only rise and fall with the sun, and my heart synchronises itself to tectonic shifts. I am willing into being an act of rapid-onset fossilisation – make me a stone, if you have any mercy, and fix me here for all time. I'm thinking of the ruins of Pompeii, of the citizens frozen in mid-flight, and how I envy them, and what I wouldn't give to trade places, to be a rock, a statue, solid, immovable, just me and her.

I'm thinking how you don't even know yet that she's a girl – you have a daughter. Had a daughter, for a moment at least. Hold on to that. I am thinking how we refused to plan for this. If the worst happened. If the worst happens, I said, no plan will make it better, but at least we'll have each other. I never imagined a world in which you wouldn't be here.

Has anybody called you yet? Is that something somebody will do? I would call myself but I am a stone. I have calcified. We are marble now, mother and daughter, hewn from the same monumental slab, no join, no seam, no hair's breadth between us, so how can I ever break myself away? How can I ever look you in the eye and say the worst has happened, my love, the very worst. I am thinking how in the days and weeks and years to come I will have to remember how hard this must be for you too – the not being here – the banishment – the lurking in the hospital car park waiting for the phone to ring. I am thinking how your existence hasn't been shattered yet, which is unfair and wonderful and horrifying and unforgivably cruel, and of Schrödinger, and cats in boxes, and how if I never leave this room, and you never hear from us again, then in your reality she could still be alive, and I am angry – angry – angry at you, for making me bear the weight of this alone. I will have to learn to be good and patient and generous, but for now my grief is selfish, and my mother's love is selfish, and my sitting here is selfish, while nurses check their watches and machines ping impatiently and bodies pile up in the corridors and I am not moving. I will not. I cannot. I am still.

I need to go back. Take me back. Not long, just an hour or so. Suspend me forever in that blinding pain as my flesh tears and blood pools and every nerve ending burns and she is still alive. Just keep her alive.

I am thinking of Italy. Of Naples and pizza and wine, and the world before the world ended.

I am remembering that your world hasn't yet ended.

I am thinking of Italy, and I wish you were here.

I wish you were here.

I wish you were here.

Into –

20. If Only I Could Touch You With My Hands (SONG)

COMPANY. I light a candle cos I know that it will comfort me
It's not a calling from above
It's only something I can see
If only I could touch you with my hands palpably
If only I could touch you with my hands

These hands that wash my body wash my face
These legs that somehow took me to this sacred space
This mouth that drank the wine that ate the date
If only I could touch you with my hands
If only I could touch you with my hands

Don't tell me what happens tomorrow
Just help me to get through tonight
I'll give you my own little blessing
Console you with warmth from this light
With warmth from this light

And soon the sun will rise and in the morning will I be
Still burning brightly or fast fading with fragility?
And if I'm burning then the pain proves this is real to me
My body might just melt away into the sea

These lips determined oh the words that they recite for me
I say a prayer whatever that might mean to me
These arms self-soothing now where someone else once would have been
If only I could touch you with my hands
If only I could touch you with my hands

Don't tell me what happens tomorrow
Just help me to get through tonight
I'll give you my own little blessing
Console you with warmth from this light

Don't tell me what happens tomorrow
Just help me to get through tonight
I'll give you my own little blessing
Console you with warmth from this light
With warmth from this light
Light light light light light
Light light light light light

This is our story
We will find the glory
This is our story
We'll hold on tight
This is our story
I'll tell my January self to hold the glory oh
This is our story
We'll hold the light

I light a candle cos I know that it will comfort me
It's not a calling from above
It's only something I can see
If I could only touch you with my hands palpably
If only I could touch you with my hands

Ends.

HUNGRY

Hungry was first produced as a co-production between Paines Plough and Belgrade Theatre Coventry, and first performed in the Roundabout, as part of Coventry City of Culture, on 30 July 2021, before performances at the Edinburgh Festival Fringe and on tour of the UK. It was revived in the Roundabout in 2022, with performances during the Edinburgh Festival Fringe and at Soho Theatre, London. The cast was as follows:

LORI	Eleanor Sutton
BEX	Leah St Luce
Director	Katie Posner
Designer	Lydia Denno
Lighting Designer	Richard Howell
Sound Designer	Kieran Lucas
Movement Director	Kloe Dean
Dramaturg	Sarah Dickenson

The play was revived in the Roundabout in 2022, with performances during the Edinburgh Festival Fringe and at Soho Theatre, London, with the same cast and creative team, except for Mel Lowe playing Bex.

Characters

BEX, *twenty-two, Black*
LORI, *late twenties/early thirties, white*

Note

There are two distinct modes in this play – NOW and THEN. It's useful for us to always know when we're in the present and when we're in the past.

In the present, Bex and Lori are setting up for a gathering. This plays out almost in real time.

The scenes in the past span a couple of years.

1. THEN

LORI. Service!

BEX *appears.*

This way round, yeah? Spoons at two o'clock.

BEX. Sorry?

LORI. Towards the diner, not you.

BEX (*glancing at her watch*). It's nine-thirty.

LORI. What?

BEX. The time, it's –

LORI. The plate.

BEX. What about it?

LORI. Seriously? (*Sighs.*) Okay, so a clockface – picture a clockface –

BEX. Why?

LORI. That's the plate – the plate is the clock. Spoon at two o'clock – like this – when it goes in front of them. Now go.

BEX. Show me once more.

LORI. Plate. Spoon. Clock. Spoon is the hand.

BEX. Big hand or little hand?

LORI. Big hand! Big hand at –

BEX. Thing is I'm more digital.

LORI. It isn't –

BEX *can't keep this up any longer. She cracks up.*

BEX. Your face.

LORI. Right.

BEX. I'm on it. I'm Bex, by the way.

LORI. I'm busy.

BEX. Okay.

LORI. And these are melting.

BEX. Got it.

LORI. So you can dick around on your own time, yeah? Not while we're in service.

BEX. Yes, chef.

LORI. You get that? This is a time-sensitive operation. I'm not… Can you just take them please?

BEX. Sorry. I wasn't –

LORI. Now, please.

BEX. Yep.

BEX *starts to go.*

LORI. I'm Lori. It's Lori.

BEX (*smiles*). Yes, chef.

Into –

2. NOW

BEX. What've you got there?

LORI. Sandwiches.

BEX. Why?

LORI. I said I'd bring sandwiches.

BEX. And I said I had it covered.

LORI. I don't mind.

BEX. I do. What is that?

LORI. Chicken.

BEX. Is it though?

LORI. Yes! It's a turmeric chicken with Scotch bonnet aioli and a kohlrabi slaw.

BEX. Why is it black?

LORI. It's an activated-charcoal flatbread.

BEX. No food should be black.

LORI. It's dramatic.

BEX. No one's going to eat that.

LORI. You'll like it. It's practically Nando's. (*Beat.*) Try one. It's the same dressing we use on the ribs.

BEX. I'm not hungry, thank you.

LORI. It's nice.

BEX. I know it'll be nice. It's not about *nice*, it's about Mum.

LORI. I know. It's only chicken.

BEX. Is it though?

LORI. And some pulled jackfruit for the vegetarians.

BEX. We don't know any vegetarians.

LORI. How is that possible?

BEX *shrugs.*

It's here now, anyway. It was no bother.

BEX. I didn't ask you to.

LORI. Didn't have to. (*Beat.*) Y'know this could be a good, um, proof of concept for us as well. See what they make of it, because it's this sort of thing –

BEX. Use my family as guinea pigs?

LORI. Not like… But a customer base –

BEX. So that's why you're here?

LORI. No! I'm sorry. No. I'm here for you.

BEX. Okay.

LORI. It is. It's going to be okay.

Beat.

BEX. Give them here then – I'll get them in the fridge.

BEX *takes the tray. Into –*

3. THEN

LORI. Clean plates?

BEX. Clean plates, big grins.

LORI. Good.

BEX. What was the green gunk again?

LORI. Excuse me?

BEX. Y'know – the dribble round the edge.

LORI. That is a basil fluid gel.

BEX. On a pudding?

LORI. Any complaints?

BEX. No, just someone asking.

LORI. They liked it then?

BEX. Yeah – oh yeah – too much if anything. Had this one old dude telling me how chocolate was a… a what-do-you-call-it – an aphrodisiac.

LORI. Jesus.

BEX. Then he tried to sit me on his knee and feed me a spoonful of his mousse.

LORI. Marquise.

BEX. Hmm?

LORI. Not a mousse – it was a chocolate marquise.

BEX. I think you're missing the point of the story.

LORI. Did you tell people it was a mousse?

BEX. Did I tell you he had a visible erection?

LORI. Anyway – thank you for tonight.

BEX. No bother.

LORI. There's not much left to do. You could start wiping down the sides for me?

BEX. Sure.

LORI. And take a drink if you want one – open bottles over there.

BEX. We allowed?

LORI. No, but if we don't it has to go down the sink, which is criminal, so…

BEX. Right.

LORI. Go on – the white tastes like piss but the red's decent.

BEX. Nah, you're alright. Is there a boiling water tap in here though?

LORI. What're you after? I think the tea and coffee got packed away, but –

BEX. No, just… I've got a Pot Noodle in my bag.

LORI. Excuse me?

BEX. Didn't get a chance to eat before we started, so –

LORI. Are you serious?

BEX. I'll keep my fork at two o'clock, if that helps.

LORI. Absolutely not. Not on my watch.

BEX. Oh. (*Beat.*) Right, um. That's fine. I'll have it when I get home. Sorry.

LORI. You will not – you'll chuck it in the bin where it belongs. Now – any allergies – intolerances? Real ones, not made up.

BEX. What's happening right now?

LORI. You don't bring a Pot Noodle into a professional chef's kitchen – it's an insult.

BEX. Sorry.

LORI. I should hope so. You clear those counters – I'm making you a snack.

BEX. Nah –

LORI. Five minutes.

BEX. Seriously?

LORI. It's my civic duty.

BEX. You must be knackered. Everything's packed away –

LORI. Just do as you're told and stop answering back, alright?

BEX (*with a smile*). Yes, chef.

LORI. And pour me another red. Five minutes and I'm going to blow your mind.

Into –

4. NOW

LORI. When do they get here?

BEX. Soon. Should be soon. Dad said he'd only take them for one, but…

LORI. They in The York?

BEX. Yeah.

LORI. You didn't want to?

BEX. Hmm?

LORI. Join them? We could go and –

BEX. Nah.

LORI. You could, I mean. Go have a drink – leave me to sort everything here.

BEX. Everything's sorted, so.

LORI. I just mean you can leave me by myself – put me to work – you don't have to worry about me.

BEX. I'm not worried about you.

LORI. Okay.

BEX. I'm not worrying about you.

LORI. I just meant if you wanted to go –

BEX. Then I'd be there, wouldn't I? I wouldn't be waiting for your permission.

LORI. Sorry.

BEX *doesn't entirely accept the apology.*

Just tell me what I can do. Anything you need, just… (*Pause.*) What am I today?

BEX. How do you mean?

LORI. I wasn't sure whether… Am I a friend, or co-worker, or – ?

BEX. Oh.

LORI. I don't mind if –

BEX. No – no, girlfriend. Girlfriend is… That's fine.

LORI. Yeah?

BEX. Yeah. They're not… That's not a problem.

LORI. Okay. Good. (*Beat.*) Good that… not good that I'm still your girlfriend, although that is good, but good that it isn't –

BEX. Can we not – ?

LORI. I just didn't know whether all your family – if extended family – whether that might be –

BEX. They're not dickheads.

LORI. I just wasn't sure.

BEX. If they were dickheads?

LORI. What the deal was, that's all.

BEX. Got it.

LORI. So if it was easier to just be platonic-work-friend-business-partner-tea-lady then…

BEX. Then what?

LORI. That'd be fine.

BEX. That'd be weird.

LORI. Whatever you need. Today is about you –

BEX. Today's about Mum.

LORI. Yeah.

BEX. But she's dead, so. (*Pause.*) You don't have to be here.
I didn't ask you to be here. So if you're not up for an afternoon of small talk with my possibly homophobic relatives you can just unwrap your fruit platters and piss off.

LORI (*softly*). Whatever you need.

BEX. They're fine though, actually – for the record. For a bunch of dickheads.

LORI. I don't think your family are dickheads.

BEX. Yeah, well you've not met them all yet.

LORI. What can I do?

BEX. Go. Stay. Suit yourself. I've got to get on.

Into –

5. THEN

BEX (*brightly*). Hey!

LORI. Hey! You again!

BEX. Me again. You miss me?

LORI. Uh –

BEX. It's Bex.

LORI. I know. I know, I hadn't –

BEX. It's okay. Lori, yeah?

LORI. Yeah.

BEX. Queen of the Midnight Feast. Blew my mind. Just like you promised.

LORI. Right.

BEX. You don't even remember!

LORI. No –

BEX. Bet you do it for all the girls.

LORI (*blushing, trying to move past this*). Great. So. Great to have you back on the team. Do you know what we're doing tonight?

BEX. Is it serving dinner?

LORI. So it's going to be really easy on you guys. We've got a series of sequential sharing plates for structured grazing. It's all plant-based and low-carbon.

BEX. Uh-huh.

LORI. Everything comes from within a fifty-mile radius of the kitchen – a lot of it's grown right here. All our suppliers are listed. We've got hand-outs for anyone who asks. Did you have any questions?

BEX. Yes. What exactly is the heritage of the heritage tomatoes?

LORI. Is that a real question?

BEX. Are they related to the Queen, or – ?

LORI. Any serious questions?

BEX. Did Prince Charles grow them?

LORI. They come from Essex and they're organic and they're very good.

BEX. What do they taste of?

LORI. Tomatoes.

BEX. Got it.

LORI. You'll be serving some ingredients you're unfamiliar with. If you're asked something you don't know don't guess, check in with the kitchen, yeah?

BEX. Oh, one other thing – pickled turnip, sprout tops and cobnuts?

LORI. What about them?

BEX. Bet you a fiver no one touches it.

LORI *thinks for a second.*

LORI. You're on.

BEX. So what're you going to make me tonight then?

LORI (*ignoring this*). First plates go out at six, on the dot. The trout's chilled and the kitchen's hot, so I need you to be on it.

BEX. Yes, chef.

LORI. Anything else?

BEX. No one likes cold fish either.

LORI. Tuck your shirt in. Are those the shoes you're wearing?

BEX. Looks like it.

LORI. Okay. Try to keep up. It's going to be a long night.

Into –

6. NOW

LORI *is fixing* BEX*'s collar or picking a bit of fluff off her sleeve.*

BEX. What're you doing?

LORI. Making you respectable.

BEX. Good luck.

LORI (*clocking her shirt*). Have you ironed this?

BEX. Doesn't need ironing.

LORI. It absolutely does.

BEX. It's fine.

LORI. Will there be one here?

BEX. What?

LORI. An iron?

BEX. No one cares.

LORI. No, *you* don't care.

BEX. No one's going to care today.

LORI. They will! Someone will tut or frown or give you a funny look and then… I'll do it – I don't mind doing it. Pass it here.

BEX. You trying to get my clothes off already?

LORI (*deadpan*). You saw right through me. Strip off.

BEX. Make me.

LORI. Bex –

BEX. Look at me. All crumpled. I'm a disgrace.

LORI. I wasn't –

BEX. Come teach me a lesson.

BEX *pulls* LORI *towards her, her hands on her shirt. Into –*

7. THEN

BEX *and* LORI *have just had sex. They kiss.*

LORI. Jesus.

BEX. You okay?

LORI. Yeah.

BEX. You sure?

LORI. Yeah, I'm… Wow. I might just need a… (*Beat – a new thought.*) Oh, before I forget –

LORI *rummages around in her pockets until she finds a five-pound note – she tosses it towards* BEX.

BEX. Uh, what the fuck?

LORI. What? (*Realising.*) Oh, shit, no – cobnuts –

BEX. What?

LORI. Fucking pickled-turnip bullshit.

BEX. Oh!

They are both now near hysterical.

LORI. From the… You bet me a fiver no one would touch it.

BEX. Right.

LORI. I wasn't –

BEX. No.

LORI. Sorry.

BEX. I did wonder. For a second.

LORI. I'm really sorry.

BEX. Thought 'wow, I've misread this.'

LORI. I just – I saw the jar of cobnuts up on the shelf.

BEX. Right.

LORI. It reminded me.

BEX. And honestly, if I was charging I reckon a fiver seems quite low.

LORI. Yeah. Yeah, absolutely. I mean I wouldn't know, but –

BEX. I mean, I'll still take it.

They giggle again.

LORI. They really hated that dish.

BEX. Told you so.

LORI. It tastes good! (*Off her look.*) It does – I swear! Did you try it?

BEX *doesn't answer.*

Right – you're going to taste it now.

BEX. You're alright.

LORI. Just a mouthful.

BEX. I've already eaten.

LORI *gives her a look.*

I do shifts for Ollie at The Lime Tree sometimes. He does charred sprouts with bacon and chimichurri. They banged.

LORI. Right.

BEX. I mean if you pick the sprouts out and just eat the bacon.

LORI. Ollie's a hack.

BEX. Just saying. Problem is your pickles. You do pickles and greens you need something richer than a cobnut to balance it. Something creamy or fatty, something emulsified. (*Beat.*) What? Don't worry, I'll give you some pointers next time and we won't end up scraping so much of it into the bins. Cos it's not very eco, is it – all that wastage?

LORI. Shall we have another drink?

BEX. I'm okay.

LORI. Are you sure? I think I might. Do you mind? I just… I don't make a habit of this. To be clear.

BEX. Right.

LORI. I've never… This isn't the kind of thing I do.

BEX. That's a shame.

LORI. Was it okay?

BEX. More than okay.

LORI. No, I mean okay like… You didn't feel pressured? I wasn't abusing my power?

BEX. What power?

LORI. You were working for me tonight.

BEX. Yes, chef.

LORI. It wasn't inappropriate to – ?

BEX. Was fingering me in the walk-in fridge inappropriate?

LORI. I just –

BEX. For a workplace environment?

LORI. I wouldn't want to… I'd hate it if you –

BEX. I was off the clock. (*Beat.*) I don't make a habit of it either. So you know.

LORI. Have another drink with me. Just one, just… Come on. This is not a… a normal shift, and I would like to… Something nice. Let's open some two-hundred-pound, some five-hundred-pound bottle of… Write it off as a breakage. Get some waiter fired. Martin, maybe. Twat. I would like a paddling pool of claret. A swimming pool – an Olympic swimming pool full of… Do you know about the wine lake? There used to be a wine lake somewhere. And a butter mountain. In Europe. All the excess – all the extra… Because of the… the… the EU – the restrictions on… So they'd end up with all this surplus, just piled up somewhere. I'd like to go live in the butter mountain. Go skiing down the butter mountain. Smear myself in it. Not in a… You're thinking in a sexy way but that's not how I mean it. That's your mind. I mean it very wholesomely actually. I want the freshest bread and the creamiest butter and the reddest wine. I want a pain de campagne the size of a double bed, rip the crust off while it's warm and soft and just snuggle up inside it. Butter pillow. Butter bedsheets. Bed and butter. Breakfast in bread. Is that…? I'm not drunk, I just haven't eaten today. Bread and butter and wine – that's all you need. Not all this faff – 'dining concepts' – trends and tweezers – and no pickled turnips, I promise. No cold fish. Just bread and butter and wine – and you. What bread do you buy? This is important. Do you buy good bread? You have to buy the best you can. Not from a supermarket – never – not even the Finest, the Taste the Difference – no – *real* bread. No plastic shit. You are never to eat shit bread again, do you understand me? I'm serious. I forbid it. I'll never buy you flowers because flowers are pointless – you just sit them there and watch them die – but I will bake for you, any hour of the day or night. I'd watch you eat. I'd eat you up. Look at you. You get it, don't you? You're *real*. You know what matters. Simple things. Bread and butter and wine and you. Sorry. I'm being weird. I thought I was being romantic but I'm just being drunk and gay. Do you want something to eat?

8. NOW

BEX *has just (half-heartedly) come on to* LORI. *It's awkward.*

BEX. Right. Forget it.

LORI. Sorry.

BEX. Doesn't matter.

LORI. I wasn't… Just because of how we left things, whether –

BEX. Yeah.

LORI. Or if… if… People could be back any minute, you said – your dad, so –

BEX. Not exactly the best time for a quickie.

LORI. No.

BEX. Stupid. I'm stupid.

LORI. You're not.

BEX. I am.

LORI. Come here –

BEX *moves away.*

BEX. I just thought… y'know, you said 'anything' – anything I needed, so…

LORI. Yeah. Okay, yeah.

BEX. And maybe it would bash some of the sad out of my head for five minutes, but… You're right. Bad idea.

LORI. I'm sorry.

BEX. It's fine.

LORI. We have… How much time do you think we have?

BEX. Moment's gone.

LORI. We could make out for a minute. Or just cuddle? Might be nice to –

BEX. It's alright.

LORI. It's just that you said space – to give you space – not to… And that's been really hard.

BEX. Sorry.

LORI. I'm not saying be sorry, I just… I wanted to come round sooner. I did. (*Beat.*) I was glad when you invited me today.

BEX. Yeah, well. Didn't ask you to cater it, but…

LORI. It's good to see you. Come here. (*Beat.*) Please. If that's okay.

BEX *moves towards* LORI. BEX *allows herself to be held.*

You've lost weight.

BEX. Have I?

LORI. I think so, yeah.

BEX. Do I need to change?

LORI. No, you're fine. You're great.

BEX. It's one of those shirts you don't have to iron, actually.

LORI. Right.

BEX. That's what the label says.

LORI. You're lovely. You look lovely.

Into –

9. THEN

BEX. You're wearing a skirt.

LORI. I am, yeah.

BEX. Should I have worn a skirt? Is this a skirt place?

LORI. You look great.

BEX. Is this a dickhead place?

LORI. It's nice. You're going to like it.

BEX. If you'd told me where we were going –

LORI. It's a surprise.

BEX. You just said seaside. So I thought layers.

LORI. Felix is a mate. You can wear whatever you like. (*Beat.*) Now, we've got the wine flight with dinner, but did you want a cocktail to start?

BEX. You didn't have to do all this.

LORI. I wanted to. Champagne, obviously the classic choice with oysters, but a trailblazer such as myself might do a Fino sherry –

BEX. I don't do oysters.

LORI. First time for everything. Ooh – or Black Velvets! Guinness and champagne cocktails – have you ever…? (*To an unseen waiter.*) Hi! Incredible. And can we get two Black Velvets and two glasses of the Valdespino? Brilliant. (*To* BEX.) I figure you try both, and I'll just drink whatever's left over. (*Beat.*) Go on.

BEX. Do I have to?

LORI. They're not a punishment, they're a rite of passage. They're a proper aphrodisiac – you know that?

BEX. Says who?

LORI. Everyone. Very sexy. Very erotic.

BEX. How are these sexy?

LORI. You know – because they look like a…

BEX. A what?

LORI. You know!

BEX. A fanny?!

LORI. Ugh!

BEX *cackles.*

BEX. Really?

LORI. Yes!

BEX. Do they though? Do you think they do?

LORI. I don't know. Maybe.

BEX. What kind of fucked-up fannies have you been looking at?

LORI. It's a thing!

BEX. Is that what my fanny looks like to you?

LORI. It's just a thing – a known thing – that they're said to… Oysters, clams, any kind of… bivalve.

BEX. Bivalve?

LORI. Try one.

BEX. Is that why you like them? Why you're so proficient?

LORI. Stop it.

BEX. Dab hand with them – know how to open them up, give them a good slurp –

LORI. Alright –

BEX. A pro with a clam, hasn't got a clue what to do with a carrot.

LORI *looks away.*

Do I taste like an oyster? (*Beat.*) Because that's a thing, isn't it? About girls tasting fishy. Which is – don't get me wrong – actually just bullshit peddled by incels with a fear of cunnilingus – but – fish isn't meant to be that fishy either, is it? You go into a fishmongers and it reeks of fish, you know something's wrong. It's supposed to smell of the sea. Do I taste of the sea?

LORI. Try one and see for yourself.

BEX *considers it.*

BEX. Ugh, no, I can't.

LORI. How will you know whether you like it until you try it?

BEX. You know that's the argument my first boyfriend used to talk me into anal.

LORI. Fine. Fuck it – fine – do whatever you want.

BEX. Are you mad at me?

LORI. I'm just trying to… There is a world beyond chicken nuggets, you know?

BEX. Nothing wrong with a chicken nugget.

LORI. No, actually there is.

BEX. Agree to disagree.

LORI. I'm trying to do something nice. Something special. I let you rip the piss when we're working but actually I've put a lot of thought and time and money, as it happens, into tonight, so I could really do without… It isn't cute. It's actually really boring when you're like this. It makes you seem small.

BEX. Okay.

LORI. Not like… I didn't… Are you drinking that?

BEX *shrugs a 'go ahead'.*

Let me try again. Have I told you about Normandy? Normandy. I was fourteen. First ever time abroad. We were flat broke back then, but my parents had been saving up for years. A proper holiday. Massive deal. We're staying in some shitty tumbledown BnB where we all got fleas – genuinely – and it's rained the whole week, but then on the last night we go down to this little place on the harbour and the air is warm and the stars are out and Dad says I can order anything I like. I want oysters. I don't know what they are exactly, but I want them, and we've got this cartoon of a snooty French waiter who gives us this look like 'fuck off, all of you – she doesn't want them – he can't afford them', which just makes both of us more determined, so out they come, and I don't know what I was expecting, but I try one and it's just… They taste of everything I didn't even know I wanted. Magic. Unforgettable. I want you to have that. I wanted us to sit by the window so you can see the sea and the boats coming in and it's there – it's *right there.*

BEX. They're that good then?

LORI. I want you to experience things you never otherwise would, because I think… You turn your nose up at all this because you think it's not for you, but it is – it can be for you! You deserve it! You're special! But waiting tables isn't special. Chicken nuggets aren't special. The life you have right now isn't special and it should be. (*Beat.*) Forget it.

BEX. Right then.

LORI. I'm sorry.

BEX. Okay, you slippery bitch. Let's see what all the fuss is about.

LORI. You don't have to.

BEX. Do you just sort of knock it back, or – ?

LORI. Leave it.

BEX. I want to.

LORI. No, you don't.

BEX. No, I don't, but I'm going to. Just… (*Still dithering with the oyster.*) Just for the record though – this isn't normal. Oysters aren't normal. Having a spiritual experience with seafood aged fourteen isn't a normal thing to do.

LORI. I don't think you're normal either.

BEX. And it's a myth about chicken nuggets – McDonald's did those ads. There's nothing weird in them, just chicken.

LORI. Doesn't matter. Genuinely. Just leave it.

BEX *does.*

BEX. You should have them. You love them – you have them.

LORI. I'm not going to sit and eat a plate of oysters all by myself – I'll feel like a Roman emperor or something.

BEX. Okay.

Pause.

LORI. I've really fucked this, haven't I?

BEX. No! No, it's going to be great. (*Beat.*) It's not all raw, is it?

LORI. No.

BEX. Good. (*Beat.*) Thank you for… I'm sorry. And anything you put in front of me from now on, I'll eat it, I promise. I'll do better. I'm excited.

LORI. You hate it here.

BEX. It's perfect.

LORI. No, it's perfect for me. I should've known –

BEX. I love it.

LORI. You called it a dickhead place.

BEX. I'm sorry.

LORI. Come on let's go.

BEX. What?

LORI. I mean it. We're going.

BEX. Haven't we got like six courses left?

LORI. Doesn't matter. What time is it? (*Glances at her watch.*) Good. Still plenty of light. We're having fish and chips on the beach. We're going to The Seagull because they use proper beef dripping and we're going to wait and make them cook it from fresh. We're going to pick up two bottles of prosecco from M&S on the way.

BEX. We can do that any time.

LORI. But we're doing it now. Three bottles – one for me, one for you, one for the road. And we'll come back here later for pudding and cocktails at the bar. All the fucking puddings. Just normal, delicious puddings. And all the booze.

BEX. Won't your mate mind?

LORI. No. I'm going to get him to put a sparkler in it and everything. I'm going to make everyone sing.

BEX. I will hate that.

LORI. You've got to give me something.

BEX. You've planned a whole thing.

LORI. I'm going rogue.

BEX. You're wearing a skirt.

LORI. So you'd better remove it at the earliest opportunity.

BEX. It won't be special.

LORI. It's with you – of course it's special.

BEX. I'm sorry.

LORI. What for?

BEX. Spoiling things.

LORI. You've not spoiled anything. I love you.

BEX. What?

LORI. You heard me.

BEX. Say that again.

LORI. I love you. No biggie. And you don't have to say it back if –

BEX. I love you too.

LORI. Happy birthday.

BEX *smiles. Into –*

10. NOW

BEX. What else have you brought then?

LORI. Nothing. (*Beat.*) Barely anything. A couple of salads. Some more fruit.

BEX (*without enthusiasm*). Great.

LORI. And some of those home-made peanut-butter-cup things.

BEX. The ones that tasted of sand?

LORI. Just thought it'd be good to have a bit of variety. (*Beat.*) Are you eating? Properly eating, not…? I could do some meal prep, bring some things round.

BEX. We're fine.

LORI. I'd like to.

BEX. We've got every auntie for fifty miles bringing us casseroles, we're alright.

LORI. Okay, good. That's good. (*Beat.*) Just for balance though. Something with veg, pulses, the proper stuff. Maybe just for the freezer – for you and your dad, so –

BEX. Freezer's full.

LORI. What if we had a sort through? Because it's probably all her stuff, isn't it? You don't have to eat like that any more. We could –

BEX. Stop it.

LORI. I just mean you can have a bit more control now – over what you –

BEX. Right.

LORI. Might be good. Might be liberating.

BEX. Uh-huh.

LORI. In your own time. Whenever you're ready. Just to –

BEX. I won't end up like her.

LORI. I know.

BEX. Isn't that what you're afraid of?

LORI. I never –

BEX. I'll reach forty and just… The look on your face the first time you met. You tried to hide it, but I saw. We didn't have sex for a fortnight afterwards, did you know that?

LORI. She was an incredible woman.

BEX. Who ate herself to death?

LORI. I… I know she struggled with…

BEX. I'm not chucking anything out. It's all good – won't waste it. There was some pretty green malt loaf in the back of her dresser, but otherwise…

LORI. Okay.

BEX. I'm still finding her little stashes – thought I knew them all. Cheesy Wotsits in the airing cupboard, Jammy Dodgers under the bathroom sink. Pulled out a box marked 'Christmas baubles' and it was just full of Matchmakers.

LORI. Classic.

BEX. I wish she was catering this. She'd have known exactly what to put out – how to get everyone smiling. How many meals – thousands – tens of thousands – served at this table and no one ever left it hungry. Can you always say that?

LORI. Tell me what you need.

BEX. I need my mum.

LORI. Why don't you sit down for a minute? Just sit still for a minute and… What have you eaten today?

BEX. I'm fine.

LORI. Let me fix you a little plate, just to keep you going. Something simple.

BEX. I'm really not hungry.

Into –

11. THEN

LORI *has just got in.* BEX *is in high spirits.*

LORI. What is all this?

BEX. You alright?

LORI. What're you doing?

BEX. Wouldn't you like to know? There's beer in the fridge. Those fancy Dutch ones you like.

LORI. What for?

BEX. If you're not pissed already?

LORI. I just had the one closing down.

BEX. Well, I hope you didn't eat.

LORI. No.

BEX. Good.

BEX *pulls* LORI *in for a kiss.*

I'm cooking.

LORI. You don't cook.

BEX. I'm expanding my horizons.

LORI. I could've brought something back.

BEX. I know. Fish stew – Normandy-style. Got Anton to give me some instruction on the sly. Look – nothing frozen – all fresh. He did the filleting for me, cos I didn't fancy the trip to A&E, but one step at a time.

LORI. Okay…

BEX. Grab a beer. Go on. No shortcuts, no packets, no artificial whatever. All responsible and sustainable. And check this out – pain de campagne – the good stuff, from that beardy place. And I'm going to toast crumbs of it in garlic butter – real French butter – and then you sprinkle them on top. Had to do a test run to get it right and they're fucking incredible. Oh – and a green-bean salad too, to stop it getting too lardy – very balanced.

LORI. Right. (*Beat.*) Sorry, am I missing something?

BEX. How do you mean?

LORI. I haven't… It's not an anniversary, or – ?

BEX. No.

LORI. Then what?

BEX. And then – the pièce de résistance, slightly less on-theme – Rice Krispie brownies. Sounds trashy, but it's actually a Nigella thing, and Nigella is the only white woman I truly trust, so.

LORI. Wow. Stone cold.

BEX. I would let her do things to me.

LORI. Is everything alright?

BEX. Do you want to taste? Tell me if it needs any…? No – don't actually. I'm feeling good. I want to get it right by myself.

LORI. Y'know what, this looks… incredible. Like actually incredible.

BEX. Try not to sound so surprised.

LORI. What happened?

BEX. Had a day off.

LORI. Yeah, but –

BEX. It's only dinner.

LORI. No, it isn't.

BEX. I dunno. You're always telling me I have these hidden depths and I'm not saying you're right or anything but…

LORI *smiles.*

Shut up! You've not tasted it yet. Lower your expectations. And don't look at anything too closely, it's a state, just… I know you have this catalogue in your head of every meal that's changed your life, and so I thought, well, if I'm serious about us maybe it's time I made the list.

LORI. Thank you.

BEX. But you can't watch me. Sit down. Put your feet up. I've got it all covered.

LORI. Yes, chef.

Into –

12. NOW

BEX. You do know you're like two hours early?

LORI. Sorry?

BEX. And obviously everyone else will be late.

LORI. I wanted to help set up.

BEX. I didn't ask for that.

LORI. You don't have to.

BEX. I told you it was covered. I was super clear. I said this is the deal – come pay respects or whatever – and you said 'can I bring anything?' and I said no, and you said it's no bother and I said no, and then you said sandwiches, and I said no – I've got it covered.

LORI. I just thought –

BEX. What?

LORI. Maybe you'd –

BEX. Have fucked it all and need rescuing?

LORI. Maybe you wouldn't want to be alone. (*Beat.*) Maybe you'd have successfully banished everyone else, but actually when it came down to it you could use some company from someone who doesn't mind it when you scream at them. Maybe I'm the last person you'd want to see but I'd still be better than no one.

Pause.

BEX. Doesn't mean I want your fruit platter.

LORI. Your mum used to love my fruit platters. (*Off her look.*) She did! Never touched them herself but she said they made her look good – put one out every time she had a house visit. She told me.

BEX *isn't amused.*

Oh, I know she hated me. (*Beat.*) That's okay. It's not like I've got a pathological need for approval or anything.

BEX (*grudgingly*). She didn't hate you.

LORI. She used to call me 'skinny flat white'.

BEX *laughs.*

I've had worse. (*Beat.*) I wish she could've seen it – the restaurant. She'd have been so proud. Not that she wasn't proud of you already, but –

BEX. She wouldn't be seen dead.

LORI. She'd have loved it. (*Beat.*) I've got some other bits and pieces in the van too. Business stuff. Nothing important, just… If you could sign the lease agreement though, it means I can start hiring contractors.

BEX. Right.

LORI. Just a signature, that's all. Because everything's in both our names. But I brought some of the fun stuff too – branding mock-ups, sample menus – just in case. I emailed you, but –

BEX. I saw. Haven't looked yet.

LORI. Okay.

BEX. Sorry.

LORI. That's okay. Just wanted to keep you in the loop. Looks even better in the flesh, so… I think Kerry's really come through.

BEX. Great.

Beat.

LORI. Anyway, you tell me – you let me know what level of involvement you're ready for with anything – no pressure – and I'll just keep cracking on.

BEX. Yeah.

LORI. If you don't let me know what you need from me I'm just going to keep guessing, which is fine, but evidently I'm not getting much right so far, so… (*Pause.*) I can't imagine what you're going through. Losing a parent is… I can't imagine. But I can listen, and I can look after you, if you'll let me, and…

BEX. I'm fine.

LORI. You're not.

BEX. Of course I'm fucking not. So what're you going to do – make me a salad?

LORI. No.

BEX. None of this helps.

LORI. If you… There's science in… If your body isn't getting what it needs it can't heal.

BEX. I know you put a lot of faith in kale, but it can't resurrect the dead, so.

LORI. I know.

BEX. Today isn't about healing. Today was never about healthy choices. Today is about eating our feelings and getting wasted and maybe even having a bit of a laugh if we can manage it, and if you're not on board with that, you really don't have to stay.

LORI. Okay.

BEX. I mean it. Might turn into a bit of a session later, so.

LORI. I'm fine.

BEX. Yeah?

LORI. I promise.

BEX. No one asked you to turn up with a stick up your arse and a van full of tofu.

LORI. I didn't know what else to do.

BEX. Right.

LORI. I cook. I cater. It is literally my job – what else was I going to do? Why wouldn't you want my help?

BEX. Because I don't need it.

LORI. Okay.

BEX. What?

LORI. I'm not going to fight with you.

BEX. Stop being a twat then.

LORI. You've done brilliantly – getting anything out is brilliant –

BEX. But?

LORI. Okay! But now we actually have some variety, not just whatever beige shit was in your freezer.

BEX. This is how I want it.

LORI. Right, so it's a… a sentimental thing, I get it – that's not a criticism. But surely it's better to have a range – have some colour –

BEX. Your chicken's black.

LORI. I've got other stuff.

BEX. And bringing black chicken to a wake – I don't know if that's you working to a theme, or –

LORI. If you'd talked to me – if you'd told me what you wanted –

BEX. I told you it was covered.

LORI. Not just the food – if you'd talked to me about anything… (*Beat.*) Do you want me here at all?

Pause. BEX *can't answer.*

Right. (*Beat.*) So why even invite me?

Pause.

BEX. I thought you were working.

Beat.

LORI. What?

BEX. I spoke to Tony and he said you were doing some big wedding this weekend. Thought you wouldn't be able to make it.

LORI. Oh.

Pause.

BEX. Sorry.

LORI. Yeah. I was, yeah. I pulled out.

BEX. Right.

LORI. I wanted to –

BEX. You must have lost –

LORI. A few thousand. (*Pause.*) I set them up with Zainab though – she could really do with it. She'll be great.

BEX. I'm sorry you did that.

LORI. I was happy to. Really happy when –

BEX. I'm sorry.

LORI. Why? (*Beat.*) I know you're dealing with a lot, but I really do think I'm allowed to ask you why now.

BEX *looks away.*

Cos I've tried to be patient, and respectful, and not to trample over your grief or whatever. I'm not perfect, I know that – I'm annoying as fuck sometimes – but it really has felt like I'm being punished for something and I don't think it's entirely fair. (*Pause.*) I've stopped drinking. Not *stopped*, but… cutting back, anyway. So you know.

BEX. That's good.

LORI. And we've got so much planned right now – big things – exciting things – like proper life-changing things between the two of us that I must've done something pretty awful to make you hate me this much.

BEX. I don't hate you.

LORI. What is it then?

BEX. My mum died.

LORI. I know.

BEX. I don't need anything else. You can go now.

Into –

13. THEN

LORI. So…?

BEX. Your own place?

LORI. Can't stay in catering forever. I'll be fucked if I'm doing another supper club. Shoot me in the face before I buy a food truck.

BEX. Sure.

LORI. Now's the time to get serious about it. Jonno's a wanker but he's got cash to burn. Plus I can borrow a bit from my parents maybe, and so many places are going to go bust in the next year rents will be dirt cheap.

BEX. Isn't that risky?

LORI. Not if the product's right. I know I can staff the kitchen no bother, I just need someone mega to run front of house.

BEX. Right.

LORI. Someone properly brilliant. Someone I can trust.

BEX. Yeah.

LORI. Someone I can make out with in the walk-in if it gets quiet.

Beat.

BEX. You mean…?

LORI. What do you reckon?

BEX. Me?

LORI. Who else?

BEX. But… What do I know about any of that?

LORI. You'd learn.

BEX. You must need qualifications, or –

LORI. Maybe. So get them. Plenty of night courses – college courses – all that sort of… No rush – we can take our time, and you can get a grant, or a loan, or –

BEX. No, this is actually mad.

LORI. Talk to Tony. Talk to Freja, actually, because she's a total badass, and she might mentor you. Or if she can't I bet she'll know someone who could.

BEX. I still add up on my fingers, you know that?

LORI. You'll get better! What else are you doing? I can hardly have you waiting tables in my own place, can I?

BEX. Why not?

LORI. Wouldn't that be embarrassing?

BEX. For who?

LORI. Just think about it – our own place. Not mine, *ours*. Somewhere round here. Local. Unpretentious. Comfortable. Somewhere you could take your mum.

BEX (*a little wary*). Right.

LORI. I mean it. But not, y'know, not junk – still healthy and eco-conscious and sustainable, just without making a big deal about it. Big flavours – bright, fresh, punchy – and – get this – I was thinking we do Soul Food.

BEX. Really?

LORI. With our own twist. Because what is Soul Food, actually, or anything that comes out of that sort of diaspora? It's community, right? It's traditions, not trends. It's this honest sort of elbows-on-the-table, lick-your-fingers, sit yourself down and get yourself fed.

BEX. Right.

LORI. And people love it, because it's got comfort and history, but actually the exciting thing about a… a jambalaya, or a jollof, or a jerk whatever – is the flavour, right? It's only flavour –

BEX. Okay. None of those things are Soul Food though.

LORI. Don't be pedantic. It's British. Contemporary British. Which is anything. It's roasted plantain with chip-shop spice. It's Dublin Bay prawns with gumbo butter. It's… You remember that place we went with Emma for curry goat?

BEX. I think so.

LORI. So I've been working on this thing – it's a bit cheffy, sure, but you swap out the goat for hogget – British-reared – slow roast in a firepit with a spice rub then smoked over Earl Grey tea. So it's a bit Caribbean, a bit Texas barbecue, and then Earl fucking Grey – the most English thing! Magic.

BEX. Got it.

LORI. You see?

BEX. So it's just a bit of something from anywhere we've stuck a flag.

LORI. No – you can fuck off with all of that. It's *flavour*, and I understand flavour – flavour is my life. It's not *colonial* to… to expand your horizons. This is what I keep telling you. Or else you end up like my granddad, demanding liver and onions five times a week and thinking a clove of garlic is a bridge too far. That's the danger – that's the racist attitude. Racists don't eat chicken tikka masala –

BEX. I'm pretty sure they do.

LORI. Okay, they definitely do, but… Food should unite us. It's essential and universal, and it's all the same – fundamentally all the same. Protein, vegetable, carbohydrate. Salt and fat and acid and heat. No one *owns* that. We should never… 'This isn't your dish, it's mine.' 'You can't sit at our table.' No – *that* is elitist. That is the opposite of… sitting down and breaking bread and sharing something.

BEX. I'm just saying all this – this is why people don't like Jamie Oliver.

LORI. That's not why people don't like Jamie Oliver.

BEX. It's one of the reasons.

LORI. So you're not allowed pizza?

BEX. What?

LORI. You're not Italian – why are you allowed to eat pizza?

BEX. I wasn't saying that.

LORI. See – it's ridiculous. And actually, actually, white chefs *should* be learning, we *should* be looking further afield, not just idolising classical French or modern Nordic, but studying all those world cuisines banished to the deep-fat fryer and the late-night takeaway. And – and – okay, if you look at some of those cultures, those, um, people of specific ethnic backgrounds where there's a propensity towards, uh, obesity, or diabetes, or heart disease – what if that's because historically those cuisines have been neglected? What if we take them, elevate them, do something lighter, fresher, a bit different –

BEX. You want to teach my grandma how to fry chicken?

LORI. I'd probably bake it, so…

BEX *laughs at this, in spite of herself.*

BEX. You do know people will give you shit for this?

LORI. That's what I've got you for.

BEX. Can we talk about this later? Can I think about it?

LORI. Imagine we had a restaurant where your mum felt totally welcome and she could order anything on the menu without feeling bad about it. Imagine that.

BEX. Maybe.

LORI. How's she doing? You said she had another appointment?

BEX. Oh yeah. Fine. Just got her bloods checked, and a new inhaler.

LORI. And that was all – ?

BEX. Yeah, good. New doctor. Nicer than the last one.

LORI. That's good. (*Beat.*) Think about it. Just think about it. Time for a new adventure.

Back to –

14. NOW

BEX. You should find someone else for the restaurant too, obviously.

LORI. What's going on?

BEX. Shouldn't be hard. Get Emma in on it – or Zainab maybe – your little protégé.

LORI. Don't be stupid.

BEX. Just make sure they're the right shade so no one comes after you.

LORI. Forget about all that for now. Talk to me.

BEX. I'll see how much of a refund I can get from college. I'll pay you back.

LORI. Have you stopped going?

BEX. I don't want you wasting any more money on me.

LORI. It's fine to take a break – just speak to them, let them know – or I can call them, if you haven't already.

BEX. I'm not going back.

LORI. They have, don't they, um… allowances – compassionate – for things like this?

BEX. Waste of time – always was. Can't fix stupid.

LORI. You're not.

BEX *shrugs.*

You're not stupid. Stop saying that.

BEX. No, I am. Nothing sticks. Can't focus. Can't remember any of it.

LORI. So we made plans for that.

BEX. Fuck off.

LORI. Structure your time. Eat properly.

BEX. For one minute.

LORI. Exercise. Sleep. Build a routine.

BEX. Why though? No, I mean it – genuinely why? Cos it never ends. GCSEs and NVQs and BTECs and HNDs. Do this one, then that. No, you can't get that piece of paper until you've got this one. No, we don't offer that here. No, not around shift work. You don't meet our basic criteria. How long have you been out of education? Saddle yourself with what – fifteen grand of debt – twenty, thirty, by the time you've done all of it – all to go chasing after jobs that don't even exist? What's the point?

LORI. To do something better.

BEX. What's better?

LORI. We're doing it. We're so close.

BEX. Y'know I was actually happy before – before you came and told me how shitty my life was.

LORI. You were miserable.

BEX. No, you told me I was miserable. You told me so often I started to believe it.

LORI. No –

BEX. You *made* me miserable. You make my life unbearable just by the way you look at it. You know all you had to do today was breeze in and say 'well done' – take a look around and be even the tiniest bit impressed, not immediately start trying to fix things – but it's *impossible* – physically impossible for you – because nothing about my life is ever good enough.

LORI. I've only been trying to help.

BEX. Fuck your help. None of this is by accident. Smiley potato faces because we had them for Christmas dinner one year after Mum incinerated the roasties and we never looked back. Onion rings because the engagement ring Dad got didn't fit her right at first, so he ran out for a bag of these instead. Burnt half the skin off her finger but she couldn't stop laughing. We've got Sunny Delight that I had to order from fucking eBay because that's the right one. Everything here is for her. I didn't think I had stories like yours but I do.

LORI (*weakly*). I just thought you might want a range.

BEX. She'd never touch it.

LORI. I know.

BEX. So why would you…? It's about paying respects. This is fucking communion shit. You don't mess with that.

LORI. I understand.

BEX. You don't. It's my fault. This is my fault. Should've been up front with you. Shouldn't have let it get this far. But you don't get to sit with us. You don't belong at this table and you never will. That's okay. But it's enough now.

Into –

15. THEN

LORI *is drunk.*

LORI. Bex! Bex! Where are you?

BEX. Hey.

LORI. Hey – you're still up.

BEX. Yeah.

LORI. Great.

BEX. You weren't answering my calls.

LORI. Sorry.

BEX. Where have you been?

LORI. Sorry.

BEX. Do you know what time it is?

LORI. Shall we have a drink?

BEX. No thanks.

LORI. Little drink?

BEX. I'm not –

LORI. Cheeky little nightcap.

BEX. I'll get you some water.

LORI. Fuck off.

BEX. Can I talk to you?

LORI. Me first. We're celebrating.

BEX. No.

LORI. Yes. Have we got fizz? Nothing cold, right? Okay, so that's another rule – a new rule, add it to your list – fizz in the fridge at all times, in case of emergencies.

BEX. Do you want to sit down?

LORI. Right. Gotta be whiskey then.

BEX. Please.

LORI. Okay – it's late – I'm sorry – I'm terrible. I've got to talk to you.

BEX. I need to –

LORI. I've found it. The most fucking perfect… You know the dodgy chicken shop on South Street? Finally being put out of its misery. And so I know what you're thinking – too small – much too small – and yes, you are correct – but the bookie next door that's been closed for a million years? Same landlord. We can knock through, tart it up, make it incredible.

BEX. Uh-huh.

LORI. Perfect. I promise you it's perfect.

BEX (*quietly*). Great.

LORI. So, will you wipe that look off your face and have a drink with me now?

BEX. I've got something I need to tell you too.

LORI. I know. You said, and I've got… (*Glancing at her phone.*) Seventeen missed calls? Wow. Needy much?

BEX. You weren't answering, so…

LORI. I'm sorry. I'll make it up to you. Come on – a toast to us, and to the future, and then we'll get on to your thing. (*Beat.*) What? Jesus Christ, Bex, who died?

A horrible silence. Into –

16. NOW

LORI. Okay. Right, I'll… I'm just going to go then.

BEX. Yeah.

LORI. And you can do what you want with… Chuck all the… Or don't, actually – give it to some homeless –

BEX. No homeless person wants a pulled-jackfruit wrap.

LORI. Uh-huh. And you'd know, would you?

BEX. Fiver says so.

LORI. Right. Because of course you're an expert on every sort of… Forget it.

BEX. Thanks for trying though.

LORI. Actually I can't… You're grieving, so you get a free pass on a lot of this, but that is a… a very classist attitude. A very… People can surprise you. Give them a chance and people will surprise you.

BEX. Okay.

LORI. Not everybody wants the shit they're given – most people – the vast majority of people – they're not actively choosing the shit they're given, they're just given it – no other option. I tried to give you another option, and that makes me the villain, apparently. For offering something better.

BEX. Who says your stuff is better?

LORI. I'm done with this. I can't argue with you.

BEX. Go on. Who?

LORI. It is. It just is, Bex. Objectively. Um. Ethically – nutritionally – sustainably. Better for you, better for the planet, better for the people who make it – not that you've ever seemed to give a fuck about them. Do you want carbon footprint, or fairly traded, pesticide-free, low-impact, vitamin-rich… what sort of metric are you after? It's better.

BEX. If you say so.

LORI. Stop trying to make it some heritage thing, some cultural thing – diabetes isn't a protected characteristic. I am so tired of this.

BEX. Of trying to make me better?

LORI. Yes.

Pause.

BEX. Lot of judgement coming from a pisshead.

LORI. I'm not… I told you, I'm managing that.

BEX. Your liver's gotta be way more fucked than my arteries, but that's fine. At least you don't drink the cheap stuff.

LORI. I'm dealing with it. I've said sorry for –

BEX. Good luck, anyway.

LORI. Okay. I hope tonight is… I will try to leave you alone but please know you can call me whenever you want to.

BEX. Can I ask you something?

LORI. Sure.

BEX. Did you ever want me like this, or did you only want the thing you thought you could make me into?

LORI. Of course I did. I just wanted you to have more.

BEX. More like you?

LORI. Just *more*! Happier, healthier, *more*! Isn't that the whole point of…? And this – all this – I'm sorry, but I find it grotesque. It's not a tribute. It's obscene, actually. Celebrate the woman, not her cause of death. Do better. Every parent wants their child to do better.

BEX. You didn't know her.

LORI. I'm not asking you to rewrite your personality. I'm not asking you to turn your back on the people who raised you. I'm just asking you to do… something. If it's not the restaurant, fine. If it's not with me, so be it, okay, because I can't keep doing this. Plant a forest. Write a novel –

BEX. What?

LORI. Or whatever.

BEX. When have you seen me read a novel?

LORI. But suggesting that you do something – *anything* – that you don't drop out of college for a second time, that you take yourself seriously and figure out what it is you love – that doesn't make me a bad person, it doesn't make me a snob, and it doesn't make you a class traitor. It makes me a really good girlfriend, actually. So tell me what I've done wrong. Tell me why trying to be better is a bad thing. (*Beat.*) Bex? I'm waiting.

Silence.

BEX. It's not… I'm sorry. I know it's not useful to be sorry, but I am. I'm sorry I can't make you understand it. It's hard to pinpoint exactly what it is – because you've got this way, this really clever way of making everything sound so reasonable when you say it and then I think I've got everything straight when you're not here – I've got a handle on it all – but I can't…

The thing is you can't tell me I have this capacity to be better without telling me I'm shit right now – making me feel like shit. Without going 'Jesus Christ, look at the state of you, but take my hand and pull your socks up and we'll get through it.' And you do it in this really patient, caring, compassionate way – like you do really feel for me, and how shit my life is, and you want to swoop in and whisk me off to this brave new world of matcha powder and pomegranates and reclaimed floorboards, and… And that isn't…

What if I really was happy as I am? Nothing would terrify you more. Happy before you got to work on me, making me fit for your oyster bars and supper clubs and Christmases with your family. Happy without changing a hair – can you imagine the power of that? Can you imagine how incredible it'd be if that were true? And I'm not. Of course I'm not! What do you expect? And I'm not saying things aren't shit – my life isn't shit – but it doesn't mean… Aaargh! I can see the argument – it's there – it's flickering, but I can't quite… I'm hungry. I've not eaten. Sorry.

Did you ever stop to think about why my life is shit before you started trying to fix things? My life is shit because the system is shit. Because the job market is shit. Because housing is shit. Because no one on minimum wage and zero hours has the headspace to make their own yogurt. And the only solution you can offer is for me to drag myself out of it – to upgrade – to somehow become a less shit person and then the world will open up before me. So I can get off the estate, clean up my act, fix my hair, and then once you've ironed all the kinks out of me, if I ever have to talk about where I'm from, or where I'm *from*-from, it can be with this big fat line drawn underneath it, like thank fuck you got to me when you did. Thank fuck you saved me. Thank fuck I'm better now.

I think it's a waste of time trying to make people better. I know that sounds bad, but I do. I think people are always going to be people – kind and stupid and greedy and everything else between. But what you can change is the things around them. Not just saying 'be a better person – be the type of person who deserves better', but saying actually if this is… If this is… Cos if I move off the estate, someone else moves in. I get promoted, someone else takes my old spot. So you've gotta improve the estate, right, not the individual? But you can't see that. You aren't interested in that version of better. And I think maybe the proper goal of all this self-improvement – all social climbing, in your eyes – is just to get to the point where you personally don't know any poor people any more. They're still there – you sort of abstractly know that – but they don't keep you awake at night. Cos it's not you – you're not them – and everyone you know is fine.

Who is it really for? What difference would it have made? Would she still be alive – my mum – if she were more like you? Richer, quieter, whiter? Doctors would've been kinder to her, listened better, taken her more seriously. She could've hired a dietician – a personal trainer – a lifestyle coach. She would've had different tastes – learnt to eat better growing up. Or maybe not. Plenty of fat posh people. But she'd have carried it differently – dressed better – wouldn't get the same kind of stares. People might've still thought she was thick but they might've hated her less for it. Maybe she'd have made it. Had an epiphany. Turned it all around. But maybe you can't make people better. What's better, anyway?

Y'know she was always big – always had an appetite – but it only really became a problem when she felt like she had to hide it. That's when it got bad. That's what you did to her – people like you – you made her feel ashamed. And when you feel shame you seek comfort, and when you feel lesser you seek comfort, and when you feel judged for every choice you ever made and every choice that was already made for you… (*Gestures to the food around them.*) This isn't what killed her, this is what made her life worth living. You're what killed her. You. And you made me feel ashamed too – not just of myself, ashamed of her. Ashamed of this incredible woman – this kind, generous, loving… Who always had a seat at her table. Who would try anything once. Who lived more than you ever will even if you reach a hundred. She didn't want to change. She shouldn't have to. She would've been happy if only people had just *left her alone*.

And yeah, I know, it's all a con – she didn't really want it, she just got tricked into wanting it. It's this whole institutionalised, weaponised class warfare that teaches us to know our place, and take what we're given, and says 'Oh no, you don't want this – you'll never get them to eat that.' So we go 'Yeah, fuck your fancy shit – it's not for us – give us our nuggets.' We eat shit because we're treated like shit and we're all too thick to know any better, but you – you're not like that. No, you're different. You're one of the good guys. You wanted me to try everything – even the rank stuff – you said I deserved the best. Did you really believe it? But it doesn't matter, because if the best's not on offer it makes no difference whether I'm deserving. It's actually worse. It's cruel to make me want it. I'm me and you're you, so… so that's all there is to it. Waste of time. I'm right. I know I'm right. Tell me I'm right.

You can't make people better, but what if I was enough already? What if we just had to find the compromise? Is it this? Is it exactly this, me and you and a weird little well-intentioned, culturally insensitive neighbourhood restaurant? All micro herbs and community gardens and pride flags and Stormzy on the playlist? We'll do it up in matching dungarees, and it'll be slow to start cos people don't know us, but we build trust, we get the word out. You bring in the yoga mums and I go round the barbershops and nail salons with boxes of wings to drum up custom. It's a weird mix, but it works. We're a family. Queer kids come in to do their homework and paint their nails in secret. Homeless know they'll get fed, no questions asked. And if you're ever locking up late by yourself there's always someone insists on walking you home – 'Don't worry auntie, we've gotta get you back to your girl.' Like it's no big thing. No one bothers us. And we get awards and plaudits and all that but we don't care, and when some slick dickhead comes round with a shiny suit and an expansion plan you kick him out. I say 'You didn't have to do that' and you say 'Who needs it? This is us.' And you kiss me and the world explodes. No one else thought we could do it, but you did, and we do. We do. We do.

Do you like the sound of it? You should – it was all your idea – your little wet dream of gentrification. I've gone over it so many times I think it's pretty perfect now. Only there's no money, and no community, and the yoga mums are racist and the barbershops are homophobic and my mum is dead so what's the point of anything? You can't make it better. You can't make any of this better. And I try not to think about it any more because it just makes me so sad.

I don't know what I want. That was always the worst thing. It would be so much easier to walk away if I had something to walk towards, and I don't. I don't want to write a novel. I don't want to run a restaurant, not really. Never did. I don't have a… a passion for animals, or a longing for the great outdoors, or any sort of… and that made me think I was stupid and broken and it's the kind of thing you can't admit to anyone so it was easier to just let you make plans for both of us, but it's gone too far now. You want to make me better – you do – but it's only ever been on your terms. You want me to blossom into something else and I think that's love – I genuinely think it is – but it's not reasonable. Love is unreasonable, maybe, but I just want to feel like enough, and I don't – not when I'm with you. I feel like I'm failing, and that was you. It's not me, it's you. And if I can't find a way to love you and love myself at the same time then I know what I have to do, because this can't be what it should feel like. Like I'm always having to hold my breath when I'm around you.

I'm sorry. I'm sorry I didn't tell you any of this sooner. I'm sorry I can't even tell you all this now. It's too exhausting. It'd take too long. You wouldn't understand. That's okay, but that's on you. Let that be your burden. I'll be fine. I'm young. I'm smart. I'm hot. I was always enough – that was your mistake. Maybe my mistake as well. It's okay to want different things, value different things, but I value myself, so… You can't fix something that isn't broken. I refuse to break.

LORI. Bex? Are you okay? You haven't said anything for a really long time.

BEX. Yeah, I'm fine. Just hungry. I'll be fine.

Into –

17. THEN

LORI *starts making* BEX *her impressive snack. It's possibly the first real food we've seen. It should look and smell delicious.* LORI *also has a drink for herself.*

BEX. You really don't have to go to all this trouble.

LORI. No trouble.

BEX. Honestly. I would've been happy with the Pot Noodle.

LORI. Then you need to love yourself more.

BEX. Don't worry, I love myself plenty.

LORI. Just don't expect this every time we work together.

BEX. You'd have me back then? (*Beat.*) Is that mashed potato?

LORI. It's Vada Pav.

BEX. It's what?

LORI. Vada Pav? It's an Indian street food. Well, this is a sort of inverted Vada Pav actually, because traditionally it's a sort of fried croquette in a soft bun, but I'm just going to toast it in the pan.

BEX. Right.

LORI. So you'll get crispy outside, fluffy middle, rather than the other way round.

BEX. Is it a mashed potato sandwich?

LORI. No, it's a twist on –

BEX. Because that is the best thing I've ever heard in my life.

LORI. Oh. Really?

BEX. Are you kidding? Did you invent this?

LORI. Um. Sort of. It's just…

BEX. And just how drunk were you at the time?

LORI. It's a real… Although it is really good for soaking booze up actually. Double-carb, but that's… you know, that's fine, every once in a while. Shouldn't be eating it this late – shouldn't be eating anything, but… I don't know. I think everything tastes better after midnight.

BEX. So true.

LORI. Yeah?

BEX. Chicken nuggets on the night bus – can't beat it.

LORI. If you knew where those chickens had… (*She stops herself.*) Sorry, that's not…

BEX. So hold on – it's not just a mashed potato sandwich, is it? It's a mashed potato toastie!

LORI. No, it's –

BEX. Fuck. I think I'm in love.

LORI. It's nothing, it's… so you've got your spiced potato in the middle, green chutney on one slice, red on the other, butter both outer sides.

BEX. My mum used to do me toasties when I was sick – still does sometimes. Ham and cheese and Heinz Tomato Soup. Gotta be Heinz.

LORI. Great taste.

BEX. Yeah, she's alright.

LORI. Mine does lentil – big vats of lentil soup so thick you can stand your spoon up in it.

BEX. Poor you.

LORI. No, it's great. And it's not about the taste, or the… the nutritional value. It's care, isn't it? Nurture. Comfort. It's… a salve against the injustices of the world. (*Beat.*) Sorry – I'm being a massive wanker, apparently. I'm not always like this.

BEX. No?

LORI. Maybe I am. I don't know – shit at first impressions. Anyway, right. Here we go. It'll be pretty hot in the middle, so… Go ahead. I won't watch you eat – that'd be weird. I'm going to go and check in on… Hope you like it. Let me know if… Bon appétit. Fuck's sake. Sorry. Enjoy.

BEX. Thank you.

LORI *smiles awkwardly and goes.* BEX *grins. She looks at the sandwich. She takes a big bite. Maybe we watch her eat the whole thing. It's good. She is happy.*

End.

~~NOT~~ THE END OF THE WORLD

~~Not~~ the End of the World was first performed as *~~Kein~~ Weltuntergang*, translated into German by Gerhild Steinbuch, at the Schaubühne, Berlin, on 4 September 2021. The cast was as follows:

ANNA	Alina Vimbai Strähler
UTA/LILLY	Jule Böwe
LENA	Veronika Bachfischer

Director	Katie Mitchell
Assistant Director	Lily McLeish
Set and Costume Designer	Chloe Lamford
Sound Designer	Donato Wharton
Assistant Sound Designer	Joe Dines
Dramaturg	Nils Haarmann
Lighting Designer	Anthony Doran

Characters

ANNA, *thirties, Black*
UTA, *fifties to sixties, white*
LENA, *twenties, white*
LILLY, *forties to sixties, any ethnicity*

Setting

At some time in the past, Uta interviews Anna. At some time in the future, Anna is cross-examined by Lilly. From another place, Lena talks to us.

The primary location is Uta's office at a university campus in the heart of Berlin. Anything naturalistic in its presentation might gradually break.

Note

Two asterisks (*   *) represent a jump or a reset.

PART ONE – INTRODUCTIONS

1.

UTA*'s office.* UTA *welcomes* ANNA.

UTA. Miss Vogel?

ANNA. Doctor Vogel, yes.

UTA. I'm sorry?

ANNA. Doctor Vogel.

UTA. So you are.

ANNA. This is a post-doctoral position?

UTA. Yes

ANNA. So that would be a prerequisite?

UTA. Yes, yes.

ANNA. Therefore not surprising?

UTA. Miss Vogel – *Doctor* Vogel, by all means –

ANNA. By all means?

UTA. Whichever you prefer.

ANNA. Only one is accurate.

*   *

2.

UTA. Doctor Vogel?

ANNA. Yes.

UTA. Come on through.

ANNA. Thank you. And please, call me Anna.

UTA. If you insist. Please call me Professor Oberdorf, in the interest of maintaining professional boundaries.

ANNA. Oh.

*   *

3.

UTA. Doctor Vogel?

ANNA. Yes.

UTA. I'm afraid we're running behind. I can't see you today. If you speak to Marianne on your way out, she can reschedule.

*   *

4.

UTA. Doctor Vogel? Is there a Doctor Vogel waiting? (*To* ANNA.) Can you check at reception? And a black coffee, two sugars, if you please?

*   *

5.

ANNA. Professor Oberdorf?

UTA. Yes?

ANNA. Anna Vogel, I'm your eleven o'clock. You're running behind so I thought I'd let myself in. Here, is it?

*   *

6.

LENA. It's difficult, knowing where to begin.

*   *

7.

UTA. Doctor Vogel, I presume? Do come in. I am Professor Uta Oberdorf, as I'm sure you're aware. I am the Head of this Institution. I hope you shan't think it rude if we get straight down to business? I have rather a lot of people to see today, and you are rather less qualified than the majority of them, so I don't intend to waste much of either of our times. Sit, by all means. If you were intending to impress me, you really should have started by now.

* *

8.

LENA. Knowing what is significant – what matters in the end.

* *

9.

UTA. Ah, Doctor Vogel.

* *

10.

LENA. When we talk about greatness, everything is significant. It all matters. No detail is too small.

* *

11.

UTA. I'm Professor Oberdorf.

* *

12.

LENA. When a great man dies – whenever a great man dies – there is always a reckoning.

* *

13.

LILLY *with* ANNA.

LILLY. Anna, is it?

ANNA. Yes.

LILLY. Lilly Draxler. Thank you for meeting me.

ANNA. Of course.

* *

14.

LENA. My mother was a great woman.

* *

15.

UTA. Please. Come on through.

* *

16.

LENA. So today there must be some kind of reckoning.

* *

17.

LILLY. You were the one who found her?

ANNA. Yes.

LILLY. On the ice?

ANNA. Yes.

* *

18.

LENA. For the life that was lived, and the life that might've been. All the permutations along the way. So.

* *

19.

UTA. Anna, is it?

ANNA. Yes, that's right.

UTA. I'm Uta.

ANNA. Thank you for seeing me.

UTA. Not at all.

* *

20.

LENA. I'm still trying to make sense of it all. That's what we do – what all scientists do. Look for patterns. Cause and effect. Order from chaos. There is no such thing as a random act, only a pattern we haven't understood yet. How did we get here? How might this have been avoided?

* *

21.

UTA. Have you come far?

ANNA. Not far – just the other side of the zoo.

UTA. Not far at all then. You walked?

ANNA. No, I took a taxi.

UTA. Oh.

ANNA. Yes, I… I hadn't left quite enough time. And with the weather…

UTA. Mild, I thought.

ANNA. A bit muggy. Close.

UTA. Is it?

ANNA. And rain later. They're saying thunderstorms. I didn't want to get caught out – arrive looking like…

UTA. I see.

ANNA. You can feel the city heating up already. In a few weeks' time it'll be unbearable.

UTA. And in a few years uninhabitable.

ANNA. I don't make a habit of it.

UTA. The running late, or the taxis?

ANNA. Either – I promise.

*   *

22.

LENA. How might we do better?

*   *

23.

UTA. Please, take a moment – catch your breath.

ANNA. I'm sorry.

UTA. Can I get you some water?

ANNA. No, I'll be fine.

UTA. There's no rush.

ANNA. I walked. Well, strode. Didn't quite realise –

UTA. Where from?

ANNA. Lichtenberg.

UTA. Oh, that's… ambitious.

ANNA. I'm just trying to be less reliant upon… I try to go everywhere under my own steam. I underestimated just how far –

UTA. Very conscientious.

ANNA. I try.

UTA. Of the planet, if not my time.

*   *

24.

LENA. If we were to change our path –

*   *

25.

UTA. A joke.

ANNA. I am sorry.

UTA. And you swam here, I see?

*   *

26.

UTA. Have you come far?

ANNA. From Kreuzberg.

UTA. That's not so bad.

ANNA. No. A train and then a bus, but the train was delayed.

UTA. I see.

ANNA. An accident, I think. Maybe a protest. Somebody on the line.

UTA. Oh.

*   *

27.

LENA. Where might it take us?

*   *

28.

ANNA. I do normally leave a lot of time – a lot of contingency –

UTA. Well, you're here now at least.

*   *

29.

LILLY. Doctor Vogel?

ANNA. Yes?

LILLY. I'm afraid I need to ask you some questions – about Professor Oberdorf.

ANNA. Why? Has something happened?

LILLY. Please. Perhaps you should sit.

* *

30.

LENA. Where did we go wrong? How might we put things right?

* *

31.

ANNA. From Friedrichshain.

UTA (*perking up*). Ah, I have a sister there.

ANNA. Oh?

UTA. Very fashionable these days.

ANNA. I like it.

UTA. But some distance.

ANNA. It's not so bad. I cycled.

UTA. Ah, very green.

ANNA. It's blue actually.

UTA. Hmm?

ANNA. My bicycle.

UTA (*chuckles*). Very good! Yes, very good. (*Gesturing to a seat.*) Please.

* *

32.

LENA. A sculptor stands before a vast block of marble, chisel in her hand. She frets. She hesitates. She knows whatever she does next cannot be undone.

*   *

33.

UTA. Doctor Vogel?

*   *

34.

LENA. A passing philosopher approaches and tells her not to worry – whatever marks she makes are indelible, but also inevitable. Every moment since the dawn of time has led her to this point, and everything that follows is already set in stone. This is the law of the universe. There is only one possible outcome. But still the sculptor hesitates.

*   *

35.

UTA. Shall we make a start?

*   *

36.

LENA. It is at this moment that a quantum physicist wanders over. 'I'm sorry to interrupt, but might I tell you about the multiverse? You see, this is not the only plane of existence – we are just one of an infinite number of alternative worlds. Every time you make a mark on this marble a brand-new universe is formed. Every atomic movement gives birth to a fresh version of reality. Every time you go one way, another you goes another. Every time we act – '

*   *

37.

ANNA. Hello, I'm Professor Oberdorf. (*Beat.*) Sorry, *you're* Professor Oberdorf, I don't know why I… Doctor Vogel, yes. That's me. Anna. Hello.

* *

38.

LENA. ' – the universe divides and the world has changed. Everything is inevitable because everything happens somewhere. Somewhere you fail. Somewhere you succeed. Somewhere you are Michelangelo.' And the sculptor sets to work, not knowing whether or not she has been comforted.

* *

39.

UTA. Did you want to sit? I'm afraid we don't have much time.

* *

40.

LENA. I know I should be trying to offer words of comfort. I understand that is the traditional function. I'm not sure if I find the traditional things comforting, so you might have to bear with me. This is the only way I know how to pay tribute. I'm doing the best I can.

* *

PART TWO – CHILDREN

41.

LILLY. What was Professor Oberdorf like, the first time you met her?

ANNA. I don't know.

LILLY. You don't remember?

ANNA. It was years ago.

LILLY. But your first impression?

ANNA. They were running late – we didn't have much time together.

LILLY. What did you talk about?

ANNA. Lots of things. The role. My research. Her family.

LILLY. Why her family?

*   *

42.

LENA. I wonder what I can tell you then, about my mother?

*   *

43.

ANNA. Are these yours?

UTA. The twins, yes.

ANNA. Beautiful.

UTA. Yes.

ANNA. Just the two?

UTA. More than enough.

ANNA. I'm sure.

*   *

44.

LENA. You know her work, of course. Her reputation. Her brilliance.

* *

45.

LILLY. Anna? Wake up. You have to wake up. Uta is dead.

* *

46.

LENA. You know a version of her. Not my version.

* *

47.

ANNA. Just the two?

UTA. And Matthias, you see – my eldest – up on the bookshelf.

ANNA. He's handsome.

* *

48.

LILLY. Did that strike you as strange – unprofessional?

ANNA. Not really.

LILLY. No?

ANNA. I brought it up. I think. I can't remember. Maybe.

* *

49.

LENA. And so I am mourning, I suppose, not just the woman she was, but the woman she could've been. All the women she could've been, or was, perhaps, somewhere else.

* *

50.

ANNA. Just the two?

UTA. No, no, not at all. Six now – a grand total of six.

ANNA. Gosh.

UTA. Anything is possible, Doctor Vogel, if you put your mind to it.

* *

51.

ANNA. We talked about her family. To break the ice.

LILLY. What family?

* *

52.

LENA. Death robs you not only of the life you had, but of all the lives you can now never have. I'm trying to make space for them – for every imaginable inch of her. Even if that leaves no space for me.

* *

53.

ANNA. Are these yours?

UTA. The twins? No – my nieces.

ANNA. You don't have your own?

UTA. No. (*Beat.*) Does that surprise you?

* *

54.

ANNA. You don't have your own?

UTA. No.

ANNA. I can't make my mind up. I used to worry about overpopulation, but now if anything they think the opposite, don't they? Fertility rates plummeting, because of all the chemicals in the water, in plastics, packaging, pesticides, radio waves, mobile phones in trouser pockets, diet, lifestyle, soybeans. Just another thing to worry about. But maybe it's a blessing really.

* *

55.

ANNA. You don't have your own?

UTA. No.

ANNA. No. You can't, can you? I don't know if I could ever. Not even one. I could adopt, I suppose, to lessen the impact, but even then… I can just about get through each day knowing the storm that's coming for us all, but if I had a child – if it was coming for my daughter… I don't think I could bear it. Not for her. How could I look her in the eye and say this is the world I leave you with? Knowing she could see the end of this century.

UTA. A lot could happen in that time.

ANNA. That's what I'm afraid of.

* *

56.

ANNA. You don't have your own?

UTA. No. I had a child. A son. He died.

ANNA. I'm so sorry.

* *

57.

LILLY. Lilly Draxler. I left messages for you. I –

ANNA. Yes – I'm sorry, I can't stop. I have to pick up my children.

* *

58.

UTA. You don't have your own?

ANNA. Not yet. (*Beat.*) What?

UTA. Nothing.

ANNA. I still have time.

* *

59.

UTA. You don't have your own?

ANNA. Not yet.

UTA. Good. Best to keep it that way.

* *

60.

UTA. You don't have your own?

ANNA. Not yet.

UTA. I'm a firm believer that everyone should have a child – even if only one – be responsible – but something to root them here – a buy-in – a commitment. Without that, how can I ever trust you?

ANNA. So the childless are…?

UTA. Adrift. Does that offend you?

ANNA. No.

UTA. Have a child, Doctor Vogel – nothing shall provide you with greater motivation. We should all have a genetic stake in the future.

* *

61.

LENA. I think sometimes it is impossible to be a truly great person and a truly great parent. I think my mother would have agreed.

I think she was a great person, so… That's what really matters in the end. Our lives are short and we have to make the most of them.

* *

62.

UTA. Don't have a child, Doctor Vogel, whatever you do. If you ever want me to take you seriously, you must promise you shall never have children.

* *

63.

ANNA (*to* LILLY). We talked about the future.

* *

64.

UTA. I cannot hire a thirty-year-old childless woman – you do understand that? Trust me, I am speaking from experience. I might get what – two, three, five years out of you, maximum, before your biological clock starts ringing and you're no more use to me. No use pulling that face – those are the facts. Facts that cannot be ignored to spare your feelings, I'm afraid.

* *

65.

LILLY. When did you last see her alive? (*Beat.*) Forgive me, I'm just trying to build up a picture.

ANNA. Uh… It would've been about a week before she died. We talked in the lab just before she went away.

LILLY. Had she changed? Thinking back to that first time you met – was she a different person? Was she still recognisably her?

ANNA. I…

LILLY. Did she strike you as someone who was near the end?

* *

66.

LENA. The average life expectancy of a human being is seventy-two-point-six years as of 2019. This is the global average. This is ten or twenty years shorter than that of a blue whale, two to three hundred years shorter than the Greenland shark, sixty-two million times shorter than the earth, infinitely shorter than that of the *Turritopsis dohrnii*, also known as the immortal jellyfish, which can cycle back and forth between its mature and immature states seemingly indefinitely, meaning technically – *technically* – it need never die, so long as there are still oceans for it to inhabit. The lucky *Turritopsis dohrnii*, who perhaps comes closer to experiencing life in the multiverse than any of us, given the chance to go again and again and again, continually resetting the clock.

*   *

67.

UTA. Thank you for coming in today. Can I get you tea, coffee, water?

*   *

68.

LENA. Seventy-two-point-six years is approximately half the lifespan of the world's oldest known lobster, caught off the coast of Maine in 2012. Lobsters, contrary to popular belief, are not in fact immortal. A lobster can regenerate repeatedly, replacing its entire exoskeleton in the process, growing bigger and bigger each time, but the larger the lobster grows, the more energy it must expend to moult, until this simply becomes too much effort. The exoskeleton can't be repaired, only replaced. If it can't be replaced, it starts to degrade, cracks form, bacteria sneaks in. Now trapped within its own shell and unable to summon the strength to escape, the lobster begins to rot from the inside. This is what I think of every time I hear that a long life is a blessing. I still don't know if any of this is a comfort. I don't know if comfort is my goal. I was never taught how to grieve but I was taught science, so…

*   *

69.

LILLY. Did you expect to see her again?

* *

70.

LENA. The lobster's tragedy is its inability to live within its means. If it could heal itself without growing larger it could theoretically carry on forever, but it exists in a constant state of expansion. Bigger and bigger and bigger and bigger and bigger. An unenviable end. It is a concrete law of the universe that a lobster will always eventually run out of space.

* *

PART THREE – PINK SNOW

71.

UTA. I take it you're broadly familiar with the work we do?

ANNA. I am.

UTA. We are the undisputed vanguard of climate research. The facilities we have here are unparalleled. You might earn more elsewhere, but you'll never do anything more important.

ANNA. That's why I'm here.

UTA. You've just come back from the Alps?

ANNA. That's right. Last year, a group of us were –

UTA. I was reading your paper, on the… what's your name for it? The watermelon snow.

ANNA. Not my name for it, but –

UTA. 'Blood snow' isn't it – more commonly?

ANNA. Yes, sometimes, although the colour –

UTA. Friendly advice – the 'watermelon' makes you seem frivolous. Very impressive, all the same.

ANNA. Thank you.

UTA. Phenomenally impressive, really, to persuade your faculty to fund a research expedition to a ski resort. You'll have to tell me how you did it.

ANNA. Well –

UTA. You'll find our work here to be a little more serious.

*   *

72.

LILLY. Tell me about your expedition.

ANNA. We were studying the retreat of the glaciers, in the Arctic Circle. Well, that was one aspect of it.

LILLY. You'd been before?

ANNA. No. Uta had.

LILLY. But this trip was your idea?

*   *

73.

UTA. I was reading your paper, on the… what's your name for it? The watermelon snow.

ANNA. Not my name for it, but –

UTA. Right.

ANNA. *Chlamydomonas nivalis.*

UTA. Yes.

ANNA. The name of the algae.

UTA. Yes, yes.

ANNA. The most common one, anyway – or that's what people thought. But actually we found –

*   *

74.

UTA. The watermelon snow.

ANNA. You read it?

UTA. I glanced. It's nothing new, you know.

ANNA. I'm sorry?

UTA. The *Chlamydomonas nivalis*. Aristotle beat you to it.

ANNA. Yes, although we did find –

UTA. You don't mention him. Aristotle – he's not cited.

ANNA. We were looking at the microbiology.

UTA. You should read him.

ANNA. I have.

UTA. Everyone should read Aristotle. But also consider updating your sources.

*   *

75.

UTA. Watermelon snow.

ANNA. You read it?

UTA. And that's because of the colour?

ANNA. And the smell – it even smells sweet.

UTA. Yes, but the colour – you call it Millennial Pink?

ANNA. Yes, it's –

UTA. I haven't the first idea what that means.

*   *

76.

ANNA. Is this for the insurance? (*Beat.*) You funded the expedition, didn't you?

LILLY. In part.

ANNA. That must be embarrassing.

LILLY. Why?

ANNA. Whenever someone dies wearing a snowsuit you sponsored, I imagine that must be fairly embarrassing.

LILLY. We're very proud of our partnership. She was a very important woman.

ANNA. Yes.

LILLY. And so all I'm trying to do is… When someone of her stature passes away it can't just be ignored. It has an impact. It reverberates throughout the community. (*Beat.*) Have you been offered counselling? Any form of therapy? There's the option of compassionate leave, if –

ANNA. I'm fine.

LILLY. You've been through a highly traumatic experience.

ANNA. I'm not traumatised.

LILLY. With respect, you might not be qualified to make that statement.

ANNA. And you are? Because you're not a doctor, are you? Not an actual doctor.

* *

77.

UTA. You're just back from the Alps – studying the *Chlamydomonas nivalis* – the pink snow.

ANNA. *Sanguina.*

UTA. I'm sorry?

ANNA. It's a different algae. There's been quite a lot of research already into the *Chlamydomonas*, and we used to think that was the main cause of the coloration, but actually there's this new genus, *Sanguina. Sanguina nivaloides* and *Sanguina aurantia.*

UTA. I see.

ANNA. *Nivaloides* is red and *aurantia* is orange – a sort of orange, anyway. It's much less common.

UTA. Not pink?

ANNA. They can still look very pink.

UTA. Right.

ANNA. It's all the same sort of –

* *

78.

LILLY. Doctor Vogel?

ANNA. Yes.

LILLY. I have to ask you to complete this questionnaire on your mental wellbeing.

ANNA. Is that compulsory?

LILLY. I'm afraid so.

* *

79.

UTA. You've been studying… what was it again? Moss?

ANNA. Algae. Microalgae, in the permafrost.

UTA. You published a paper?

ANNA. Yes.

UTA. I haven't had the chance to read it.

* *

80.

LILLY. 'I am in a position to take responsibility for my actions. Strongly agree, agree somewhat, neither agree or disagree, disagree somewhat, strongly disagree.'

* *

81.

UTA. This work you've been doing in the Alps – this algae.

ANNA. Yes. It lives underneath the snow, and when it blooms it makes the snow look pink – mostly pink – sometimes other colours. It's extraordinary. You can have whole mountainsides, whole snowfields, turned this delicate pastel pink. Beautiful, but eerie. Actually quite unsettling.

UTA. You went to look at snow because it was a pretty colour?

ANNA. No, because –

UTA. Do you know how difficult it is for us to be taken seriously at the best of times?

ANNA. No – but the colour is why it's important. The coloured snow can't reflect as much sunlight, so it traps more heat. That heat melts more ice, which causes more algae to bloom, which darkens more snow, which traps more heat –

UTA. So it's a feedback loop?

*　　　*

82.

LENA. When my mother passed away –

*　　　*

83.

UTA. So it's a feedback loop?

*　　　*

84.

LENA. When my mother died –

*　　　*

85.

UTA. So it's a feedback loop?

*　　　*

86.

LENA. When I heard my mother had died –

*　　　*

87.

UTA. So it's a feedback loop?

ANNA. Definitely. And it's not going anywhere – the algae – it can survive extreme temperatures, low nutrition, acidic soil, radiation, sunlight, darkness –

UTA. And it's pink?

ANNA. It can be pink.

UTA. Millennial Pink?

ANNA. Yes, I wanted to –

UTA. Hardly scientific. Hardly relevant.

ANNA. I disagree.

* *

88.

UTA. Millennial Pink?

ANNA. Absolutely. Millennial Pink. Tumblr Pink. It's soft, it's kitsch, it's feminine. And it's sneered at – just like you're sneering now – because it's trivial, and girlish, and so obviously absurd. Because we're always sneered at, my generation – too old now to be the future but too young to be taken seriously – and we're blamed for *everything*. We're killing the restaurant industry, and the motorcycle industry, the napkin industry, the greeting-card industry. We're killing diamonds, beer, banks, soap, golf, fabric softener, plastic straws and yogurt. But Millennials aren't killing the planet – not in the way that you are – not at the same rate as our parents. Not because we're better people, just because we lack the agency to bring about the apocalypse. Still, we'll be the ones clearing up after you – entering our old age at the midpoint of the century, just as the real trouble starts – once you're all dead and gone. So what is a better symbol of our inheritance? The Earth on fire and a candyfloss mountain. The colour of the climate crisis is Millennial Pink, because what else could it be? Does that answer your question?

* *

89.

LENA. Imagine a tree. Imagine your family tree. Imagine a Christmas tree, and you are the star perched on top. Below you sit your parents, below them, four grandparents, eight great-grandparents, and so on and so forth as the branches fan out. And through this model you are always at the pinnacle – everything has been leading up to you. Their last hope. Their best chance. The one way forward. Now invert it. Picture an oak, perhaps.

Take a common ancestor – a seed – a single individual, and watch the tree grow – their children, their children's children, on and on and on. This tree is messier – lopsided – some limbs flourish while others die off completely – but eventually by the time we reach your branch, you are no longer the solitary endpoint of all your ancestor's efforts, but one bud amongst billions. So rather than this individualistic approach of you, the star atop the tree, the centre of the universe, the focus switches to the common spark that started this all. Does that make you feel any less special – less unique? Less pressure on you, perhaps. The weight of the world no longer solely on your shoulders. Both pictures are about as unhelpful as each other, because of course there is no single tree, there is only the forest – a deep, dark forest, endlessly vast, with branches weaving, snaking, interconnecting. Twenty generations – that's all it takes, on average. Twenty generations of a population breeding at random and everyone is related to everyone else. It's how every European can claim to be related to Charlemagne. We are a web, a maze, a labyrinth with a billion different ways through it. No single start or end point, just a mesh, a criss-cross jumble of wires going every which way.

The oldest tree – the oldest single tree, that we know of – is around ten thousand years old. Roughly the same age as the invention of the wheel. A baby, compared to the oldest tree colony. In Utah you'll find a grove of over forty thousand male aspen trees, known as Pando. Each tree in the colony is a clone, genetically identical to the next, all connected by one single massive root system. Therefore we can consider it a single living organism, each tree a bristle on the back of a humungous subterranean creature, a slumbering giant weighing over six thousand tonnes and dating back over eighty thousand years. Eighty thousand years, meaning it colonised North America long before Homo sapiens did, before clothes, before language, before tools. Before so much of anything. A thousand human lifetimes ago a seed takes root. And there it is. And there we are. And in the face of that, it seems absurd be believe a single human life can ever make any difference. And yet it does. Of course it always does.

* *

PART FOUR – MOTIVATION

90.

LILLY. You found her?

ANNA. What was left of her.

LILLY. What was left?

ANNA. Bears.

LILLY. Oh.

ANNA. Polar bears. They think –

LILLY. Yes.

ANNA. Didn't kill her – weren't responsible – just got to the body first.

LILLY. I see.

ANNA. They come further and further south each year, further towards human settlements. They're starving. They can roam for hundreds of miles, looking for –

LILLY. Yes, I've read.

ANNA. Or a brown bear. There are brown bears in the Arctic now.

LILLY. There are?

ANNA. They mate sometimes – the polar bears and the grizzlies. They call them 'pizzlies' – pizzly bears – a whole new species. They shouldn't exist at all, really. They never look very healthy. They'd never normally cross paths, but because we've destroyed so much of both their habitats they can sometimes end up together.

LILLY. Still, a new species though – can't be all bad.

ANNA. Oh no, it is – it's bad.

LILLY. Well, of all the reasons for leaving an employer… I have to say, 'my head of department was eaten by bears' is a new one on me. So you're looking for a fresh start?

* *

91.

LENA. Can I tell you a story? Three bears, one large, one medium, and one small, sit down for breakfast, only to discover their porridge is still far too hot, so they take a walk in the woods to let it cool. A small child breaks into their house while they're gone. She eats from the first bear's bowl – too hot still. The second bowl, for reasons unknown, is now far too cold. The third, however, is just right. She sits and scoffs the lot, every last morsel, seemingly caring nothing for the poor bear who will be left hungry.

*   *

92.

UTA. So tell me – what's your story, Doctor Vogel?

ANNA. My story?

UTA. What led you down this path?

ANNA. I want to make a difference.

UTA. Yes, but what got you started?

ANNA. You'll laugh.

UTA. Please.

ANNA. I had a bear. A little white bear – a polar bear, I suppose it was – growing up. Slept with me, went everywhere I did. Inseparable. Until it wasn't very white any more. And then one day I saw –

UTA. Don't tell me – the bear on the ice?

ANNA. Yes.

UTA *laughs.*

You said you wouldn't.

UTA. I'm sorry. The bear on the ice, it's…

ANNA. A little cliché?

UTA. People like to think they understand bears – that's the problem. They don't understand your algae in the permafrost or exothermic feedback loops, but they understand a bear on a piece of ice and that piece of ice getting smaller. That is real to them. I had an email once from some man – some American – I had no idea who he was, but very famous, apparently – a big movie star – action hero. It came to me through the faculty – very important – because he was very rich, you see, so it demanded attention. And the letter said 'I want to help.' 'I've read this article, watched this documentary, seen this viral something and I want to know what I can do to help the polar bears.' Nothing else – no context – no sense of cause and effect – just the idea that if we saved the bears everything might be okay.

ANNA. It'd be a start.

UTA. I wrote back to him – 'Dear whatever-his-name, thank you so much – what a wonderful example you set. If you're serious then I suggest you get yourself to the Arctic at the earliest opportunity, smear yourself in peanut butter and prostrate yourself in front of the first bear you encounter, so the poor thing can at least have a good meal.' Although I doubt the bear would've enjoyed him much. All muscle, you see – very chewy.

*   *

93.

LENA. The three bears return to find their breakfast ruined, their furniture destroyed, a stranger sleeping in their bed. Instead of stopping to clear up her mess, Goldilocks wakes and flees. Smash and grab and out into the deep dark forest without a backward glance. A spoilt little girl with no appreciation of what she had, no idea of where she's going next.

*   *

94.

ANNA. My story?

UTA. What led you down this path?

ANNA. I had an orangutan.

UTA. A real, living – ?

ANNA. Not in my house! No, in… in Borneo, I think. Somewhere. One birthday, some well-meaning aunt adopted an orangutan for me. You know the sort of thing I mean? You send a little money each month and you get updates, pictures, certificates. And detail – quite a lot of detail – on their habitat, the deforestation, palm oil, and –

UTA. I see.

ANNA. I didn't grow up with an orangutan, Professor.

UTA. And that was it? You were radicalised?

ANNA. I suppose.

* *

95.

LENA. The planet Earth exists in the Goldilocks Zone – that is the area of space around a star where life is possible, neither too hot nor too cold, where liquid water might be found. Of all the worlds that are, of all the worlds that could've been, here we have one that is *just right*. Through cosmic fluke or divine intervention, coupled with millions of years of evolution, we have been gifted a planet where we need not just survive, but thrive. We are lucky. We are blessed. We have everything we need. For now.

* *

96.

ANNA. A documentary. About fish.

UTA. Fish?

ANNA. About the fish and the slave labour and the corruption and the suffering.

* *

97.

ANNA. About Standing Rock.

UTA. The pipeline?

ANNA. And the greed, and the health risks and the tribal lands.

* *

98.

ANNA. About toxic waste. About 'Cancer Alley' in Louisianna. About how it's always the poor communities, the Black communities, the ones who can't fight back who bear the brunt of it.

* *

99.

ANNA. To impress a boy.

* *

100.

ANNA. To impress a girl.

* *

101.

ANNA. It's a growth industry.

UTA. Yes, I suppose it is.

* *

102.

ANNA. I stopped sleeping.

UTA. Completely?

ANNA. More or less.

UTA. And why was that?

ANNA. It wasn't one thing. The heat, in part. It's getting hotter.

UTA. Yes.

ANNA. Harder to breathe.

UTA. You mean the – ?

ANNA. In the city, especially. Around people. Too many people.

* *

103.

UTA. What led you down this path?

ANNA. The town where my parents were born is underwater now. I didn't choose this path, I just left for higher ground.

* *

104.

LENA. Here is an alternative explanation for our charmed existence. We're not in the Goldilocks Zone by chance, or because some deity decreed it. If all this seems too good to be true, maybe that's because it is. Maybe we are living inside our own fairytale. The Simulation Hypothesis suggests that in the future, technology will be able to produce artificial realities indistinguishable from the 'real world'. And if that is the case, it then becomes statistically almost certain that the world we consider real is in fact a highly sophisticated computer simulation. A simulation full of artificial people having artificial thoughts imagining further artificial worlds. And if we could sit outside of it, edit the code, tweak a few key variables –

* *

105.

ANNA. A bear.

* *

106.

LILLY. What were you doing in the Arctic?

* *

107.

ANNA. An orangutan.

* *

108.

LILLY. What were you doing in Borneo?

* *

109.

ANNA. A documentary.

* *

110.

LILLY. Did you suggest the trip to North Dakota?

* *

111.

LENA. We can reboot the experiment and try again.

* *

112.

LILLY. You were the one who found her, in the jungle?

* *

113.

LILLY. You found her – by the digger?

* *

114.

LILLY. You found her – in the water?

* *

115.

LENA. It doesn't matter how many times the simulation fails – none of this matters if none of this is real. But the theory relies on the simulation being flawless – on us never being able to tell. If it feels real then it is real, surely? The bear doesn't know he only exists in a story, he only knows his porridge has gone. That is real to him. His home has been ransacked and he has been left hungry. That is real. So the big bear wipes the tears from the baby bear's eyes, picks up the broken furniture and begins to tell a story – a story of soft beds and full bellies, a story where obnoxious little girls get their comeuppance. For he is a bear of great vision, and the little bear will have to carry on his work when he's gone.

*   *

116.

ANNA. Bears?

LILLY. I heard –

ANNA. Who told you that?

LILLY. I thought I read somewhere – her wounds – it looked like –

ANNA. There aren't any more bears.

LILLY. I know, but –

ANNA. No bears can survive in the Arctic now – not even the hybrids. There's nothing for them.

LILLY. I must've misunderstood.

ANNA. She had cuts – lacerations from the fall. They think she fell.

LILLY. I just thought… I don't know. Maybe there would still be bears out there somewhere.

ANNA. That's a fairy tale.

*   *

117.

UTA. What let you down this path?

ANNA. It wasn't just the one thing. It was the Hyperobject.

UTA. The Hyperobject?

ANNA. Yes. You know the term? Something so big it's impossible to comprehend in its entirety. It was *everything*. And you think 'okay, let me take it piece by piece', you try to break it down into manageable chunks – but there's nothing manageable about it. It's all screaming for your attention, and I'm craning my neck trying to take it all in. The Environmental Hyperobject. Climate change is a Hyperobject. Ecology is a Hyperobject. Oil as a Hyperobject – not the oil contained within a single barrel, but all the oil that has ever and will ever exist throughout all of time, in all its many forms, seeping, pooling, smothering. I can't tell you what got me started because it's been like this always. There's no escape from it.

* *

PART FIVE – THE ANTHROPOCENE

118.

UTA. Yes, I suppose you were rather born into the eye of the storm. It's funny – you call yourself 'Millennial', but in actual fact you are first-generation Anthropocene – the age of human interference.

ANNA. Oh, I think our interference goes back a little longer.

UTA. No, but as the dominant force –

ANNA. We've dominated for hundreds of years.

UTA. You misunderstand me.

ANNA. No, I don't.

UTA. As the *dominant* – this isn't up for debate – the era in which mankind is the *most significant* force affecting the planet. I'm speaking scientifically – as a geological epoch. This is a brand phenomenon. Industrial Revolution? Not really – not comparatively. Atom bomb? Yes, to an extent. The seed of the Anthropocene is in the atom bomb. 'Now I am become death, the destroyer of worlds.' But the Anthropocene proper only goes back thirty years.

*   *

119.

ANNA. I saw what happened in Geneva. Chaos, but incredible. That was all you?

LILLY. There are a lot of us out there.

ANNA. I'd like to help. I think I can help.

*   *

120.

ANNA. Thirty years?

UTA. As the dominant force.

ANNA. No –

*   *

121.

LILLY. So you understand the tactics we use?

ANNA. Yes.

LILLY. You understand the risks?

ANNA. I believe so.

LILLY. If you're arrested –

ANNA. It wouldn't be the first time.

LILLY. If it requires more than that? (*Beat.*) I want your eyes to be open.

ANNA. There isn't much choice, is there?

*   *

122.

UTA. As the dominant force.

ANNA. No, it's earlier. You have to start much earlier.

UTA. So when would you like to start?

ANNA. 1492.

UTA *laughs.*

The *Santa Maria*. The *Mayflower*. The *Golden Hind*. The claiming of a New World that was in no way new.

UTA. I see.

ANNA. The colonisation of an entire –

UTA. Columbus wasn't the first coloniser.

ANNA. But he sets in motion –

UTA. The Anthropocene refers to a very specific –

ANNA. You posed the question – when did the destruction start?

*   *

123.

LILLY. Can you unbutton your shirt? (*Beat.*) I need to see if you're wearing a wire.

*   *

124.

UTA. So why not Alexander?

ANNA. I'm sorry?

UTA. Alexander the Great? Why not start there?

ANNA. No, but –

UTA. The First Persian Empire? The Abbasid Caliphate? The Ming Dynasty? Always building great big walls – hardly progressive, by today's standards.

ANNA. My point is –

UTA. A scar still visible from space.

ANNA. My point is that the European colonisation of the Americas –

UTA. Part-built by slaves too – the Great Wall. Although I understand it's far more fashionable to only point fingers at the Western oppressors.

ANNA. That isn't what I'm saying.

UTA. Or would you be happier if none of us had ever left Africa? We all should've stayed put in the Cradle of Life hunting zebra and picking wild fruit and staying out of trouble.

ANNA. With respect, Professor Oberdorf, you asked me a question.

UTA. And you gave a foolish answer.

ANNA. You haven't allowed me to answer yet.

*   *

125.

LILLY. Why now?

ANNA. It wasn't one thing. But I haven't been sleeping – I don't think I know anyone who's sleeping, do you? It's the heat but it's more than that.

LILLY. Go on.

ANNA. And they don't follow the law, so why should I? They don't care who gets hurt. Somebody has to stop them.

*   *

126.

ANNA. One hundred million dead.

UTA. What?

ANNA. One hundred million.

UTA. Where?

ANNA. Approximately one hundred million Indigenous people have been killed or died early between 1492 and today. Killed by invasion, by conquest, by colonisation. Killed by foreign diseases, destruction of habitat, crop failure, poisoned water. Killed by poor education, by poverty, by want, by violence, drug abuse, suicide, police brutality. Killed for their land. Killed for convenience. Killed because they could be.

UTA. One hundred million?

ANNA. At best estimate.

UTA. Whose estimate? How could you possibly – ?

ANNA. One hundred million lives cut short. Ninety-five per cent of all Indigenous people.

UTA. Even if that were true –

ANNA. It is.

UTA. Even if it were, we're talking about measurable impact on the planet, not whatever social justice campaign you're –

ANNA. And why can't we talk about justice?

UTA. Because we're talking about science – pure science!

ANNA. We're talking about destruction! Their lands were taken. Their lands were developed. New crops, new species, new diseases. The American Frontier – Manifest Destiny – the ecology of a continent fundamentally and forever shifted – that is geological change.

UTA. That isn't what I'm talking about.

ANNA. Then why not?

*   *

127.

LILLY. No. I know your sort. Nice girls like you. All you do is *study* destruction. Measure destruction, record destruction. Write your reports, submit your recommendations, take your Big Oil blood money to build your laboratories and lie to yourself that maybe one day they'll change.

ANNA. Yes.

LILLY. But you want to make a real difference?

ANNA. Yes.

LILLY. And you know what that means?

ANNA. Yes. I know what has to be done. I know how –

*   *

128.

UTA. Because none of that is relevant.

ANNA. Why? Why are their lives irrelevant? Why don't they interest you? You don't have to answer – we both know the answer. For centuries Black bodies, brown bodies, poor bodies pile up and nobody bats an eye because it's what we expect those bodies to do. Born to suffer. Good for nothing else. But ninety-five per cent! Surely there comes a time? There's a statistic – do you know it? – about the oceans: at one-point-five degrees of warming, ninety per cent of all coral dies. Ninety per cent – just imagine – we can't let that happen. But ninety-five per cent of a people… I am telling you that mass destruction is nothing new, you only notice it when it's on your doorstep – even then you'll just move house. You'll head to higher ground. Goldilocks will colonise Mars before she cleans up her own mess.

UTA. With respect, doctor, I've been fighting this battle since you were a child.

ANNA. Then why haven't you done better?

UTA. Drink some water. Take a breath. Now could we be serious for a moment – serious and scientific? Could we return to the matter at hand? Here's what I know: more carbon has been released into the atmosphere since your birth than in all of human history before you – that is a new phenomenon – that is the Anthropocene in action, and it did not begin in 1492. That is wilful destruction unlike anything the world has ever seen. The Earth is literally shifting on its axis because of the rate at which we're melting glacial ice. We have proved, beyond a shadow of a doubt, that we as a species are responsible for heating the planet, and that is *fantastic*, because if we're the ones doing it then we can stop it. If we are to avoid two degrees of warming it will take a superhuman collective effort on an unprecedented global scale, and that – *that* – must be our focus. Anything else is a distraction.

*   *

129.

LILLY. Okay, you've got two minutes – talk.

ANNA. Uta is dead. (*Beat.*) They're calling it an accident, but –

LILLY. Good.

ANNA. But –

LILLY. So they're cancelling the expedition? No more drilling? No more exploratory studies?

ANNA. For now, but –

LILLY. That was the goal, wasn't it? What you were pressing for?

ANNA. We talked about protest – about blockades. I didn't want her to die.

LILLY. That was her choice. To finally do something meaningful.

ANNA. I never –

LILLY. What does it matter? Everybody dies.

*   *

130.

LENA. I wonder where Goldilocks' parents are in the story. I wonder if she'd just lost her mother too. I wonder if as she fled into the deep, dark forest she realised for the first time that there was to be no more porridge, no more rocking chairs and soft beds, that she was on her own from now on. Mother cannot save you – you have to save yourself. We all must take responsibility in saving ourselves.

*   *

PART SIX – PRIVILEGE AND SACRIFICE

131.

UTA. Perhaps we could start again.

ANNA. If you'd like.

UTA. For us to have any hope of a happy future, we must show resolve, resourcefulness, and sacrifice. Tell me, what have you sacrificed?

ANNA. For what?

UTA. The survival of the species.

ANNA. I…

* *

132.

LENA. The Paris agreement of 2015 gives us two small numbers amongst a slew of terrifyingly large ones – two and one-point-five.

* *

133.

UTA. Nothing?

ANNA. I don't drive.

* *

134.

LENA. If warming increases by two degrees Celsius, life could become unbearable, at one-point-five merely unpleasant.

* *

135.

UTA. Good. That's a start.

*   *

136.

LENA. Half a degree of difference would make water shortages twice as severe. We would lose twice as many plants, three times as many insects.

*   *

137.

ANNA. I recycle.

UTA. Everything?

ANNA. Most things.

*   *

138.

LENA. We would see an extra one hundred and fifty million deaths from air pollution alone.

*   *

139.

UTA. But not everything you could?

*   *

140.

LENA. We could see an increase in flash floods and tropical cyclones.

*   *

141.

ANNA. Probably not every single… The facilities around me are okay – not brilliant.

UTA. And you don't drive.

ANNA. No.

*   *

142.

LENA. The Arctic would be free of sea ice one summer in ten, rather than one in a hundred.

*   *

143.

UTA. Tricky, isn't it?

ANNA. No. No, not at all.

*   *

144.

LENA. It would mean – and here is the real incentive – an additional twenty trillion dollars lost from the world's economy –

*   *

145.

ANNA. I don't fly.

UTA. No?

ANNA. Not for years now.

*   *

146.

LENA. As our land becomes less fertile and our resources grow scarcer and we must constantly rebuild after disaster after disaster after disaster.

*　　*

147.

UTA. You might have to fly. A lot of our research requires –

ANNA. If it was necessary – professionally necessary, then –

UTA. For the greater good?

*　　*

148.

LENA. In 2021, the IPCC updated their findings. There now seems to be no scenario in which one-point-five degrees of warming is not exceeded by the middle of the century.

*　　*

149.

UTA. You chose to come in today.

ANNA. Yes.

UTA. In person. We offered the option of video conferencing, but you –

ANNA. Yes. I find for first impressions… And my Wi-Fi isn't always –

*　　*

150.

LENA. In their 'very high' emissions scenario, temperatures could plausibly rise by as much as five-point-seven degrees by 2100.

*　　*

151.

ANNA. I walked. That was partially why I –

UTA. Why you were late?

ANNA. You were running over, professor – I was on time.

*   *

152.

LENA. To put this into context, at three-point-seven degrees of warming, the financial burden to humanity is estimated at five hundred and fifty-one trillion dollars, or roughly twice all the money that currently exists in the world.

*   *

153.

UTA. Pets?

ANNA. Not allowed in my building.

UTA. Bitcoin? Do you own any Bitcoin?

ANNA. No.

UTA. Or another other cryptocurrency?

ANNA. No.

UTA. Because the energy involved in –

ANNA. Yes, I know.

UTA. People don't often take into account their digital footprint, but –

ANNA. I do.

*   *

154.

LENA. Of course at these temperatures, society as we know it will almost certainly collapse, so it seems churlish to worry about who's going to foot the bill. I'm sorry. I don't know how this part is meant to be comforting. Maybe it only comforts those who are no longer with us.

* *

155.

UTA. – prepared to sacrifice?

ANNA. I don't eat red meat. Or pork. Or soya. I don't drink coffee, only herbal tea. I grow my own herbs – only herbs, no space for anything else. I eat seasonally, locally, sustainably. I collect a vegetable box every week of all the things the restaurants were going to throw away.

* *

156.

LENA. But what can you do?

* *

157.

UTA. Sacrifice?

ANNA. I fitted a box to the showerhead so it uses less water.

* *

158.

LENA. I'm asking – what can any of us do?

* *

159.

UTA. Sacrifice?

ANNA. In winter we stick layers of cling film over the window frames.

UTA. Sacrifice?

* *

160.

LENA. I have a capsule wardrobe. I collect rainwater.

ANNA. I buy everything second hand.

LENA. I own two mason jars, a clay pot and a wooden spoon.

ANNA. I donate blood.

LENA. I collect my urine in one of my two mason jars and use it to water my urban allotment.

ANNA. I –

*   *

161.

UTA. Sacrifice?

ANNA. I make placards.

LENA. I switched my energy supplier.

ANNA. I write to my representatives.

LENA. I opened an eco-friendly pension fund.

ANNA. I planted an orchard.

LENA. I plant seeds in the cracks in pavements.

ANNA. I chain myself to pipelines and lie down in front of bulldozers.

LENA. I raised a colony of twenty thousand bees and released them into the headquarters of ExxonMobil.

ANNA. I am plotting to kidnap the first-born sons of the chief executives of the world's largest automotive companies and execute one child each day until all production halts.

LENA. But it doesn't help. I don't know how to help.

*   *

162.

UTA. Sacrifice?

ANNA. Nothing. I've done enough.

UTA. We'll all have to –

ANNA. I've already sacrificed. I'm not the one who has to sacrifice.

UTA. Surely everyone must –

ANNA. I've done enough – more than enough. Was sacrificed. Had no say in it. My security, stability, dignity. My parents, who sacrificed. My ancestors, who were sacrificed – never willingly. My generation, who aren't allowed to own things any more, from our homes to our music to our identities. Sacrificed. Uploaded. Shared digitally. If you're not paying for it then you become the product. Commodified. Marketed. Sacrificed. My generation is the one bred for life amongst the ruins. I am the precariat. I have given enough already.

UTA. Doctor Vogel –

* *

163.

ANNA. What have you sacrificed?

UTA. I… I offset. We plant trees. We insulate. We have solar panels and a heat pump.

ANNA. Is that all?

UTA. I advise governments on –

ANNA. But personal sacrifice?

UTA. I practise what I preach. This whole institution is carbon-neutral at my insistence. We have ponds teeming with biodiversity, living plant walls to maximise vertical space. We have our own beehives, for fuck's sake!

ANNA. And you feel that as a sacrifice, do you?

* *

164.

UTA. Sacrifice?

ANNA. Nothing.

UTA. Nothing?

ANNA. It's a lie. The Carbon Footprint was marketed by British Petroleum as a way to pass the buck on to the consumer. They spent two hundred and fifty million dollars promoting it. So we get neurotic about disposable cutlery while they extract four million barrels of oil a day. But we have to sacrifice?

UTA. We can push for reform while still –

ANNA. No – I'm sorry, but no. This isn't about individual responsibility, it's about collective pressure – holding those with real power to account. Our governments – Big Business – Big Tech – Big Oil – that's who we have to get through to. Structural overhaul. A top-down, fundamental shift from… We had a global pandemic and the whole world stopped – air travel down ninety-seven per cent, cougars roaming the streets of Santiago, dolphins swimming up the Bosporus. And you know what? It did nothing. It made no difference, because any society running on fossil fuels can never be a healthy one, and in that society, individual choices mean *nothing*.

*   *

165.

LENA. And there are trees that are eighty thousand years old and bears who don't know they're in stories and three-quarters of a billion of us in Europe all related to Charlemagne and the sculptor doesn't know whether she's comforted or not.

*   *

166.

LILLY. What can you tell me about Professor Oberdorf? What can you tell me about what happened to her?

*   *

167.

LENA. To know that every mark she makes is inevitable. To know that every mark she doesn't make is made by another sculptor in another world.

* *

168.

UTA. Nothing?

ANNA. Nothing. Anything I do means nothing. That's the truth, isn't it?

* *

169.

LENA. But the sculptor knows this is the only reality she will ever see. This is as real as it will ever get. This is the only chance she'll get.

* *

170.

LILLY. And she was already dead when you found her?

ANNA. Yes.

LILLY. On the ice?

ANNA. Yes.

* *

171.

UTA. Aren't you grateful to be here?

ANNA. Grateful?

UTA. Yes! Instead of lamenting your fate or pointing fingers, stop for one moment to consider the astronomical implausibility of your existence. Consider how lucky you are to be standing here today. Not here in my office – not *only* here in my office – but here on this planet. Consider the probability of conditions being just so – the stars being so perfectly aligned that human life can thrive – infinitesimally small. And not just that, not only that – that we have breathable air and arable land, and oceans full of water, not hydrochloric acid – but that as individuals we both came into being in this place and in this time, in these bodies, that our parents and our parents' parents and every one of our ancestors came together at exactly the right moment so that we could meet each other today and have the genuine opportunity to make a meaningful difference – how, in consideration of all those things, could you be anything other than unconstrainedly grateful?

ANNA. To you?

UTA. To the universe! (*Beat.*) And yes, as it happens, also to me.

ANNA. With respect, professor, I believe you're talking from a position of privilege.

UTA. Oh, I'm privileged, am I?

ANNA. I believe that someone with your background – your status – perhaps sometimes you forget –

UTA. And you're not privileged, I suppose?

ANNA. I don't believe so.

UTA. No. No, no, no.

ANNA. With respect –

* *

172.

LILLY. 'I am grateful for the opportunities I have been given.'

ANNA. Is this necessary?

LILLY. Strongly agree, agree somewhat, neither agree or disagree, disagree somewhat, strongly disagree.

ANNA. I don't know.

* *

173.

UTA. You see this – exactly this – this is where I find fault with you. Your entire generation. Here you are, blessed with the greatest privilege of all – the immense and implausible cosmic privilege of *existence* – and you would split hairs quibbling over whether anybody else was born into greater advantage than you. Petty. Obnoxious.

ANNA. Professor Oberdorf –

UTA. I haven't finished. I find it offensive. Unacceptable. An unforgivable excuse for any woman to use today. And especially now – now when we see how delicately things hang in the balance – when half a degree is the difference between comfort and oblivion –

ANNA. I should be grateful?

UTA. Grateful. Responsible. Fearful. Proactive.

ANNA. Fearful?

UTA. Focused on the task at hand. It is unbelievably frustrating. Because this – the challenge of our collective lifetimes, that so dwarfs anything else – this is entirely solvable. We could halt climate change within a generation if we really wanted to – if we all sacrificed, if we prioritised, if we stopped getting in our own way. It isn't too late for us yet. We could turn the tide if only we stopped squabbling with each other and all pulled together. And I simply don't have time, doctor, to cater to your trivial grievances. They are insignificant. The ice caps don't care what colour your skin is, so stop playing the victim and start taking responsibility.

ANNA. If I could finish –

*   *

174.

LENA. What else can I tell you? What is important? Lobsters are not in fact immortal. We have chopped down three trillion trees since the start of the industrial revolution. The Deepwater Horizon oil spill covered an area of ocean the size of Oklahoma. Watermelon snow doesn't really smell of watermelon, but it does smell sweet. The bears are starving. Native American organisers were successful in shutting down the Dakota Access Pipeline. The possibility remains that none of this is real.

*   *

175.

LILLY. You'll be wanting a change of scene, I imagine, now the professor is dead. We're funding a new lab in Massachusetts – or something in the marine centre? Have you been following their work with the algae? You were the algae girl, weren't you?

ANNA. Yes, I've looked at –

LILLY. Great guys. It's the future of biofuel – which is the future of everything.

ANNA. Stop it.

LILLY. Or Sydney – I've got a gorgeous team out in Sydney – get you warmed up. Beautiful this time of year.

ANNA. I don't want to work for you.

LILLY. Yes you do – of course you do. You want to keep doing the work, yes? The work is vital. Doesn't matter who pays for it.

ANNA. Yes it does.

LILLY. Better we fund your projects than spend it on fracking. Better to be part of the conversation. Nothing is more important.

*   *

176.

LENA. We will suffer more than our parents did. Our children will suffer more than us. I don't know how to offer comfort. Shall I keep going?

*   *

177.

UTA. Immensely privileged.

ANNA. Immensely privileged?

UTA. Immensely.

ANNA. Privileged?

UTA. Undoubtedly.

ANNA. If I could –

* *

178.

UTA. Immensely privileged.

ANNA. If you could let me –

* *

179.

LENA. One of the problems with the complexity of the Hyperobject is it isn't always possible to spot linear cause and effect, at least not until it's too late.

* *

180.

UTA. Fortunate, yes? Immensely privileged.

ANNA. Privileged?

UTA. Immensely privileged.

ANNA. If I could –

UTA. Privileged. Yes. Immensely.

ANNA. Please –

UTA. Immensely privileged.

ANNA. Can I – ?

UTA. Fortunate, yes? Immensely privileged.

ANNA. If you'd let me –

* *

181.

LENA. A positive feedback loop is a process of accelerated response, where, for instance, a hotter planet means more forest fires which means more carbon is released into the atmosphere which means a hotter planet which means more forest fires which means –

*   *

182.

ANNA. Privileged?

*   *

183.

LENA. An accelerated response, where, for instance, a hotter planet causes forest dieback, which means less carbon absorption, which means a hotter planet, which means –

*   *

184.

UTA. What's your story, Doctor Vogel?

*   *

185.

LENA. Where, for instance, a hotter planet means warmer oceans, which contain less oxygen, which kills the phytoplankton, which releases more carbon, which warms the planet

*   *

186.

ANNA. My story?

*   *

187.

LENA. Which warms the planet which warms the planet which warms the planet.

*   *

188.

UTA. If you were intending to impress me, you really should have started by now.

*   *

189.

LENA. So we go again we go again we go again.

*   *

190.

UTA. Doctor Vogel?

*   *

191.

UTA. Doctor Vogel?

*   *

192.

UTA. Doctor Vogel? I take it you are still interested in this position?

ANNA. No.

UTA. No?

ANNA. Not any more.

UTA. I don't understand.

ANNA. It's nothing personal. I just can't go through this again.

UTA. What do you mean?

ANNA. I can't keep going with you being the one who decides my fate.

UTA (*more amused than offended*). That does sound rather personal. You're lucky I'm in a good mood, or –

ANNA. Don't you see that shouldn't be what makes the difference?

UTA. I was rather looking forward to meeting you. I wanted to talk about your wonderful paper – the pink snow. *Millennial* Pink – it's very clever.

ANNA. I can't. I'm sorry.

* *

193.

LENA. We might never know what did it – what finally tipped us over the edge. Death by a thousand paper cuts. I'm told they can't say for certain what killed her – my mother – so that's another thing for me to live with.

* *

194.

UTA. And what have I done, exactly?

ANNA. It's not what you've done – it's what you are.

UTA. Which is?

* *

195.

LENA. But that is the nature of the Hyperobject. It was everything. She died of everything.

* *

196.

ANNA. The Hyperobject. You're the Hyperobject.

* *

197.

LENA. There are environmental Hyperobjects, like oil and styrofoam and radioactive plutonium.

* *

198.

UTA. The Hyperobject?

ANNA. Yes.

* *

199.

LENA. And societal Hyperobjects too. Colonial Hyperobjects, imperial Hyperobjects, patriarchal Hyperobjects, stretching throughout time.

* *

200.

ANNA. Not just you in this room right now, you in all rooms forever, since forever.

* *

201.

LENA. Woven into our every waking moment, impossible to perceive in its entirety but equally impossible to ignore.

* *

202.

ANNA. Trying to impress you, or someone like you. Appease you, flatter you, win your approval.

* *

203.

LILLY. You understand the risks? You understand the tactics we use?

* *

204.

ANNA. But I can never see all of you at once. You're the faculty, the university, the rule of law –

* *

205.

LILLY. Doctor Vogel? I'm afraid I have to ask you some questions.

* *

206.

ANNA. You are so vast you have no idea.

* *

207.

LILLY. You want to keep doing the work, yes?

* *

208.

LENA. And now is the moment – this is what my mother taught me – when unstoppable force meets immovable object. Man versus nature, Wall Street versus glacier, Amazon versus Amazon.

*   *

209.

ANNA. That's why people don't like to think about the environment – it's not that they don't care, they just don't know where to start. There's too much of it.

*   *

210.

LENA. And you will feel small. And you will feel worthless.

*   *

211.

ANNA. I can't even bring myself to look at you.

*   *

212.

LENA. And you will feel like there is no point in carrying on.

*   *

213.

ANNA. I'm sorry. I thought – it's stupid, but I had thought you being a woman might be the thing that made the difference, but it doesn't, it can't, because it isn't really *you*, it's everything. I can't win. I can join you, or I can fight you, but what good is either? Either way I'm consumed.

*   *

214.

LILLY. Nothing is more important than the work. You are nothing, Doctor Vogel, without this work. By yourself, you are nothing.

* *

215.

ANNA. You won't understand. You can't – you're too imbedded. I barely register. I don't expect the sun to understand what it feels like when I burn. But I can't do this. I want to help, but I don't know how. I want to run to the hills, but the hills are on fire. I don't know what to do.

* *

216.

LENA. But the truth is you are more powerful than you know. Each of us is a Hyperobject too. We are infinite. Our possibilities are limitless. There is a privilege in that.

* *

217.

UTA. I think we're about finished here, don't you?

ANNA. Yes.

* *

218.

LENA. I find it comforting to think of the billions upon billions of other Anna Vogels floating around the multiverse, but only one of them was my mother.

* *

219.

UTA. I must say I have found this all very disappointing.

* *

220.

LENA. My mother, who was kind, who was stubborn, who was furious.

* *

221.

UTA. When I think of all the others who would've been grateful to take your spot.

* *

222.

LENA. Who adopted me, despite the advice of her parents, despite being mistaken for the nanny, despite everything else she knew it would entail.

* *

223.

UTA. Ah well, I've said my piece.

* *

224.

LENA. And for that I am privileged, yes. Immensely privileged. Fortunate. So fortunate.

* *

225.

ANNA. Thank you for your time. Don't worry about me, professor. I haven't finished yet.

*   *

226.

LENA. Not featured in my eulogy is the Anna Vogel who won a Nobel Prize. Not featured in my eulogy is the Anna Vogel who was awarded the Order of Merit. Not featured in my eulogy is the Anna Vogel with cystic fibrosis, with motor neurone disease, fibromyalgia, chronic fatigue, who missed her interview due to a flare-up, a caring emergency, a mental health crisis. Not featured is the Anna Vogel whose life expectancy did not make post-doctoral study feasible, whose individual carbon footprint is shameful, due to the variety of energy-guzzling contraptions keeping her alive, the plethora of medicines produced in exotic far-off places, who is too incurious to investigate the working conditions or environmental practices of the Bangladeshi sweatshops producing the small molecule inhibitors treating her carcinoma. Not featured is the Anna Vogel in rehab, in remission, still shielding inside due to an autoimmune condition or long undiagnosed trauma, the Anna Vogel who must keep every light in the house blazing because of undisclosed events that happened in the dark. Who never had children, who never graduated, who never recovered from her bout of childhood measles or that one university house party. All I can tell you about is the Anna Vogel I knew, who never gave up, who was never given her due, who suffered, and was expected to suffer. Who made a difference. Who did good. Who wanted to do so much more. In a world of uncertainties, these are my concrete absolutes. This is unchangeable. She is gone now, but she was here, and she mattered. This is my comfort.

*   *

PART SEVEN – ANNA'S DEATH

227.

UTA *and* LENA.

UTA. Miss Vogel?

LENA. Yes.

UTA (*somewhat surprised*). You're Anna's daughter?

LENA. Yes. (*Beat.*) Adopted daughter.

UTA. Oh. Yes, yes. I remember.

LENA. She didn't want to…

UTA. Hmm?

LENA. To make things worse. Contribute to –

UTA. Good for her. (*Beat.*) Lia, isn't it?

LENA. Lena.

UTA. Yes, of course. Please, sit.

LENA. These are yours?

UTA. The twins? My granddaughters.

LENA. Beautiful.

UTA. Aren't they?

They both speak at once.

LENA. / I was just wondering if you could tell me –

UTA. / I'm afraid I don't have very much time.

LENA. Sorry. Please.

UTA. Yes. I'm afraid I can't spend much time with you today. A very busy afternoon.

LENA. Of course.

UTA. You wanted to see where she worked?

LENA. Yes. Your colleague Doctor Lundberg showed me around the laboratories. The work you do here is…

UTA. Nothing is more important.

LENA. Yes.

UTA. What exactly can I help you with, Lena?

LENA. It was your expedition.

UTA. Ah.

LENA. What happened to her?

UTA. An accident. I believe an accident.

LENA. But how?

UTA. Sometimes accidents happen. Very unfortunate, but… I am of course very sorry for your loss. There isn't much I can tell you that isn't in the report. You have seen the report?

LENA. Yes.

UTA. And I should be clear – you will have read this already, but the university accepts no responsibility in what was a deeply unfortunate –

LENA. Yes, but –

UTA. *Deeply* unfortunate, but an independent investigation found no wrongdoing, no malfunctions, no failures in health and safety protocol.

LENA. But she died, so –

UTA. Yes. And I truly am very sorry.

LENA. How?

UTA. Hypothermia.

LENA. You were the one who found her?

UTA. No.

LENA. Oh, I thought –

UTA. No, no, not at all. I planned the expedition, but I wasn't there with it. I don't tend to spend as much time out in the field these days. I was overseeing operations from Berlin.

LENA. Oh.

UTA. So I'm afraid I really can't be of much help to you.

LENA. Still, you worked together.

UTA. She worked within my department, yes.

LENA. What do you think happened?

UTA. I think the Arctic is a very hostile environment. I think it's surprisingly easy to get lost, or disorientated, or fail to take the necessary precautions. I think we might never know exactly.

LENA. Because she was alone?

UTA. I think –

LENA. Was she alone? When she died?

UTA. As I've said, Miss Vogel, I'm afraid I wasn't there. I don't think I can tell you anything you don't know already. (*Beat.*) Was there anything else?

LENA. Yes. Um. Yes, there's going to be a service, next Saturday. At the moment I'm the only one speaking. I wondered if maybe you'd like to say anything.

UTA. Oh.

LENA. I know you worked together for so long –

UTA. I think… No. I don't think that would be appropriate.

LENA. But –

UTA. With no disrespect, I have a lot of people working under me.

LENA. I see.

UTA. I can't get close to all of them. (*Beat.*) You have my deepest sympathies.

LENA. You'd still be very welcome to attend, even if –

UTA. Yes. I'll check my diary. Leave the details with Marianne on your way out.

LENA. Okay. Thank you.

Beat.

UTA. I'm afraid I really must get on.

LENA. Yes, of course.

UTA. The work is… There is nothing more important than the work. The work has to come before everything else, you see?

No matter what the cost. Otherwise there's no hope for any of us. Good luck, Lia.

LENA. Lena.

UTA. Yes. Good luck.

* *

228.

Perhaps this feels like a pep talk ANNA *is giving to a young* LENA.

ANNA. Imagine a tree. Imagine the tree at the centre of the universe, the multiverse, where each branch represents a different road taken. Some right, some wrong, all inevitable, in their own way. So we go one way and another us goes another. Everything happens somewhere. Everything is inevitable. And what good is that? The multiverse is the scientific equivalent of a bedtime story – a quantum comfort blanket. Everything happens, so nothing matters. No. What we do here matters – I have to believe that.

One tree, yes. Or an entire forest, connected by the roots. One single organism of infinite complexity – infinite possibilities, but only one actuality – one version of events – one path chosen. So on we go, climbing ever upwards, an axe between our teeth, and every time we choose a branch we hack all the others away – every other option vanishes. And every time we swing the blade it's possible – it's entirely possible – we miss what we were aiming for, we slice through the branch we've been clinging on to, and plummet down into the nothingness beneath us. That's it. That's life. That's the system we're dealing with. And that's okay – I like that much better than everything happens and nothing matters. Give me the axe. Let me choose the branch. I think that's wonderful.

UTA *appears.*

UTA. Doctor Vogel? Please come through. I've been dying to speak with you and I'm afraid we don't have much time.

Ends.